ZOMBIE SEED AND THE BUTTERFLY BLUES

Social Fictions Series

Series Editor
Patricia Leavy
USA

The *Social Fictions* series emerges out of the arts-based research movement. The series includes full-length fiction books that are informed by social research but written in a literary/artistic form (novels, plays, and short story collections). Believing there is much to learn through fiction, the series only includes works written entirely in the literary medium adapted. Each book includes an academic introduction that explains the research and teaching that informs the book as well as how the book can be used in college courses. The books are underscored with social science or other scholarly perspectives and intended to be relevant to the lives of college students—to tap into important issues in the unique ways that artistic or literary forms can.

Please email queries to pleavy7@aol.com

Zombie Seed and the Butterfly Blues

A Case of Social Justice

By

R.P. Clair
Purdue University, West Lafayette, IN, USA

SENSE PUBLISHERS
ROTTERDAM / BOSTON / TAIPEI

A C.I.P. record for this book is available from the Library of Congress.

ISBN 978-94-6209-306-5 (paperback)
ISBN 978-94-6209-307-2 (hardback)
ISBN 978-94-6209-308-9 (e-book)

Published by: Sense Publishers,
P.O. Box 21858, 3001 AW Rotterdam, The Netherlands
https://www.sensepublishers.com/

Printed on acid-free paper

PRAISE FOR
ZOMBIE SEED AND THE BUTTERFLY BLUES

"*Zombie Seed and the Butterfly Blues* is a gripping story about corporate conspiracy and exploitation, relational violence, and the value of social research. A masterpiece of literary technique and thick description, this book illustrates how lives can connect in complex and unnerving ways—from everyday interactions with strangers, friends, and partners to authorities, histories, and institutions riddled with corruption and neglect. An ideal text for courses on relationships, organizational life, and narrative research, and a must-read for anyone interested in environmentalism, creative writing, and social justice."

—Tony E. Adams, Author: *Narrating the Closet:
An Autoethnography of Same-Sex Attraction*

"*Zombie Seed and the Butterfly Blues* is not only a wonderful read, it's compelling and thought-provoking. I loved it!"

—Donald Bain, Author: The "*Murder, She Wrote*" novels.

"*Zombie Seed and Butterfly Blues* is a rare book! A compelling story of social justice and a detective story! It will also make an excellent text for outside-the-box courses in organizational rhetoric and qualitative methods."

—Dr. Dean Scheibel, award-winning researcher
and teacher, Loyola Marymount University

"Robin Clair uses fiction to teach us—scholars, teachers, and students of human communication—how to bring social research closer to the richness and complexity of lived experience. Ethnographic fieldwork is not only a method of putting oneself in the shoes of another, but also a way of using our experience in another's world to reflect critically on our own. Clair shows that one of the best ways to do this is to tell a good story, one that could be true. *Zombie Seed and the Butterfly Blues* takes students on a journey reminiscent of fieldwork, one that will broaden their horizons and enable them to see connections where once they only saw divisions. Clair realizes that the actual may not be as important as the possible and that the greatest deficiency of social science is its lack of imagination. She wants us to pay attention to the world and to enlarge our sense of responsibility and conscience. *Zombie Seed and the Butterfly Blues* offers a corrective to social science's obsession with producing a mountain of facts bereft of truth. Through the canon of fiction and the mystery novel, Clair evokes the sound and feel of lived reality, filling the gaps that normally exist between author and reader, fact and truth. The result is a story that encourages us to keep pressing the case for higher standards of justice and truthfulness."

—Arthur P, Bochner, Distinguished Professor of
Communication, University of South Florida

"Clair has beautifully woven narrative threads from present day academia, classical and modern myth, and critical environmental discourse into an educational and thrilling story. The resulting complex tapestry provides educators, or those simply seeking to enjoy the journey with Delta, a unique and exciting opportunity to engage."

—Dr. Rebekah Fox, Assistant Professor, Texas State University-
San Marcos Editor, *Communication Law Review*

"Robin Clair's novel, *Zombie Seed and the Butterfly Blues*, is a great read … Clair uses her natural gift of narrative and her in-depth knowledge of social science's ethnography to unfold quite an amazing story, from quite an amazing voice. The novel is destined to be a must read in classrooms, discussion groups, and book clubs."

—Leonard Cox, Producer, playwright, and award-winning, documentary filmmaker—River Films Senior Officer, Columbia University

"There is much talk about the 'novel of ideas'—*Zombie Seeds and the Butterfly Blues* is an illustration of the great power of this genre. It is about ideas certainly: our ideas about science, about nature, about history. But it is also a narrative about the idea of narratives: what stories can and should be able to do, whose stories get told clearly and whose must wait for others to re-tell them, and the dissatisfactions of stories that don't turn out the way we hoped.

As an excellent narrative encourages, I started to chart its relation to other narratives and designed multiple courses in my head about the role of narratives in and around science and biomedicine. I will be teaching *Zombie Seed and the Butterfly Blues* in courses with science and literature students as this is a story with much to offer students across the University.

As I read the concluding chapter, the daily news tells me that there are more lawsuits about herbicide resistant crops, more concern about genetically manipulated crops escaping the boundaries we hoped to set for them. I do hope that there are Delta Quinn's out there with the courage to find the stories that are not in the news, or at least more authors like Robin Clair who insist on the power of narrative in the age of technoscience."

—Dr. Joan Leach, Science Laureate Director of Teaching and Learning, English, Media Studies and Art History Convener, Science Communication Program, University of Queensland-Australia

"Storytellers are not onlookers in this battle; we are, if anything, its grand strategists. The dispute over genetic engineering involves facts, to be sure. But its parties disagree far more passionately over the story. They quarrel over the nature of the characters, over the plot, and over the editing. They also feud over the unknowable: the ending."

—Daniel Charles, author of *Lords of the Harvest*

DEDICATION

To Activists, Artists, and Awakening Zombies

… and to Soul-Searching Scientists

TABLE OF CONTENTS

PREFACE

In *Zombie Seed and the Butterfly Blues: A Case of Social Justice* students from a liberal arts class help Professor Delta Quinn and reporter, Caleb Barthes, uncover the political and corporate story behind the scientific development and implementation of the *zombie seed*. As the secrets of the seed are revealed, so are the secrets of Delta's tragic past which explain her desire to study the sequestered stories of domestic violence, which may lead the reader to ask whether there is a connection between cultural violence and interpersonal violence, and more importantly, whether such knowledge will awaken the zombie in all of us.

Socrates' oft quoted maxim—the *unexamined life is not worth living*—speaks to the current image of the zombie who walks through life without critically thinking, without addressing political issues, without participating in civil discourse or democratic entitlements. *Zombie Seed and the Butterfly Blues: A Case of Social Justice* is meant to engage the college student, to have students address and discuss issues of relevance to society at large. Whether in anthropology, business, communication, English, history, organizational communication, philosophy, political science, psychology, religion, rhetoric, sociology or women' studies the novel is intended to provide a teaching tool to professors who are looking for novel ways to awaken students.

Zombies are far more than a cultural cliché; they are a symbolic icon of crucial importance in the history and practice of oppression and resistance. As such, a zombie theme can be used quite constructively to explain important issues relevant to the college classroom. For instance, zombie stories have a historical, cultural and religious connection to the physical and mental brutality of slavery, especially related to Haiti. This same serious symbol has been used to perpetuate stereotypes of Africans and African diaspora. Overtime the zombie's symbolism was applied to the mind-numbing aspects of repetitive, tedious and monotonous labor of any kind—a symbol of workers' angst and alienation. The meaning behind the zombie symbol was expanded during the early 20th century. In 1932, the movie *White Zombie* introduced an additional element by casting a young, white woman as a character who is turned into a zombie by a white man who wants to marry her against her will. Adding white women to the already existing economic exploitation, racial oppression and sexual violence of Africans and their descendants made clear the sexual lust and licentiousness of the Haitian plantation owners and the expanding use of the zombie symbol.

Contemporary society is teeming with zombie movies, books, games and various paraphernalia. Young people, from high school to college students, are drawn to the zombie discourse. In part this zombie rhetoric captures their attention because it speaks to the mind-numbing aspects of the traditional educational system. There are reasons why the cannibalism associated with zombies is so often directed toward images of eating the human brain. College students fight against the zombie takeover and zombie apocalypse through symbolic games from internet and Xbox games to physically charged games of zombie tag. Students are acting out, performing their own resistance. Or are they? Zombie movies, games, and books also provide entertainment grounded in violence. This violence may provide a cathartic release, especially when humor is laid over the zombie thrill, but it may also encourage aggressive behavior when rewards are attached to the 'killing of the undead.' Whichever the case may be, zombies are a part of culture today and deserve to be discussed for their societal implications under the rubric of cultural studies. Using the zombie theme fosters such discussions in the college classroom.

Some professors may not have heard of academic novels and others may have never considered using supplemental texts in the college classroom. I have been using fiction and nonfiction books to stimulate discussion, increase knowledge and connect the drier textbook material to the real life of students for many years and with stunning results. But this is the first time I have written a novel to be read in the classroom and which I hope will have impact beyond the halls of academe.

I say "beyond" because some of the book selections I have made in the past have connected students with their parents in rather special ways. After sharing passages from Studs Terkel's book, *Working: People Talk About What They Do All Day and How They Feel About What They Do*, particularly the chapter entitled, *Who Built the Pyramids,* which is about a factory worker who is saving money to put his children through college so that they can have a better life, one student told me that he called home and thanked his parents for paying his tuition. Other students have told me that they have shared synopses of the books that we read in class with their parents and it opens dialogue and begins an exchange of ideas. Some of those books include *Down and Out in Paris and London* by George Orwell, *Lakota Woman* by Mary Ellen Crowdog (and Richard Erdoes), *Rivethead: Tales from the Assembly Line* by Ben Hamper and *Enrique's Journey,* a Pulitzer prize-winning accomplishment by Sonia Nazario. *Enrique's Journey* sparked a conversation between a student and her mother; the mother revealed the family history of immigration to her college-age daughter, a story the daughter had not before known. Most of the books that I have assigned have something to do with the meaning of work, work identity, or the role that organizations play in society and the influence that corporations wield. Social justice novels, like *The Jungle* by Upton Sinclair, are especially excellent sources for discussion in the classroom. I select these kinds of books because the courses I teach often deal with work, such as Organizational Communication, Diversity at Work and Rhetorical and Critical Approaches to Public Relations. I hope that professors teaching courses like sociology of work, industrial psychology, organizational behavior, and organizational ethics will find *Zombie Seed and the Butterfly Blues: A Case of Social Justice* an excellent means of stimulating classroom discussion. And although people do not live at work, they may take work home or they may take the rewards or the wounds of work into their personal lives. *Zombie Seed and the Butterfly Blues* includes dialectical stories of work: one story of how work changes the life of a young man to the detriment of those around him and another story of one man's love of his work that brings him great joy and closer to his wife and children. In other words, *Zombie Seed and the Butterfly Blues: A Case of*

Social Justice need not be restricted to courses related to work. Courses such as interpersonal communication, psychology, and women's studies classes may also benefit from the book's use as a supplemental text.

The protagonist of the novel, Professor Delta Quinn is described as an ethno-rhetorician who studies sequestered stories mostly from the world of work, but her studies lead to an overall portrayal of the world of work as a rhetorical creation and a cultural enterprise and professors from rhetoric and anthropology may find the book stimulating. I have designed a syllabus for the course Rhetoric in the Western World that uses the "zombie approach." In addition, one of the early studies that guided this book based on a small-farm, farm-family culture and the rhetorical construction of identity received the Best Article of the Year award from the ethnography division of the National Communication Association, supporting its possibilities for use in ethnography and rhetoric classes.

In addition, cultural diversity undergirds this book in multiple ways, from exploring the history and cultural heritage of Haiti to the religious intersections between voodoo and Christianity which come together through the lives of the characters in this novel and through Delta Quinn's revisionist narrative interpretation of the miracles and the magical aspects of religion. I believe *Zombie Seed and the Butterfly Blues: A Case of Social Justice* might stimulate dialogue if not debate in diversity and intercultural college classrooms, which was one of my goals in writing it.

Although all of this seems like a perfect fit for courses in the humanities, I believe there is more to *Zombie Seed and the Butterfly Blues* as it crosses the divide between liberal arts and the physical sciences. The books that I have assigned most recently include *The Boy who Harnessed the Wind* by William Kamkwamba and *The Immortal Life of Henrietta Lacks* by Rebecca Skloot, both of which provide us with true stories of how the physical sciences intersect with the humanities. *Zombie Seed and the Butterfly Blues: A Case of Social Justice* also unites these often bifurcated areas. For science is meant to touch and improve our lives, not alienate us from ourselves. Social problems cannot be so easily segregated these days.

We are no longer naïve concerning the arena in which social problems exist—they exist entangled within every aspect of society. And although we can and do address social problems within narrow parameters, and often times for good reasons, I suggest that we need to add a polysemic approach to our repertoire of literary educational tools. *Zombie Seed and the Butterfly Blues* is just such an educational-literary novel. Specifically, it crosses traditional academic boundaries. Unconstrained by the invisible barriers that separate science and liberal arts, *Zombie Seed and the Butterfly Blues* draws students into a world that demonstrates the interrelatedness of the narratives we live and the problems we face.

Interdisciplinary studies may provide the means to finding creative and alternative solutions to contemporary world problems, especially where social-political issues are entangled in the material remedies. This can only be achieved if a dialogue of social justice engages both the physical sciences and the liberal arts. Students of science and students of liberal arts have far too long been divided, not recognizing their interconnectedness. Liberal Arts students lament the technical jargon of the physical sciences and students of the physical sciences express dismissiveness concerning the Liberal Arts, not recognizing the role that anthropology, art, communication, economics, history, literature, philosophy, political science, religious studies, sociology and women's studies, for instance, play in science. These overlapping worlds have been treated as distinct for far too long. Bringing seemingly disparate fields together through novel approaches may give new insights into the entangled worlds in which we live, giving social justice a chance to surface and spread.

Zombie Seed and the Butterfly Blues: A Case of Social Justice is a novel informed by academic research which is grounded in narrative theory. As a scholar of narrative, I explore a wide variety of stories and their means to create reality, but I sincerely hope that what I have created here is an enticing story, and a good read that encourages dialogue concerning a controversial topic.

ACKNOWLEDGMENTS

My deepest appreciation to all of the authors listed in the bibliography, without their dedicated efforts my work would not have been possible. Visits to the Newberry Library and the Illinois State Museum Chicago Gallery located in the James R. Thompson Center were crucial to the novel and made possible by my spouse who never hesitated to go on these adventures with me. I am grateful to Judith Burson Lloyd Klauba, Associate Curator, Illinois State Museum Chicago Gallery for our conversation about the archived farmers' narratives. Many thanks to Ray Little for being Ray Little and allowing me to include him in the novel. My thanks go to Felicia Roberts for correcting my French; Jeffrey Ooms for input on publicity; Brian Britt for formatting and Diana Livingston for her assistance. I owe a huge debt of gratitude to Renée and Donald Bain who gave me advice on an earlier version. Their energy and passion for writing amazes me. Without their comments the novel would never have moved with such speed and coherence. I owe my entire family my gratitude as they encouraged me in numerous ways to complete this project—thank you, Tim, Cory, Calle and Shea and to my siblings, Candy, Kate, Jo, Betsy, Bob, Jim, and Drew. Special thanks to my sister, Elizabeth (Betsy) Alder, author of the *King's Shadow* and other books, for all the phone conversations filled with encouragement, grammar lessons and writing tips. I am ever so grateful to my partner, Tim, because of him this is a better book in so many ways—thank you for taking trips to Chicago with me, editing the manuscript and providing me with support. To those friends, family, colleagues, and students who encouraged me along the way, especially—Pam and Jim Finucane, Jill Vaught, Devika Chawla, Shirley Simpson, Marv Diskin, Ralph and Ginny Webb, Leonard Cox, Rebekah Fox, Deb Leiter Nyabuti, Isaac Holyoak, Tammy Halsema, Sarah Mooney, Sam and Heather McCormick, Carole Harris, Theon Hill and, of course, Jill Rudd—thank you. I am very grateful to Keith Berry who invited me to present my first study of a farm family at a preconference at the National Communication Association annual meeting, later invited me to co-author a special edition of *Cultural Studies ← →Critical Methodologies* with him, and nominated my work for recognition that led to my receiving the Best Article of the Year award for the study. In addition, Keith introduced me to Tony Adams who quickly put me in touch with Patricia Leavy, Series Editor for Sense Publishers. Patricia believed in my work unconditionally and her phenomenal spirit and keen eye in terms of editing made this book a sharper project, indeed. I am thrilled to have my work accepted for publication by this cutting-edge series on academic novels. To Peter de Liefde, founder and owner of Sense Publishers, I am grateful that he took a chance on an academic novel with the word *zombie* in the title. Great thanks to Bernice Kelly for her professional production management and for sharing her unique information about the type of butterfly seen on the cover of this book. Also, I would like to thank Purdue University for providing Human Subject clearance for this project and allowing it to be presented as either scholarly research or fiction. To my students, I say, thank you—your youthful spirits give me energy and your curiosity drives me to learn more. My gratitude would be incomplete without giving tribute to the farm-family whose story set the stage for the first study and acts as the backdrop to this book. However, their names must remain anonymous in order to protect their privacy. Finally, I would be remiss not to mention my parents, who encouraged me as an artist and a writer, may they rest in peace.

PRELUDE

In 1772, an Ethiopian carried a secret in the form of a seed so powerful that he would lay down his life rather than share it with the uninitiated. But his dire circumstances left him no choice. He had been schooled in the properties of the plant—the root, the stem, the leaves, the pollen, the seeds—so as to understand the medicinal contributions of each part. He had been instructed never to say the name of the plant aloud, but rather to simply call it *the butterfly* as if its power were that of a tiny creature rather than a tiger. It was not only disguised under the name of *the butterfly*, but it was also literally hidden from view. Ethiopian men of medicine never carried the butterfly seed in the open or even within an herb pouch; instead, upon ordination into the spiritual and physical medicinal arts, they sliced the heel of the sole of the left foot with a burning knife, inserted the seed, and tightly stitched the skin together. So it was for the Ethiopian who carried the seed hidden under his skin to this day, this deplorable day.

Now he lie thinking of the words he had been told so long ago— *this seed brings forth the plant that is the salvation of the people, if ever the people are faced with flood or famine or disease, plant this seed. It will restore life.*

The Ethiopian smelled death and decay all around him. He needed to pass the seed to the next generation before the ghosts invaded his body and swallowed his spirit. His only hope was the boy who lay shackled next to him.

The boy was neither Ethiopian nor Nubian. His facial features were not as delicate as an Ethiopian's, not as proud as a Nubian's and his body was more compact, although thin and bony from starvation, his frame was clearly wider, not long like an Ethiopian's body.

Head to feet, feet to head, the man and boy lay curled next to each other on a hard, wooden plank within the dark, dank confines of a slave ship. The ship rocked and pitched as did the elder's stomach. He, who was born of the line of the great King Piye, wretched repeatedly over the side of his plank bed. Naked and bruised, he

1

knew that his captors were not the captors of his world, where slaves were the result of battle and were freed every seven years to return to their families. No, he knew that the future was lost to him; his legacy would vanish. After all, he had disappointed himself and probably his parents—his Nubian mother and Ethiopian father—by his capture, by falling prey to a nefarious and pernicious plot, which had been simple, effective, and deceptive. He had been accosted by a wayfarer who sought his help. The traveler explained that his companion had taken ill only a short distance away—a kilometer or two—from the village. The dark stranger asked the man for medicine to help. Without hesitation the Ethiopian had grabbed his pouch and headed down the path with the stranger. Just outside of the village, the Ethiopian was struck by a blinding light from a blow to the back of his head.

He awoke hours later to find an ox's yoke about his neck, his hands bound in front of him, and he was linked to others who were likewise restrained. How many times had he told the children of the village not to wander off alone; he berated himself his error. Now, no descendants would honor him, nor could they even if they wanted to, for he knew, he would never be buried with his ancestors, no Abyssinia rose petals would decorate his grave. Nor would he ever again see the emerald-spotted wood doves, waterbucks and warthogs by sparkling pools of blue, nor gazelles and zebras racing across land. He knew this, he had heard stories; there is no return for those who disappear. He accepted his fate with a cold sweat, never to see his homeland, mother Africa, again.

Jerking upward abruptly, on a bony elbow, he reeled vomit without warning; foam lingered on his lips. Slumping backward, he realized that his death was imminent and that the boy next to him represented his only hope.

The chains that connected the shackles to the wooden posts were long enough to allow the priest of an auspicious heritage to extract the seeds from their hiding places; his hair, his ears, his nose, his navel and so on. This is where he had hidden the contents of his pouch after his capture at an opportune moment when no one watched him. Now, in the slave ship that rocked and heaved, he pulled the seeds from their hiding places. With each extraction he

2

placed the seeds into the corresponding orifices of the boy; with each seed came a word of instruction, in a language that the boy didn't understand. The older man continued nonetheless to burrow into the boy's hair, burying seeds and talking to him until only one seed remained to be exchanged. This one seed, which had been sewn into the calloused heel of the man's foot, carried the power to resurrect a people, but the man had no knife with which to free it.

Clanking the heavy iron shackles as he pulled his frail legs tightly toward his swollen and aching abdomen, he tore at his calloused skin with his fingernails; but his fingernails broke away at the tip. Frustrated but intent, he stretched his legs, dug deeper, scraping the nubs of his toenails of his right foot against the spot on the bottom of his left heel in hopes of freeing the final seed, but the calloused tissue was too tough, his toenails too brittle and frail; what was left of the toenails crumbled like dried parchment when grated against his foot. After several attempts, the waning priest fell back exhausted. A small cry escaped his lips.

The boy watched. Although he understood not a single word the older man had uttered to him, he clearly knew the man's plight. Without a sound, the boy pulled himself closer to the man's feet. The priest could feel the boy's breath on the arch of his foot, and then his heel.

The boy ferociously bit the man's foot.

Gasping with shock and reeling with pain, the captive's body arched, revealing the underside of his briny-covered body, the salty sea powder disguised a once bold figure of a man, a black man, who did not cry out. The ship heaved and moaned; the planks creaked and screamed; the waves slapped and beat the sides of the ship. The man remained silent; he swallowed hard as the boy continued to bite. The boy gnashed his teeth, until the man's foot bled forth the final seed. At last, the boy, with blood trickling from his white teeth, lifted his head with pride and showed the older man the salvaged seed that sat between the tips of his teeth.

With that painful pleasure, the priest from the line of Piye nodded gently to the boy before lowering his eye lids for the last time.

PART I

CHAPTER 1

Tuesday, August 10, 2010—West Lafayette, IN

A jarring force accompanied by a loud bang sent the blue 2004 Honda Accord flying forward. Professor Delta Quinn barely had time to react as she saw herself fast zeroing in on the rear end of a semi. She instinctively turned the wheel to the left with surprising speed. With the wheel turned sharply, the car flew past the semi and sailed over the edge of State Route 52 above the median—airborne over a wide, deep gulley. Delta gripped the wheel of the car as it soared through the air and banged back to earth. Bouncing uncontrollably, the squat compact careened upwards and onto the other side of the median, landing directly in the path of oncoming traffic. As the car banged to the ground, the driver's head slammed against the headrest.

Delta felt as if she were falling downward, as if she were falling from a cliff on a moonlit evening, darkness surrounded her. For a moment, she succumbed to the gentle, seductive warmth of the darkness, like a bedroom in which the draperies had been carefully drawn together sealing out the light, allowing one to slip into nocturnal dreams. Downward, downward, ever downward. She felt a vague sensation that she should stop this downward trajectory. Although the car seemed nonexistent and the professor felt as if she were free floating in space, she nonetheless attempted to press her foot against what she thought was a brake. It was all so strange. The velvety, dream-like darkness enveloped her; the physical sensations existed as if in her mind only; she floated untethered from reality, while pressing her foot against nothing. Indeed, her foot wasn't even moving.

As if awakening from a dream, she heard a rapping on the car window that grew to a loud knocking. A voice called to her as a pain shot through her right side, a real pain. She tried to lift her arms but they refused to cooperate; they barely moved. She struggled as if trying to get out of bed after a long illness—disconcertingly weak. She reached for her right side.

"Are you okay?" She heard the voice from the other side of the window.

"I, I'm ... the seatbelt, it's hurting my ribs," she stumbled over the words.

"No, stay put," the voice told her. "I need to direct oncoming traffic around your car. Don't move until I tell you."

Delta let her head slip gently back against the headrest, not noticing any pain from the presently emerging lump. *On coming traffic? What oncoming traffic, s*he wondered.

Slowly she began to feel a sense of clarity return. *It's really quite bright*, she realized. *A sunny afternoon. Not dark at all.* She attempted to lift her arms again; this time they moved. Slowly. A dream-like sensation lingered. She rolled the window down and caught the fragrance of English lavender and wild sage that grew along the highway as it wafted on the breeze of the late August air. Milkweed plants that hugged the guard rail had lost their summer flowers—the pink pom poms of spring. A monarch butterfly fluttered above the green leaves. Delta's thoughts continued to flutter as well in languid lucidity, landing here and there. *Where am I? Wasn't someone just speaking to me?* She breathed in the fragrance of the fields again; the lavender smelled soft. Everything else evaporated. She closed her eyes again. She didn't hear the sirens of the police car nor did she have an awareness of the ambulance's flashing lights as it arrived. She had no conception of how much time elapsed before hearing another voice.

"Are you okay?" A new voice asked. The car door was being opened. Regaining her strength, she released the seat buckle and swung her legs out tentatively.

"Yes, I think so," she said putting a hand to the back of her head, amazed at how quickly a lump had sprouted on her scalp under her dark hair.

"Do you know what year it is?"

She hesitated. "... 2010." It sounded right, but she felt as though she had guessed the answer.

"Do you know where you are?"

She thought for a moment, "No, I'm not sure, but I think I was on my way home from work."

"Where do you work?"

Again the young woman considered the question put to her, "… I'm a professor. I work at Purdue University."

"Who's the president of the United States?" *Odd question to be asking*, she thought. "It's not Bush," she answered, stalling for more time, unable to recall the President's name.

"No, it's not Bush," the man agreed with her. Again she waited, pursed her lips, longing for a lucid answer, but her memory felt fuzzy. She struggled to find the answer. The man turned away.

"No, wait. It's Obama," she answered without further hint of hesitation.

"Let me help you out. I'm Sheriff Turner," he said offering his hand to her. "Do you think you can walk?" The sheriff had a plain face, simple features, nothing too big or too small, nondescript, mostly with thinning brown hair the color of chaff. He looked like a man who worked out in order to eat hefty meals of meat and potatoes, resulting in a thick waist that tested his belt, but also gave him a sturdy stance, rooted in a Midwestern mien.

"Yes, I think so," she answered, taking the sheriff's hand to steady herself. He retrieved her purse and handed it to her. She slung it over her shoulder and flipped her long dark hair from under the strap before taking a step. Delta wobbled a little as the sheriff and the EMT, who had just arrived, escorted her to the waiting ambulance on the opposite side of the median. She was dressed in cream-colored, Katherine Hepburn-style trousers with a brown silk blouse and heels that were not exactly made for hiking up or down the grassy knoll of the gulley. No one would describe her shoes as sensible, even on a good day. Upon reaching the ambulance, the medic assisted her up and into the back of the portable emergency room where a second medic felt the back of her head with his latex-gloved hand. He then provided the professor with an ice pack after discovering the large lump under her sable-colored hair.

"Yeah, she's got a bump all right," the first medic told the second.

"Concussion?"

"Probably."

They offered to drive her to the hospital, but Delta declined. Instead, she pulled her cell phone from her purse and pressed *favorites*. The medics looked on disapprovingly. They listened as Professor Quinn spoke: "Mona, … Yes … Have you left the office yet…Could you do me a favor? I've been in a bit of an accident. No, no I'm fine, but the car isn't … Could you pick me up and give me a lift home … State Route 52, close to the bridge … Ten minutes … You're an angel." The disappointed medics gave the professor less attention now; they had had a rather boring day; using the siren again would have given them something more to talk about later. They were hoping, at the very least, to drive her to the hospital.

"You should really have that bump looked at," the EMT who had helped her across the street told her.

"Thanks, but I'm okay, really. I just need a good night's sleep."

"Unh, unh. That's not gonna happen," the other EMT, the one with a twang to his voice, told her. "You have a concussion. You need to be checked every two hours for 24 hours. You got to have a friend check on you. Wake you up every two hours."

Delta slumped. She hadn't slept well in over a week: first, she had been at a conference in NYC and she never slept well in hotel rooms—unfamiliar places always made her uncomfortable; second, the return flight had been delayed several hours—airports are not exactly designed for dreaming; and worse yet, she missed her ride back from the airport. When she finally did get a chance to sleep she received annoying prank phone calls; somebody kept calling and hanging up. But most disconcerting of all were threatening messages left on her voice mail. She had angrily erased them. All she wanted was one decent night of serious sleep. She sighed.

"You got somebody to check on you?" She heard the EMT asking.

She nodded as she thought of Mrs. Rushka, her neighbor, who was the kind of person—motherly, nurturing, who'd gladly check on Delta, but Delta being Delta probably wouldn't bother the elderly woman. She knew that Mona would check on her, if she were to ask, but she probably wouldn't do so. *It's just a bump on the head.*

The medics let Delta sit in the back of the ambulance as the county sheriff took the report. He had used his own cruiser to block traffic as he moved her vehicle off the road. When he had returned he asked for her "driver's license," which she gave him; "registration," which she told him was in the glove compartment; and "insurance," for which she produced a card and a number. The sheriff asked a few general questions before actually inquiring about the details of the accident.

"What happened exactly?" He handed the keys to the car to her, a car which now sat so brutally beaten that it would be dragged away like a losing pugilist from the ring—coach and trainer under each arm, toes dragging on the ground. She sighed.

"Someone rear ended me. That's all I know, Sheriff."

"Wow, the back of your car is pressed like apples to cider," the second EMT announced. "Jimmy, did you see?" He addressed his partner.

"Yeah, yeah, I saw. Lady, you're going to need a cemetery plot for that little coup," the other EMT looked at his watch and gave his medical opinion of the car, pronouncing, "Time of death, 4:20 p.m." Delta sighed again at the thought of it.

Turning her attention back to the sheriff, she asked, "Who helped me before you got here?"

"That was the trucker. He heard the bang and saw your car go veering off from his rear view mirror."

"Did he see who hit me?"

"A yellow Hummer, newer model, but he didn't get the license plate. After hitting you, the driver took off."

She readjusted the ice pack, switching it to her left hand and warming her right hand by slipping it between her thighs. Water condensation dripped down the back of her neck. Her hair felt matted. She began to recall a few details—the yellow Hummer in her rear view mirror, how it seemed to have been accelerating toward her, and turning the wheel to keep from hitting the semi in front of her.

"It'll be pretty hard to hide a yellow Hummer, especially one with blue paint on it. We've got a bulletin out on it," the sheriff assured her. He stepped out of the ambulance as a second sheriff's car arrived. After conferring with the deputy he climbed back into the ambulance to talk with Delta. "There aren't any tread marks,

Professor Quinn. My guess: they weren't paying attention, texting maybe, and didn't see it coming."

Maybe, Delta thought.

Less than ten more minutes passed when static, coming from the sheriff's walkie-talkie, interrupted their conversation. Delta listened as the crackling voice on the other end informed the sheriff that a patrol officer in the next town had already found the Hummer at an exit near I-65. Abandoned. The officer had called in the plates and was waiting to hear whether it was a stolen vehicle.

"Likely it's a stolen vehicle, abandoned by thieves after they hit you," the sheriff said, shaking his head. "Sorry."

"Couldn't you try to get prints off the steering wheel?" she asked.

"Prints? Not for a hit and run with a minor concussion for an injury. Actually, the county doesn't even have a lab. It'd be six months before we'd get results back from fingerprinting. This isn't CSI, you know. Anyway, it was probably some joy riding kid and the county doesn't have the money to track a teenage hoodlum. Sorry."

The professor slumped. She wanted to tell Sheriff Turner that she didn't think it was just a hit and run, but she was pretty sure he'd think she was crazy if she told him what she was thinking.

Somebody intentionally ran me off the road. They could've killed me. Whoever it is, I think they're doing this because of my research. Research? What kind of research, the sheriff would ask. Narrative research, I'd answer. Narratives? Like bedtime stories, he'd say with an incredulous look on his face. Sort of, I'd say, but more like sequestered stories. I think maybe I've stumbled onto one that's more dangerous than I realized; I just don't know which one. Or why. Worse yet, I don't have a scrap of evidence. I never should've deleted those voice mails? The only thing I know is that all this started right after I returned from New York City eleven days ago. I know that's not much help. No, I doubt very much that the sheriff would believe me. And why should he?

"Do you need a ride home?" Sheriff Turner asked.

"No," the professor said. "I think that's my ride pulling up now."

CHAPTER 2

Wednesday, August 11, 2010—West Lafayette, IN

"How's your head? Are you feeling okay?" Mona Barthes asked her academic advisor.

"I've had better days," Delta answered and then followed by thanking her graduate advisee for the ride as she settled into the front seat of the little green Geo.

"No problem, professor," Mona replied.

"And thank you for picking me up last night after the accident, too."

"Really, no need to mention it. So, what's the status on your car?" Mona asked as she drove down the road.

"I think the insurance company will declare it totaled."

"And you?"

"I guess I made out better than the car. Just a minor concussion."

"Maybe you should have stayed at home," Mona suggested.

"No, no. I need to get a few more things ready for classes. I'll be fine."

"Do you want me to help you?" Mona adjusted the rearview mirror as she spoke.

Delta didn't answer. Instead, her thoughts drifted to the threatening phone calls she had received over the last week or so, yesterday's car accident, Sheriff Turner's questions, the EMTs' comments, and the chat she'd had with her neighbor Mrs. Rushka.

"A man came by to see you, dear," Mrs. Rushka had said.

"Really? Who was it?"

"He didn't leave his name."

"What did he look like?"

"Look like? Well, he looked a little blurry to me. I didn't have my glasses on when he came to the door." Mrs. Rushka had been of little help to Delta as she tried to figure out who had stopped by to see her and whether it had anything to do with the strange events of the last week and a half. *Why would anyone send threatening messages or try*

to run me off the road? Maybe, 'the accident' was just an accident.
Maybe, I'm just being paranoid.

"Professor Quinn, … Delta … Delta!" The voice persistently grew louder until Delta responded. She turned. Now, facing Mona, who looked at her with concern, Delta apologized.

"I'm sorry. What did you say?"

"I asked whether you want me to help you with anything today?"

"Oh, no thanks. I'll be fine. I've just had a lot on my mind lately."

"Obviously. Do you want to talk about it?"

"No, it's nothing."

"I've seen you preoccupied before, but not like this," Mona pressed as she drove them west on State Road 26. "Usually you're preoccupied with your research or—"

"Let's change the subject."

"Fine," Mona said with mild exasperation. "How was the conference? It was an interdisciplinary conference, wasn't it? Rhetoric, anthropology and economics?"

"Yes. It went well. A few people asked for the paper."

"Did you get any phone numbers?" Mona asked in a teasing tone.

"I gave my business card to one man when he asked about the study, but he never called. I wouldn't have gone out with him anyway. I mean, he was a total stranger."

"When you're at a conference you're allowed to get a little wild," the younger woman encouraged her advisor. "So you talked to him after the presentation?" Mona said with curiosity.

"Yes, he wanted to know more about the study."

"The one about the farm family?"

"Yes."

"Hmm, was he from Rhetoric, Anthropology or Economics?"

"He never said. And then I lost track of him. He sort of disappeared into the crowd," Delta said without emphasis, dismissing the event and memory of it.

"Yeah, I bet he wanted a date and got too nervous to ask you. Was he handsome?

"I don't know, maybe. He had blond hair, medium height, thirtyish; he was okay."

"I wish I could have gone with you. I love New York City, but don't tell my brother I said that; his loyalty lies with Chicago."

Mona glanced over at Delta expecting a reply, but Delta had become quiet again, which worried Mona. Delta's thoughts were clearly in another place and time. Mona glanced again from the road back to her advisor—the woman with dark wispy hair that fell in lustrous strands over her shoulders gazed out the front window; her green eyes, which usually seemed bright and engaging, were now focused far away, making her appear distant and preoccupied. Delta had been Mona's advisor for nearly a year and still Mona felt as if Delta was a mystery, always helpful, but never very forthcoming about herself. She had shared that she had been from a large Irish-Catholic family one day when the two of them had met over a drink at a local patio bar to talk about Mona's fellowship possibilities. Holidays were coming up and Mona merely asked if the professor had a large family and if she would see them for the holidays. Mona had always been curious about the way the professor had said it: "I came from a large Irish-Catholic family," she had said with her voice trailing away, as if it were in the past. No amount of nudging would get her to open up further about her family. Beyond that, Mona knew almost nothing other than academic information about Delta. For now, Mona decided to focus on the fact that someone with a concussion should be watched carefully. Thus, the advisee drew her advisor back from her reverie with unimportant and somewhat annoying small talk, "So what are you teaching this semester?"

Delta took a moment to respond. "Undergraduate classes— Diversity and Narratives at Work COM 328 and Rhetoric and Public Relations COM 495."

"You almost make me wish I could be an undergraduate again. I love your stuff on narratives, especially sequestered narratives," she fawned.

"Thanks. But you need to focus on your dissertation," Delta advised amiably.

"I did say *almost* make me want to take another class," Mona smiled as she emphasized her point. "Honestly, I'm really glad to have courses behind me and when the dissertation is done it'll be like a weight off my shoulders. Hey, I never asked you what your dissertation was about."

"A whistleblower and what she faced after revealing unethical practices at her workplace."

"Fascinating stuff—sequestered stories. Did you publish the dissertation results?" But before Delta answered, Mona interrupted her own train of thought; after all, she was just trying to keep her advisor engaged when she remembered something else. "Oh, by the way, we have a faculty meeting today," Mona announced.

"How did you know that?" Delta asked.

"I'm the grad student representative this semester, remember?"

"Oh yes, I had forgotten."

"It's at 2:30, but I don't know what room we're in," Mona added.

"No problem. We'll look it up when we get to my office."

"Do you want a ride home after the meeting?"

"Like I said yesterday, you're an angel."

"Not me, I'm not even religious. Actually, I'm ..."

Delta's thoughts drifted again and she lost track of what Mona was saying as they continued driving toward Purdue University. She kept thinking of the threatening phone call, 'the accident,' and her research. The thought of the accident motivated her to turn her head to see if anyone was following them, as she did a sudden pain shot through her neck and shoulder. "Son of a ..." she said grabbing the side of her neck.

"You okay?"

"No," she confided at last gently stretching her neck to one side. Delta was exhausted, in pain, and confused about everything. "I don't think the accident was an accident." She finally blurted out.

"What? Why not?"

"Before the accident, I received a number of calls, but the person on the other end kept hanging up." She held her neck.

"Who was it?"

"I don't know. But there was definitely somebody there. I could hear breathing. And then the person hung up."

"A perv," Mona concluded.

"Maybe, but on Monday I got another call. And ..."

"And?"

"And this time a man's voice on the other end said, *Stop what you're doing.*"

"Stop what you're doing," Mona repeated. "That's weird. What did he mean by that?" Delta shook her head gently and the dangly earrings that intermingled with her midnight-colored hair, tussled from side to side.

"And then, the very next day, Tuesday—yesterday—BAM, the car accident. I'm run off the road by somebody driving a stolen vehicle. A bright yellow Hummer, no less. I have a bad feeling about this."

"A bright yellow Hummer," Mona repeated. "See that's the thing. Who steals a Hummer just to run somebody off the road? And bad guys don't steal brightly-colored anything. It's probably just a coincidence," Mona comforted Delta. She paused and then added, "But it is curious." Retracting her reassurance, she finally asked, "Did you save the phone message?"

"No, I didn't think of that. I guess I just wanted it to go away."

"Probably nothing," Mona returned to her first assessment of the situation.

After parking the car, Mona noticed the stiffness with which Delta moved and so she helped her with her bag of books. "Here, I'll get those," she said taking the bag from Delta and swinging it over her shoulder. As they walked toward Beering Hall, Delta navigated the conversation away from her own troubles and instead engaged Mona in conversation about her classes. After reaching her second floor office in the west wing of the building, Delta unlocked the door.

"Thanks, Mona. You can just set those over there," she said of the books. "Oh, and let me look up where the faculty meeting is," Delta added as she sat down at her computer and began clicking the keys. She put in her password and waited for the default page to appear and for her email to pop up. Mona now looked over the professor's shoulder. That's when they both saw it—the mysterious message:

CEASE AND DESIST!

YOUR RESEARCH IS DANGEROUS.

"Are you seeing this?" A startled Delta asked Mona.

"I am. I am," Mona reassured her. Then to their surprise, the message dissolved into a million little pixels as did Delta's hope of having evidence that confirmed that the events of the last few days were more than mere coincidence.

"Oh my gosh," Mona exclaimed. "You were right. Somebody doesn't want you to do your research. That accident wasn't an accident!"

Delta swallowed hard as her stomach nearly lifted into her throat and then she pressed her hands against her diaphragm, holding herself together. Now that Mona had witnessed it, it seemed all too real. There was no denying what was happening to her.

"You should report this to the police," Mona told her, "and to the CT people, too."

Delta couldn't stop staring at the computer screen where the message had been, a place where the frazzled dots had fizzled into nothingness. A blue screen of death appeared before her. It took a moment for Delta to recover, and then she turned to Mona.

"Okay," she said composing herself long enough to assure Mona that she would indeed call the campus police and the Computer Technology Services Center and added, "But let's keep this between us, for now." Her words seemed reasonable but her voice sounded a bit unsteady and her leg jittered up and down as she spoke. "Okay?"

"Sure," Mona promised, "You mean until you know who's behind this?"

"Exactly. So for now, we should both get back to work. There's a lot to do before classes start." Delta wanted nothing more than to figure this out and have her life return to normal. Actually, she wanted the whole issue to just disappear, but she knew that Mona was right; she would have to call the police. The problem wouldn't go away on its own. Delta sent Mona on her way after thanking her one more time for the rides and assuring her that she would call the police. And then she shut her office door.

CHAPTER 3

Wednesday, August 11, 2010—New York City

Robert Cornelius Brown sat waiting in the comfortable, burgundy-colored leather booth at La Fia's, an upscale Italian restaurant in mid-Manhattan. He had barely lifted the glass of water to his lips, when his old friend Jason Slaughtery walked through the door and removed his sunglasses to allow his eyes to adjust to the dim light. Brown gave a slight wave of his hand to indicate his presence. Slaughtery walked to the table. Brown stood to greet him.

"Downtown Bobby Brown," Jason Slaughtery addressed his friend and slapped his hand into his old college room-mate's hand, and then with a turn of his wrist, the slap became a hardy handshake. The nickname—'Downtown'—had been given to Bobby Brown because he lived in and for Lower Manhattan—the downtown business district of New York City; Bobby Brown breathed in Wall Street and never wanted to exhale.

"How 'bout them Yankees!" Slaughtery added. In return, 'Downtown' grasped his friend by the shoulder, extending their handshake into a manly hug.

"You bet, you gotta love them Yankees."

Jason glanced around before sitting down.

"Nice place," Jason decided.

"It baffles me," Brown said returning to his seat across from his friend.

"How so?" Jason asked stretching an arm across the back of the booth.

"An Italian restaurant owned by a Japanese investor. What's this global world coming to, my friend?'

"Fusion?"

"Something like that." Brown smiled.

The server arrived and delivered a second glass of water along with a rote script. "My name is Emily. I'll be taking your order today. Would you care for a drink?"

Bobby Brown nodded for Jason to order first. Brown would clearly be picking up the tab and it appeared that he could well afford it, even if Slaughtery ordered top shelf booze. Dressed in a Giorgio Armani suit with signature-style Forzier tie, Bobby clashed with his more casually-dressed friend. It's not that Jason Slaughtery didn't have the money, he just preferred a more casual, rock star, jeans-and-a-jacket-look. In addition, Bobby Brown's copper-colored skin and shaved head contrasted with Jason's naturally-light complexion and full head of blond hair. For all their differences, they shared a love for fast money, gambling, the stock market, sports, beautiful women and scotch.

"Well, Emily, I think a scotch on the rocks would quench my thirst. Make it Johnny Walker Blue."

"I'll have the same," Brown told the waitress; not overly concerned about his choice, he had other things on his mind. The waitress disappeared.

"Sorry I had to ask for your help with this project on such short notice. But I had to go out of town over the weekend." Brown told his friend.

"What's her name?" Slaughtery asked. Bobby Brown smiled.

"You know me too well."

"So, how are you handling the heat?" Jason asked Bobby.

"Do you mean the sweltering August humidity, the state of the economy, or the company's reputation?"

"Your choice," Jason Slaughtery quipped with a smile as the waitress returned with a tray and two drinks.

"May I take your order?" She asked.

"Just drinks today, sweetheart." Bobby Brown had already forgotten her name. She scooped up the menus. Brown raised his glass in unison with his friend as the waitress departed.

"Always good to see you, my friend. Business or not," Jason told Bobby Brown.

"Likewise."

Slaughtery sipped the refreshing scotch and felt the cool ice cubes against his lips. He then put the side of the glass against his forehead. "It's a hot one."

"Indeed. So how did it go?"

"It must be tough running interference for the company you work for."

"It's a steady paycheck, my friend. You should try it."

"I like the freedom of freelance, taking whatever job appeals to me at the time."

"You could work for us full-time, if you ever decided that's what you want. RichField Corporation is always looking for public relations investigators that they can rely on."

"Is that what they call it? Public Relations Investigations? That's precious." Slaughtery took another sip of his drink.

"Okay, fine. So what were you able to find out about the professor?"

He took out a flip notebook from the inside of his jacket pocket and began to read. "She stayed at the conference hotel. Woke up at—

"Are you kidding me?"

"What?"

"You still use paper notes?"

"I'm not a techno-phobe; note pads can't be hacked."

"Okay, go on."

"As I was saying, she stayed at the conference hotel; woke up at 7:00 a.m.; masturbated for … oh, no, wait, that was me."

Brown not only cracked a smile, but laughed at his friend's joke. Slaughtery was pleased with himself.

"Okay, on the level." This time he pulled his phone from his pocket and pulled up his digital notes. "She really did stay at the conference hotel. Arrived Friday afternoon. Took a walk around the city after checking in, went back to her room early. Saturday she attended two panel sessions, before presenting her own paper." Jason glanced up at the serious looking Bobby Brown. "I deserve combat pay for sitting through ultra-boring, academic presentations."

"Bore me. What did she say?"

"You can listen to the whole thing if you like. I taped it."

"Summarize the highlights for me. What does she know? What did she report?"

"That's two different things. She didn't provide her full paper. It's coming out this week in an academic journal. The bad news, what she reported on does indeed hint at, but not confirm, that something fishy is going on in the seed and chemical area of agriculture, although she didn't name RichField specifically, as she used pseudonyms throughout, it might not be difficult to connect the dots to them and their illegally testing genetically-modified organisms and possibly dangerous or at least questionable chemical compounds in U.S. farm fields. Oh and she also quoted the farmer as saying the government ag reports are falsified in favor of big corporations."

Brown wiped perspiration from his upper lip. "Pseudonyms, that much is good. Did she have any proof or can it be a he said/she said?"

"Strictly he said/she said. Are these the same farms that you and I visited as 'investigators,' a year or so ago?"

"I think so. And if so, in that case, I may need your help with damage control."

"To be honest with you, I think her focus was elsewhere. She's a rhetorical ethnographer."

"A what?"

"Ethno-rhetorician, something like that. Does it matter?"

"You tell me."

"She's focused on humanities. She's interested in rhetoric and the construction of identity. In this case, how farmers frame who they are through the stories that they tell. Discursive issues. Harmless stuff."

"Listen to you? 'Rhetoric and the construction of identity'! " This time Brown leaned back with a smug smile on his face.

"I took notes, remember?"

"We might have to do something about her."

"Like what?" Slaughtery sounded defensive.

"You know, destroy the originals … or her credibility."

"Really, I think it's harmless stuff. And don't forget she used pseudonyms; she never used the actual name of the company. RichField should be safe."

"Is she pretty?"

"Yes, but—

"Did you get her number?"

"Yes."

Brown shook his head at his friend. "Don't let your dick do the thinking." Then he leaned forward, "Did the thought cross your mind that pseudonyms come from original names. She knows more than you think, maybe more than she realizes, but I suspect, either way, we'll get word to 'investigate' further. Possibly a road trip. Are you up for that or was she so pretty that you can't think straight?" 'Downtown' suddenly appeared as if he had an epiphany.

"Oh God, did you sleep with her?"

"No, for chrissake Bobby, I'm more professional than that."

"Did you talk to her?"

"Yeah."

"What did you say?"

"I said—Your research is fascinating and you really seem to care about the farm family you studied. I'm interested in reading more. Could I have a copy of your paper? "

"That's it?"

"That's it. And for the record, I do think she genuinely cares about those people."

"Don't get sucked in. She cares about herself. She's no different from us. You know what she cares about? She cares about getting published. Think about it. Was she back in the fields actually helping that family or was she just talking about them at some conference, where nobody really gives a shit, giving a presentation, racking up vita hits for tenure; get my point?"

Slaughtery sighed, realizing that his friend was probably right.

"Now, are you in or not? I think I'll need help if we have to travel back to the heartland."

"Of course, if the money is right."

"That's my boy. Yes, the money will be solid."

"In that case, it sounds like old times. By the way, how did you know about her research before it was presented at the conference or published in the journal?"

"RichField keeps people on retainer, simply to keep us abreast of these kinds of things."

Jason thought for a moment, "You mean someone close to her?"

"Close enough. Somebody at the university, I think."

"You don't know who for sure?"

"Actually, I got the feeling that we might be the backup on this project. I'm not sure how corporate found out about her research. Let me listen to some of the tape." Brown held out his hand. Slaughtery tapped an icon on his phone, turned the sound up slightly, set the phone on the table for Brown to hear.

"Fast forward if you want. The stuff about corporate evil is near the end." Slaughtery slid out of the booth and headed for the men's room.

As soon as Slaughtery was out of sight, Brown took the phone and tapped a different icon, quickly selected the word 'contacts,' scanned for Delta Quinn's phone number and then added it to his own list of contacts before Jason returned.

CHAPTER 4

Wednesday, August 11, 2010—West Lafayette, IN

Worry was unbecoming on Delta; she didn't wear it well. Although she pulled her phone out of her purse, she didn't dial the police. Instead she sat, considered what she would say to the police and twisted her lower lip between her forefinger and thumb. She continued to rotate her lower lip into contorted shapes as she thought, *Who? Which research? Why? How would any of this make sense to the police?* It didn't even make sense to Delta who finally stopped twisting her lip. She set her phone aside and turned to her computer. She needed more time to think, or to not think about it.

She managed to get her fingers to the keyboard to type her syllabus by telling herself to *focus, focus, focus, get one done and then call the police.* But as she looked down at the keyboard she discovered her fingers were trembling in fearful anticipation of a possible new message that might come across her screen as well as the possibility that all her work files may have been erased; she wasn't sure which thought frightened her more. "Fortitude," she said forcing her fingers to type. She logged on again. This time her documents came up on the screen. She scanned quickly. Her files appeared as usual. She sighed in relief. Her eyes avoided the email; she moved the cursor and clicked.

She flipped through her calendar, checked on books—required and recommended, typed the tentative schedules and then the descriptions of the term paper and projects into her syllabus. At the bottom of the last page, she typed information about what to do in case of an emergency. Once she had finished the first syllabus she felt steadier, more in control. She took a deep breath, squared her shoulders and reached for the phone.

Even still her voice cracked a little as she told campus police her story and their nonchalance had a disquieting effect on her. "Cease and desist, you say, couldn't that have been sent to you by accident?

Maybe that's why the pixels dissolved. You should probably talk to the CT people. But we can take a report if you want."

The next ten minutes were allocated to the police report, taken over the phone, by a less than enthusiastic officer. Delta took another deep breath before calling CT as she expected to receive the same treatment. To the contrary, the CT people were definitely concerned about the pixels dissolving and maybe a little intrigued about the possibility of someone "accidentally" accessing her computer, but Delta realized that neither the campus police nor the computer techies seemed to be concerned about the content of the message or her safety. Only Mona had voiced genuine concern. *Maybe*, she thought, *I'm making too much of it. Maybe, the police are right.*

By 2:15 she was relieved to be attending a faculty meeting. *It should be the same old droll*, she thought, *a welcome to the academic year, announcements about the budget being cut again, introductions of new counselors and the new librarian liaison.* For the first time, the idea of listening to the mundane and annually repetitive orientation seemed very inviting. After asking the departmental secretary where the meeting would be held, Delta took the stairs down to the first floor classroom where the faculty was gathering. Mona Barthes was waiting for her outside the room.

"Delta, did you call the police?" Mona asked in a whisper. Delta Quinn nodded. "And?" Mona demanded.

"And they took a report,"

"What about the computer techies? Did you call them?"

"They said they could restore my email by this afternoon; it should be up and running again before the meeting is over. It would seem it's pretty hard to get through university fire walls and even more difficult to actually destroy somebody's research. They also didn't seem too concerned about the whole thing. They decided it was some prankster or a misdirected email."

The faculty meeting was beginning and the two young women took seats next to each other. The head of the department was noticeably absent. His second in charge, the Assistant Head Rory Cane stood in the front of the room, calling the meeting to order.

"Welcome to the new school year," he said, notebook and pen in hand. Next to Rory Cane stood a middle-aged man, trim with well-clipped hair; he waited to be introduced. Faculty members glanced from Rory Cane to the newcomer. The stranger stood quite at ease, one hand in his pocket, as he waited.

"You may have heard that John has been asked by the provost to lead a small delegation of faculty to China to discuss the possibility of opening a sister school in Beijing. He'll be gone for most of the semester. In his absence, Dr. Walter Steath has agreed to fill in. Dr. Steath is from Cornell University. His degrees, from Harvard and the London School of Economics, are in political economy. As you may know, Harvard retired its rhetoric program many years ago and is currently reconsidering that decision. They've asked Dr. Steath to explore the rhetoric units at Northwestern, IU and our own Purdue University and in turn Dr. Steath has agreed to oversee the department and advise us on grant getting opportunities, while he is in the Midwest. With that said, I'll turn the meeting over to Dr. Steath."

"Thank you, Rory, ..." The Acting-Acting Head of the Department said this as if he and Rory were old friends. The faculty faced this sudden regime change with silent, but serious curiosity, some shifted in their seats, others glanced at one another, but none said a word as Dr. Walter Steath began talking.

"It's a pleasure to ..."

This meeting was far from the usual ritual that Delta had predicted. Mona leaned over and started to whisper something to her advisor, but Delta gently waved her off, not wanting to talk while the new and somewhat enigmatic visitor was speaking. Besides, she could guess what Mona wanted to ask, something about the day's strange circumstances, which seemed to be getting stranger by the minute.

"... Yes, as Rory mentioned Harvard closed its rhetoric unit nearly one hundred years ago and we are just now rethinking that decision. No one ever accused us of moving too fast," he said with a smile. The faculty laughed at Dr. Steath's little joke.

"At any rate," he continued. "I promise not to get in your way while I'm here and as Acting-Head of the Department I see my duties as mostly signing the bureaucratic paperwork." He flashed another congenial smile. Then in one very smooth motion he extended his left arm just enough to raise his jacket and shirt sleeve to reveal a wrist watch. He turned his wrist over, checked the time, and turned to Rory Cane.

"Dr. Steath has to get settled in and he has a meeting with the Provost in a few minutes. So, well, welcome to the department," Rory said, "and I'm sure we'll all look forward to getting to know you in the weeks ahead." With that said Dr. Steath nodded to the group and strode out of the classroom. Rory picked up the thread of the conversation, making announcements for the up-coming semester, including who would be library liaison and other minor details, just as Delta had expected. But Delta wasn't paying attention, she was considering something. A tacit thought about Dr. Walter Steath raised Delta's curiosity. *Something about him doesn't fit*, she thought. But after the day she had had, she wasn't going to concern herself with a middle-aged academic from Harvard. *Or was it Cornell?* Delta turned around and glanced at the clock on the back of the classroom wall. Almost 4:00 p.m.

"Folks, we've got to bring our printing costs down …" Rory was still talking when Delta started to pack up her papers and Mona pulled out her phone, typed a text message and sent it. Seconds later, Delta's phone vibrated. She knew it was Mona before she even looked at it and she couldn't help but to smile at the irony of the student-like behavior she was about to engage. Delta held her phone below the level of the desk top, in her lap, and read: "My older brother will be in town tomorrow and for the rest of the weekend. I think u should meet him. He might be able to help." Delta typed a response and sent it back to Mona Barthes.

CHAPTER 5

Wednesday evening, August 11, 2010—West Lafayette, IN

The warmth and humidity of the August evening had drawn families to campus to cool off in the fountain spray. As children splashed each other and parents lounged on cement seats watching, Delta rushed past the summer scene barely noticing the peals of laughter and squeals of delight that faded behind her. She quickly made her way to the quad, the center of campus.

Taking a longer stride, she felt the weight of the tape recorder in her black bag bang against her hip. She took hold of it at the base, steadying it, before looking ahead at the expansive green space dissected by the "hello walk," a sidewalk gifted to the university by alums. On either side of the sidewalk, which transverses the commons, rich green lawn lay ready for student activities. On any given day, one would find college students playing Frisbee or hacky sack, gathering around someone playing a guitar or listening to a speaker shouting from a soap box. Tonight, however, Delta saw only one lone figure at the opposite end of the "hello walk." And that figure moved toward her with awkward, jerky movements. Stiff arms and legs carried him forward.

She could see that he was wearing a sandwich board sign. As she got closer, she could make out his painted face, white with smudgy red circles around his eyes. Fake blood dripped from his mouth; his nose appeared bent out of shape. And now, Delta could read his sign—WAKE UP.

As he approached her, he pointed to his oddly painted eyes and then he pointed at her, as if to say—*I've got my eye on you.* Delta quickly passed without a word, definitely without saying, "hello." Each walked in different directions, their backs to one another.

After passing the creature by a good distance, Delta stopped momentarily and turned around. The student dressed as a zombie walked on unaware that she had stopped. Delta read the back of his sign—IT'S NOT A GAME. Just then, he turned around, surprising her. She jerked back. He repeated his earlier message—*I'm watching you*; this time, however, he tipped his head down but stared up ominously at her. Delta turned back around and hurried across the last few feet of the "hello walk" and up the steps to Stewart Center. She didn't relax until the lobby door closed behind her. She finally breathed easily after entering the humanities library on the other side of the Stewart Center lobby, there she straightened her bag over her shoulder, took a deep breath and made her way to the back of the library.

Delta spotted Karyn sitting at the same table where they had met the last time. Putting the zombie encounter behind her, she approached the young woman and greeted her professionally.

"I'm glad you decided to come back, Karyn," Delta said this softly to the young coed who sat at the oak table situated in a sequestered corner of the humanities library. Dimly lit, and hugged by shelves of old books, this cloistered corner smelled musty. Licking her lower lip, Delta could practically taste the dust of antiquity, the ancient narratives, the rich histories that were held within these books with broken bindings and burnt umber-colored covers. It gave her a sense of security, something about their permanence. She breathed it in as she pulled out a chair and joined the girl. While Delta embraced the library, Karyn, in contrast, covered her nose and fidgeted as if she were in a dentist's waiting room.

Delta appraised their differences as she looked at the girl whom she was preparing to interview. Karyn's medium-length, straw-colored hair with pink streaks and choppy-looking style sprung wildly from under a tweed cap. The coed wore a series of eight sparkling gem earrings along the rim of her right ear and four more on her left. Her downward tipped head all but hid the eyebrow piercing, a slight silver glint from the bar gleamed through her locks. In contrast, Delta wore three hoop earrings, two on one side and one on the other, barely rebellious. As for clothing, they both wore blue jeans, but Delta complimented her jeans with a bright summery-print top, whereas Karyn, the 19 year old sophomore, layered herself in shades of black and covered the last layer with a thin, grey sweater. Although youthful in every other way, Karyn pulled the long-sleeve sweater tightly around herself as if she were a fragile, elderly, senior citizen suffering from the harsh cold of the air conditioner.

The girl looked up from her down-turned face, only her eyes moved. Delta spoke again.

"You know, you can stop the interview whenever you want, just like I told you last week when we met. Remember?"

"Yeah, I know." She chewed gum.

"So, I want to remind you that the study is about communication and the cultural understandings of troubled relationships. I won't focus on your situation personally, I mean individually, but rather I want to compare it to others in a general way, looking for framing devices used in the stories. I'm interested in the communication." Delta didn't say it, but what she was really interested in was the discursive construction of the relationship, how the abuse becomes a secret. She actually hoped the girl wouldn't ask her to explain further, academic jargon can be both onerous and strategically ambiguous—tell her what you want in a way that's so simple and yet so confusing she won't even ask questions. Delta set up the tape-recorder and clicked the record button.

"I never seem to say anything right," the younger woman mumbled. "Even when I told him I was coming here, last week, he said that I would just make things worse."

Delta jotted a note to herself—*boyfriend says, she will make things worse by talking to researcher.*

"Why do you say that, Karyn?"

"We just keep fighting, arguing," the girl said, her elbows rested on the light-weight oak table and her uplifted hands cradled her chin. She continued, "They're just little fights, but they're all the time. No matter what I say, it leads to an argument. It didn't use to be that way. Not when we were in high school. Things were good then. Our relationship worked. We were neo-punk/partial-goth together. I just want it to be like it was then. I have to figure out what went wrong."

"Where did you go to high school?" Delta asked, ignoring the reference to neo-punk/partial-goth for the moment, "and what was it like?"

Karyn began to elaborate and Delta took notes, but the researcher couldn't help but to return to Karyn's description of the current relationship as suffering from little fights and having been good in the past. Delta considered the implications—*'they're just little fights,' for example indicated that the girl may be minimizing the abuse. 'It didn't use to be that way' suggests that Karyn knows the current relationship isn't healthy. How long will Karyn persist in searching for what used to be? She certainly seems to want to resurrect the life they once had together—punk together. Ah, did they share a common enemy in high school? Perhaps, the principal? Now, somehow has Karyn's boyfriend turned her into the enemy?*

"Does he go to college, too?"

"He works at a warehouse. He couldn't wait to get out of high school so he could go to work. Get away from teachers and all that blab. He works third shift, mostly lifting, storing, and packaging seed bags. They're really big sacks. He's getting really pumped," Karyn said, pointing to her biceps and indicating that her boyfriend's arms were gaining muscle mass and she smiled. "Yeah, a lot of seed bags."

"What kind of seed?"

"Corn. Soybean. Whatever. Seed is seed."

I beg to differ, Delta thought, but realized that if Karyn was referring to how heavy the bags are then one could argue that seed is seed. But with her farm studies so recently on her mind, Delta knew that seeds are far from interchangeable, seeds are definitely distinguishable.

"How heavy are the bags?" Delta asked.

"They used to be fifty pounds."

"Not anymore?"

"There's a new packaging system. They're now 250, 000 seeds to a bag or 8 million in a boll box. I know because he gave me a tour. So now he mostly moves boxes instead of bags. He used to like it when I came to the warehouse. He'd show me around and tell me what he was doing. He was proud of his work. Now, not so much…" Karyn brushed her hair off her eye, but it plopped back down. "You know what I think? I think it doesn't take long for a factory to break a man."

The comment reminded Delta of her past research, specifically of Jim Hack, the farmer who had worked in a steel factory to save enough money to buy his own tractor so that he could become a farmer.

"He doesn't like his job anymore?" Delta asked.

"I don't know. He still lifts bags or boxes all night, and the bags or boxes, they're still close to fifty pounds. Heavy as hell. I tried to pick one up once; he just laughed at me. He can pick up bags all night. All night. Seed and grain. He moves it from one side of the warehouse to the other. It doesn't seem like it's going anywhere because there's always more. You know, he's not going anywhere either. Can you imagine how mind numbing that must be?" Karyn paused before reasserting her assessment. "No, he's not going anywhere. He complains a lot, but he's not looking around for another job. Lousy job, but good pay," she confirmed. At first, she shook her head and then she laughed.

"Is that what he says?"

"That's what I say. Now as for me, me," Karyn offered, taking a breath, "I want to be a nurse. I've wanted to be a nurse ever since I was little. A school nurse, not a hospital nurse," she said adamantly. Delta smiled at the girl.

"And high school was a good time between you two? But he didn't like high school? What about you?" Delta queried.

"Oh yeah, we would skip classes together, skip whole days and go places, like the Dunes. Neither one of us really liked school, but we loved each other."

Delta took notes as the tape recorder captured the conversation. She continued to ask questions and probe for more information following particularly interesting answers. She noted the irony concerning the fact that what the couple liked most about high school was escaping it; the best part of school was skipping school. They talked for another twenty minutes or so, when Karyn switched again from describing the relationship during high school to suggesting that she couldn't say or do anything right anymore. And that the most frustrating part is that she didn't know what she was doing wrong. She lifted her head and looked at Delta.

"Okay, so like I said, he has a job over at Jackson's warehouse. And he packs a sandwich every night. Last week he forgot his sandwich and so I took it to him and instead of being grateful, he got mad at me. And he started yelling, 'If I'd wanted you to bring me a fuckin' sandwich, I would have told you so.'" Karyn slumped in the chair; tears welled up in her eyes, but they didn't drop down her cheeks. "I just don't know what I'm doing wrong." Her voice cracked as she implored Delta to help her, "What am I doing wrong?"

Delta felt helpless. She honestly didn't know the answer to the girl's dilemma.

"Karyn, it's important for you to know that I'm not a counselor; I'm a communication ethnographer, an ethno-rhetorician." None of these terms meant anything to Karyn and now the tears began to slip forward. Delta struggled with her own thoughts of inadequacy, frustrated by the gnawing feeling that she simply didn't know how to fix the situation. "But I can give you the name of a counselor."

Delta pulled out the resource materials she had brought from the counseling center and with out-stretched hand offered the brochures to Karyn. The emptiness of the gesture filled the space between them, but Delta didn't know what else to do. Then she added, "I know you think there was one misunderstanding that snowballed out of control, but sometimes there are other reasons. Maybe a counselor could help."

Karyn glanced at the brochures in Delta's hand, straightened up, pulled her grey sweater tighter around her tiny waist, and with a crisp comment ended the conversation, "I need to go."

"Okay," Delta said, "I need to leave, too, so I can catch the bus to go home. Do you want to meet again next Wednesday night?" Delta asked hopefully. Karyn didn't reply. "C'mon, it'll be fun," Delta cajoled lightly with a smile. *What a stupid thing to say,* Delta immediately realized. Delta turned off the tape recorder. "Sorry, that was a stupid thing to say." The girl still didn't respond. Delta packed the brochures, tape recorder and notebook into her black canvas bag.

"Why are you taking the bus? Don't they pay you enough to buy a car?" Karyn quipped as she swung her backpack over her shoulder.

"I had a little accident." Delta turned to the girl, adding "Are you going to be okay?" Karyn nodded; she then smacked her gum before answering.

"Yeah, maybe this week will be better."

This time, Delta didn't reply. She was booked all day Thursday with interviews that she was sure would be as equally pathos ridden as the one she had just finished and she was beginning to wonder if she could handle the burden of the vicarious emotional pain.

CHAPTER 6

On Friday evening, Delta heard the Jamaican reggae ring tone from across the living room of her apartment. The melody reminded her of spring break; even if those days were now a distant memory. As an assistant professor, she currently used her spring breaks in pursuit of tenure. Following the old maxim—publish or perish, Delta devoted herself to her studies of discourse and culture, focusing on secret or sequestered stories. She would either be found collecting data via interviews or writing her findings—cultural implications of these narrative encounters—so that she could submit articles for publication and add to, not only a body of literature, but knowledge about subjects that had been, for the most part, hidden from view.

She had survived Thursday's interviews, but not without having a nightmare, one that she refused to bring to mind again. She told herself that she was doing something important, and refused to allow herself to quit. She sat, now, reading over her notes from the previous day. Once again the delightful reggae music, coming her from her phone, rang forth like steel drums spreading spring sunshine on an island beach, and jarring her from the dark stories of her interviewees.

Her phone sang its Caribbean tune again; this time, she answered it.

"Yes … Hi, Mona. … Thanks …. No, I don't have a car, remember? … No, why don't you and your brother come over here? I'll open a bottle of wine. Sure. See you then."

Delta set her phone down and appraised the state of her abode. She lived in a remodeled church that had been divided into several apartments. Delta had the apartment in the nave of the church, a spacious area with a loft and two bedrooms. She had turned the choir loft into a library. The loft-cum-library overlooked the expansive kitchen and living room, which still sported the stained-glass windows of the church. The religious testaments of depression-era-colored glass held together with ultra-thin lead strips had been designed into grand, perpendicular gothic shapes with wooden frames holding them in place. The delicate nature of the glass as well as the cames that separated the individual colored pieces of glass kept the developer from taking them down, although resale value would have been quite high, the cost of extricating such fragile mosaics would have been prohibitive. These artistic depictions appeared to be dedicated to the life of Mary. Delta suspected that on the wall, between the stained-glass panels, paintings addressing the life of Christ, his crucifixion, death and resurrection had hung before the church had been renovated. She pictured them on the wall space between the grand, gothic windows, and imagined a time when the faithful walked the Stations of the Cross. Delta had filled those empty spaces on the living room wall with framed posters of her own icons—Che Guevara, Emma Goldman, Albert Einstein, Frida Kahlo, and Bart and Lisa Simpson. The church had been abandoned by the faithful, as they moved to a more modern structure that was closer to town, and eventually sold to developers in the 1990s, but had only recently been remodeled and offered as apartments. This particular apartment, within the remodeled church, was no longer in the hands of the faithful; instead it was now under the care of a committed and confirmed agnostic—Delta Quinn.

A quick glance around the place suggested it could use a bit of a cleaning. She started in the bathroom. The sink held strands of long, dark hair and toothpaste splatter appeared on the mirror. Yesterday's T-shirt hung from the back of the tank and make-up containers littered the counter. Crumpled towels lay on the floor and her yoga pants and thong hung from the doorknob. She began tidying and even cleaned the mirror and scrubbed the toilet bowl. She stopped for a moment and sprayed herself with a bit of perfume.

As for the bedroom, Delta decided to shut the doors—one between the bedroom and bathroom and one between the bedroom and living room. And then she moved onto the kitchen. It wasn't too awfully cluttered, which was the direct result of the academic timing. During the semester Delta was likely to let clutter, dust, and dirt collect and at the end of each semester she cleaned. Since this was the beginning of the semester, not much had accumulated in any of the rooms—the bathroom, bedroom, living room or kitchen. After washing three of her good wine glasses—a gift set of four from a friend, of which one was already broken—that had been hanging from the notched holder mounted under the cabinet, she turned to face the rest of the apartment.

While most of the place didn't look too bad to her, there was one exception. Her office area, which was located directly under what had once been the choir loft, housed her academic work. On one side of the office a staircase led to the choir loft/library, on the other side, a stained-glass window reflected light onto Delta's stacks of interviews and articles. This office area is where Delta kept her research piles. Under, over, and on top of a large mahogany desk, which she had bought at a 'scratch and dent' sale, sat piles of papers, journals, notebooks, library books, mugs stained with tea, a couple of everyday wine glasses whose purple sediment had nearly fossilized, an array of pens, a computer and a printer. Delta sighed before tackling some of the mess.

She collected the tea mugs and the cheap, everyday wine glasses from her desk and carried them to the sink, but she only had time to fill them with water to soak as she heard the doorbell ring. The good glasses are clean; she'd use those she thought.

Upon answering the chime, Delta found Mona and her brother Caleb standing in the doorway. Mona and Delta exchanged greetings—a light hug—as Caleb took in the apartment and its contents in one long sweeping gaze to which he pronounced, "*Inspiring.*" Delta smiled as she always did when watching the expression that came across the faces of people viewing her apartment for the first time. The impressive cathedral ceiling and the stained-glass windows captured their attention and proved to be an immediate ice breaker. But his gaze fell onto Delta's visage with considerably more pleasure.

"Really, *divine*," he added.

"This is my older brother, Caleb," Mona told Delta.

"Nice to meet you, Professor Quinn," he said with a beautiful full smile while extending his hand. She replied, "Delta. Please, call me Delta."

"So I hear you're visiting from Chicago?" Delta said with a lilt to her voice.

"Yes, but I have to leave tomorrow. I have meetings in Chicago. But Mona's coming to visit me next weekend." He smiled at his sister, but barely broke eye-contact with Delta.

Nor could Delta take her eyes off Caleb Barthes. She assessed the family resemblance. Caleb and Mona had the same almond-shaped, brown eyes. They each had wavy hair which swept across their foreheads. Mona was tall, 5'7" and Caleb probably 6'1". And each had smiles that sparkled with big, white teeth. But Caleb's smile was directed at Delta and his eyes were penetrating in the best of ways.

"… Delta," Mona said, as if she had already said it.

"I'm sorry, was I staring? Jeez, I don't know what's wrong with me," she stammered. Caleb simply smiled wider.

"Come in, come in. Would you like a glass of wine?" She offered gathering her composure and moving toward the kitchen.

"You're probably still reeling from that concussion," Mona excused Delta's behavior and they followed her into the kitchen and stood on the opposite side of the island-style counter top, watching as the professor reached for the cork screw.

"Red or white?"

Caleb came around and stood next to her, perusing the labels on the bottles. His shoulder brushed Delta's shoulder.

"Let's start with the Pinot Noir," he said flashing those giant white teeth. He added, "I know you're supposed to start with white and move to the reds, but I just like to challenge authority sometimes."

"Sometimes?" Mona said sarcastically. "You're an anarchist," she added, "And a bourgeoisie anarchist, at that. Which wine—red or white?" She scoffed playfully. Delta smiled.

"Good choice," Delta interrupted the siblings' jesting. "I dressed for spilling the red," she told him somewhat facetiously, although she was indeed wearing a shear, billowy, burgundy peasant top, belted at the waist, with a pair a blue jeans.

"Here let me," Caleb offered taking the cork screw from her hand. He let his fingers brush softly across the top of her hand, just light enough to make her wonder if it was an accident or purposeful. Slightly flustered, she turned abruptly toward the freshly washed wine glasses and took them from the drainer, giving each a quick final wiping with a hand towel. As Caleb poured the wine, Delta pulled cheese from the fridge and then crackers from the drawer, a staple, as far as she was concerned, as long as she had her lactase pills. They moved to the living room where they gathered around the coffee table. Mona and her brother sat on the couch; Delta sat in the adjacent chair.

"Nice wine," Caleb pronounced after only one sip. He looked around again and then asked Delta, "So what's it like living in a cathedral, constantly surrounded by ..." He gave a wave of his hand indicating, the wide expanse, cathedral ceiling, stained-glass windows and the choir loft. "... is it *heavenly*?" He asked. Delta smiled in response; his sister groaned and rolled her eyes.

"I *confess,* I do think it's a pretty cool place," Delta countered and this time Caleb smiled. He replied, "Oh, *hell* yes, it's cool. I mean, my *God*, who lives in a church? Honestly, *gospel truth*, I thought Mona was kidding when she parked in the—"

"Actually, Caleb, we have more pressing matters to discuss," his sister Mona interrupted the volley of puns. "Delta has been experiencing some strange events."

"Yes, yes, you said on the phone that Delta had received a rather strange computer message. And from what you did tell me on the way over here, I don't see exactly how I can help," he said, reaching for a cheese and cracker, while offering a more than mildly concerned glance toward Delta. But it was Mona who responded first.

"I didn't tell you everything on the way over because I thought it best for Delta to tell you, but I was thinking that since you're an investigative reporter you might be able to give us some ideas on how to figure out what's going on," Mona explained and then took a long sip of wine. Caleb leaned forward; he became more interested with the mention of investigative reporting. Delta began her story.

"The other day, I received a 'cease and desist' message on my computer, but before that there was a phone call—"

"And don't forget the car accident," Mona inserted.

"Whoa, whoa, whoa, I think you better start at the beginning," Caleb directed as he turned toward Delta. Delta started over; she told him about the mysterious phone calls, the car 'accident,' and the enigmatic computer message that read, 'Cease and desist. Your research is dangerous!' Mona jumped in again confirming the computer message and how the stolen, yellow Hummer had plowed into the back of Delta's car and how Mona had come to her rescue or at least had driven her home that night.

"We both think it has something to do with Delta's research," Mona concluded by taking up her wine glass again.

"Well, what research are you working on?" Caleb queried.

"That's just it; I work on a lot of research at any given time. You've heard the expression, publish or perish, haven't you?" Delta addressed Caleb, but Mona asked a different question.

"How much do you have to publish in order to get tenure? And do you really lose your job if you don't publish enough?" She sounded like the stereotypically obsessed graduate student.

"A lot. And, yes," Delta answered. Mona responded with a panicky slurp of wine. "That's why you have to really care about your research and the people you study because you spend a lot of time and energy, sometimes years, dedicated to the projects you pursue."

"And what are you pursuing right now?" Caleb asked.

"My specialty is narrative theory."

"You study stories?"

"Yes, to be more specific, I study sequestered stories."

"And that means…"

"I study the stories that people are afraid to tell for whatever reasons. The stories that get—

"sequestered." Mona finished Delta's answer and then poured more wine for everyone, her own glass having been the most in need of a refill. She emptied the bottle and motioned toward the second bottle of wine. Delta nodded an affirmative to Mona to feel free to open the other bottle and then Delta continued.

"You know, for example, whistleblower's reports of corporate fraud or women's stories of sexual harassment, or domestic violence."

"So, you study the stories that people are not making public?"

"Yes."

"And what have you published most recently?"

"Interviews with farmers about their work and how corporate giants are moving in on them. But the most recent article is more about how the farmers construct their life's work as meaningful, as having a real job."

"Don't we all?"

"Yes, but this one farmer felt that farming is especially real, in contrast to say, being a professor or a—"

"A reporter?"

"No, more like a bureaucrat? He didn't like the government."

"Really, how so?"

"Well, the farmer said that the government and corporations were pressuring the small farmers out of business and that one way the government did it was by putting out falsified farm reports."

"The government ag reports?"

"Yes," the professor told him.

"And you say this article was just published?"

"Yes, actually it came out the same week I started getting the strange phone calls." Delta hadn't realized the connection until that moment; she made a face that indicated her epiphany. Mona returned with the open bottle of wine and Delta noticed they were running low on cheese.

"May I see it?" Caleb asked.

"Sure." Delta left the gathering and searched through the stacks on her desk.

"This is an extra copy," she said returning and handing the journal to him. "I presented an earlier version of this at a conference in NYC."

"When was that?" Caleb asked.

"Last weekend," she said, adding, "Before the car accident."

"Can I take it with me?" He asked, and while reaching for the slender journal his sleeve slid upward revealing a tattoo on his forearm. Delta read what she could see of it: "Never quit se..." He watched her read, noticing her raven-colored hair as it fell downward, sweeping along her cheekbone framing her soft green eyes. She looked up. His eyes locked on her eyes. She smiled softly, and then quickly averted her gaze. "So can I take this copy?" He repeated.

"Yes, of course. But I don't see how it could be that dangerous. A lot of farmers complain about the ag reports," Delta told him as she went to the fridge to replenish the cheese tray. "They didn't act like it was a big secret. Nor did anyone have any definitive proof. Sort of conspiracy theory without any meat to it."

"Ag reports?" Mona sought clarification.

"Agricultural reports," Delta told her.

"You've done other interviews with farmers?" Caleb asked.

"Yes. Why? Do you think it's connected?" She asked.

"What do you think, Caleb?" Mona chimed in.

"I'm not sure, yet?" He mused. "I mean, honestly, right now I can't imagine why anybody would run you off the road for knowing that the government embellishes the ag reports. But I also don't understand why you'd be getting harassing phone calls and mysterious messages about your research. I like to keep an open mind. So, if there's a story here, I mean a newspaper story, will you let me publish it?"

"Well, I guess so. Who do you work for, Caleb?" Delta asked while surveying the fridge; it was all but empty. Shopping had slipped her mind with everything going on, plus she didn't have a car and now the fridge held nothing more than condiments. She pulled the spicy mustard from the shelf and the rest of the crackers from the drawer.

"I freelance. But I'm working on something for the *Chicago Tribune* right now."

"He already has several investigative pieces published in very reputable papers," Mona assured Delta. Mona reached for the cheese and crackers, but hesitated.

"I'm sure he does," Delta said with a smile and then she squirted spicy mustard onto a cracker. "Go ahead, Mona, Caleb. Please, finish the cheese. I love mustard." She even squirted a spurt right into her mouth to prove it. Caleb laughed.

"You need a good hotdog under that," he told her, "One from Comiskey, well the Cell, now."

"I'm a vegetarian," Delta told him.

They shared more wine and Delta listened as Mona further confirmed Caleb's credentials; he had graduated from Northwestern's School of Journalism. He had written several exposés, one of which was published in *Mother Jones*, another in *The Nation,* a third one in the *Huffington Post.* He even had one published by *The New York Times.* He had traveled to Afghanistan and Morocco while serving in the army and had hiked across Europe after his discharge. Although Mona didn't mention the following, Caleb had been determined to smoke pot in Amsterdam, view Rodin's "The Kiss" in Paris, and run with the bulls in Pamplona. And he had completed each of these. He didn't like sitting at a desk unless it was to do research on a story.

"If anyone can help figure this out, Caleb can." Mona asserted.

While Mona praised her brother, he pretended not to listen and instead wandered about, studying Delta's apartment, looking at the magazines, books, and especially newspapers that she reads— remnants of last Sunday's *NY Times* lay in a basket near the couch, but he didn't see the *Chicago Tribune. I'll have to remedy that*, Caleb thought. He walked over to a table under one of the stained-glass windows and perused her CD collection, where he found a wide variety of music, including classics like Billie Holiday … *interesting*, he thought. "You like the blues?" He queried without looking up.

"I love Billie Holiday. *God bless the child* is one of my favorites."

"Yeah, great stuff," he commented as he continued to survey the music collection, noting the absence of burned CD's. *Good sign*, he thought. *Means there's not another man in her life.*

Caleb put an Eric Clapton CD on, after holding it up and getting the nod from Delta. Then he decided to look for additional signs of what wasn't there—like crushed beer cans in the garbage, dirty socks on the living room floor. Pointing toward the closed door, he casually asked, "Bathroom?" Again Delta nodded and Mona continued to describe her brother's life and their relationship, growing up. Mona was starting to slur her words just a tad.

Caleb entered the bathroom. The seat was down and the bathroom was clean. It smelled of perfume. He looked in the medicine cabinet; after which, he flushed the toilet and used its noise to mask his turning the doorknob to the other room. The door opened onto the inner sanctum of Delta's messy bedroom. Caleb assessed the layout, and then quickly scanned the contents of the room—the double bed, two night stands with books on only one of them, clothes flung over a chair and on the floor. A poster of Leonard Peltier hung above the bed—a quote underneath began, "I don't know how to save the world." The rest of the quote became illegible to Caleb, as the type size was too small to read from where he stood. A collage hung on the adjacent wall. In the center of the collage was an enlarged image of Michael Jackson wearing his red leather jacket with macho shoulder pads and doing his signature dance step with a slew of zombie dancers behind him—*Thriller*, and this *Thriller*-centered collage hung directly between two stained-glass windows, religious stories designed and set into gothic frames—the crucifixion with Mary weeping at the foot of the cross and the resurrection of Jesus where Mary appears to have just left praying with the other women and is standing next to a boulder that is askew of the cave opening; she appears poised at the threshold of the tomb ready to beckon Jesus to come out. Caleb shook his head and smiled at the juxtaposition of cultural statements, Zombies dancing between the death and resurrection. The other images on the collage were smaller—Louis Armstrong blasting his trumpet with words underneath that read, *I found my thrill on Blueberry Hill;* a picture of an older Judy Garland with the lettering, perhaps cut from a magazine cover, like a ransom note that read, *Over the Rainbow.* There were more images and more captions. He wished he had more time to study the collage, but he needed to get back to the conversation taking place in the living room. He started to quietly close the door when something else caught his eye. He noticed a small collection of rocks on the dresser next to the door—a piece of pink granite, a bit of grey igneous rock, a small flat fossil and a white pebble made of marble, a few more rocks arranged in a glass bowl. *Hmm,* he said in response to the little rock collection before he closed the bedroom door. Back in the bathroom, he ran a little water in the bathroom sink, simulating hand washing, in case they were listening and then he returned to the living room, where Mona was still talking.

CHAPTER 7

Friday evening, August 13, 2010—Lafayette, IN

Karyn's slender figure appeared naked. For the most part it was uncovered. Only her peach-colored thong hid her dark blonde pubic hair. The tattoo of the butterfly on her right butt cheek flew toward a brown mole on her lower back. Her small breasts were bare, although covered by her crossed arms. She tried to slide the patio door open; it wouldn't budge. She knew that her attempt would be futile; after all, she had watched him lock it after he shoved her onto the balcony, but for some reason that logic failed to register. She tried again. Of course, it didn't move.

She turned her back on the door and surveyed her surroundings. Two stories up. The apartment had a tiny balcony, so small it could barely fit the two plastic chairs they had squeezed onto it. In addition, she had placed two small plants on the railing; both coleus plants, one born of a clipping taken from the other and both of which she saw as homey and he saw as useless, because you could neither eat them nor smoke them. She had laughed at the comment. She wasn't laughing now. It was from there, on the balcony, that she viewed the familiar scenery—the parking lot mostly empty of cars as it was only 4:45 p.m. and the field beyond which gave way to the warehouse in the distance. His shiny, black truck, parked below the balcony, glared at her.

She turned again to face the patio door. She saw her reflection. Embarrassingly naked. Vulnerable. She appeared stripped, much to her dismay. Had she been inside, in front of her full length mirror in the bedroom, under different circumstances, she would have been sizing herself up in a completely different way, depending on the day, the time, the mood, the month, the time of month. She might have seen herself as petite and pixie, sexy and desirous. She might have thought on another day of the month that she was bloated, too fat, too thick. On those days, red streaks would appear across her swollen breasts, belly, and even her back following a good scratch.

47

But today she appeared neither sexy nor bloated. She appeared as an image, a specter, without clarity. After all, this was not a mirror image, this was the liminal image caught somewhere in between, between inside and outside, between self and resemblance. *A big smudge*, she thought. She slapped the glass then turned away from this ghostly image of herself, trapped on the upper deck, staring in and seeing only a reflection of herself was too much to bear.

She still refused to knock. Nor would she sit down. She turned side-ways, out of his view, if he was looking. She glanced back at the window. From this angle, she could see the TV glaring and flickering as it changed shades and intensity. She pictured him with his feet propped up, watching, but not dedicating his attention to the TV program. Her anger and embarrassment gave way gradually to confusion. She simply didn't understand how a simple discussion about grocery shopping had led to this bizarre outcome.

She had been sitting at the little kitchen table making a grocery list. He ignored her, continuing to pick something from between his teeth when she asked what he wanted from the store. He twisted the toothpick, glanced up and remained silent. She stood and said she'd let him think about it, while she took a shower. Standing in the bathroom, she had just pulled her thong half way down in order to pee, and after peeing she planned to step into the shower, when he suddenly opened the door, barged in, tossed the grocery list at her and yelled, "I don't want anything from the grocery store. I don't even want a fucking grocery list!"

The little piece of white paper had hit her in the face and then floated in the air in front of her, as if in slow motion—in front of her shoulder, curving then in the other direction it passed her naked belly with the navel piercing, a fake ruby ring in it, and eventually floated past her knees before dropping by her black-polished toenails.

He turned and left the bathroom. She pulled up her underwear and stood without having had a chance to relieve herself. She picked up the paper and followed him into the living room, shouting at his back.

"Fine, you don't want anything from the grocery store. Fine, but you don't have to yell about it. What's the matter with you?" She heard herself yelling, but couldn't make her voice do otherwise.

"There's nothing the matter with me."

"Well, it certainly seems like it."

"Just take your shower."

"I'll take my shower when I feel like it. And I don't feel like it right now." She set the grocery list on the table with exaggerated dominance, slammed the stubby pencil on top of it, and turned around and began walking through the living room. That's when he pushed her out on the balcony, shut the sliding glass door and locked it.

Shock turned into anger. Anger turned into embarrassment. Embarrassment turned into confusion. Why? Disbelief surfaced again. She tried the door again, as if it weren't really locked. Confusion and disbelief turned into excuses for him. *It's working third shift that's making him crazy. It's too much pot. It's only when he drinks too much. That professor should have been able to help me figure this out; instead, I got platitudes and pamphlets. I share my personal story and what do I get? Nothing.* Nearly twenty minutes passed before she took a step toward the door. She knocked.

There was no response. Behind her, she heard the tires of a car make its turn against the stony asphalt parking lot driveway and pull into the lot. People were coming home from work. She knocked again. No answer. She cupped her hands around her eyes and leaned against the glass, peering into the living room. She could see movement. And then nothing. She turned her back on the door, assessing her situation again.

Click! Swish! Thwack! She heard the door open, but just as she turned around she felt the sting of being hit in the face with something and then she immediately heard the sound of that same something hitting the deck floor. He re-locked the patio door after having tossed the phone at her. She picked it up.

Eventually she heard the building door, two floors below her, swing open. He made his way to his truck. She called out his name. It came forth without anger or malice or resentment, or reproach, and definitely without deference, it was just his name. He didn't turn around. He got into his truck, started the engine and drove away.

CHAPTER 8

Friday, August 13, 2010—outskirts of Lafayette, IN

"And Caleb's latest article was on Haiti."

"Haiti. What was that like? When were you there? Were you in Port au Prince?" Delta asked Caleb as he joined them again in the living room. She took another sip of wine.

"I flew into the Dominican Republic and took a bus to Haiti and then rented a little motor bike and made my way to Légânc."

"Why Légânc?"

"That's where the epicenter took place. I wanted to be at the heart of the earthquake."

"And?"

"And it was devastating. Thousands and thousands of people died in the quake. Many more injured. By the time I got there in March mass graves had been dug. And even still the smell of decay hung over the city." He shook his head. "And for the survivors, the shock hadn't worn off. Many of the survivors wandered like zombies through the crumbled ruins of houses and buildings, looking for something, not looking for money or anything like that, just looking."

"For pieces of their lives," Delta surmised.

"Yes, exactly," Caleb said, admiring her perception. He continued, "One day, I rode my motor bike to Port au Prince and on the way I met a man who was carrying a painting. I asked him where he was going and if he wanted a lift. He climbed on the back of the bike and held his painting tightly in one hand as we rode off. I took him to a refugee camp."

"What was that like?" Delta asked.

"Crowded with hundreds of tents and thousands of people, Haiti had collapsed, crumbled into dust. Dirt blew continually across the encampment of tents that were set up on the gravel-covered ground. You had to keep your face covered against the blowing dirt. Sometimes, it was hard to breathe.

"But for all the death, it was a colorful place in a strange way. The tents were brightly decorated. Well, the tents were gray, but layered with bright orange and blue tarps to help keep the rain out. The man with the painting—the one I had given a ride on the scooter—he directed me to his tent as if it was his street address. He told me that he shared the tent with twelve other people. He explained that this is a good number because of Jesus and the twelve apostles. And then he showed me the painting that he had carried all the way from the ruins to the refugee camp—*The Last Supper*. He set the painting against the tent and then he took a packet of holy cards out of his pocket. They were all of the Virgin Mary. He laid them around the cot in the tent, saying 'Mother Mary will keep the bad voodoo spirits away. The *houngan* is dead; he was better than the priest, but now the priest is dead, too. Holy cards will have to do; we have no one else to protect us. If we don't do this we will become zombies.'"

Delta shook her head, speechless, at the description that Caleb provided of the devastation of Haiti.

"Do they really believe in zombies?" Mona asked.

"Do Christians really believe that Jesus rose from the dead?" Caleb asked her. Mona responded by rolling her eyes.

"It's the holy cards and the painting that fascinate me," Delta said.

"How do they get by day to day?" Mona wanted to know.

"Barely," Caleb told her. "The relief organizations were so poorly coordinated that people couldn't get clean water. So they cooked rice and beans in whatever water they could find. And the frustrating part, supplies are there, in warehouses, waiting to be distributed, but between the disorganization and the politics, people are getting nothing. It's fucking crazy," Caleb's anger surfaced. "It's all fucking politics."

"What politics?" Delta asked. Caleb shook his head with disgust as if it was too much to try to explain.

"It's a long history. There are competing factions. Both groups saw their chance to ingratiate themselves with the people by being the ones to distribute food and water. While the two groups fought over who should do it and how to do it, the people were forced to scoop up contaminated water from puddles for cooking water and for drinking. That's what led to the cholera outbreak."

"Couldn't the Red Cross or the U.N. help?"

"The U.N. is the U.S. and the U.S. is half the problem," Caleb told them. Delta didn't understand. "It's a long, political story," Caleb told her. "I'll give you a copy of my article, if you want."

"Yes," Delta said emphatically.

"But we should get back to your problems," he said.

Just then Delta's phone rang. Caleb picked up her phone from the coffee table and looked at it.

"Delta, it's a blocked number," Caleb said with concern, hesitating to hand it to her. He stood up.

She reached for the phone. "I'll take it in the other room," she told him. Caleb kept it in his hand; he took a step back.

"You shouldn't answer it at all," Mona directed. Caleb agreed.

Delta reached out again. "I have to. It might be—"

"Who?" Caleb asked tightening his grip on the phone. She reached for it again without answering him. He moved his arm back. The Jamaican song ceased to ring. Her outstretched hand fell to her side; her jaw tightened and she said nothing. A tense silence scorched the air between them; it stood still like tropical heat, until she took a deep breath. And then she extended her hand, once again, open, palm up. This time, he contritely put the phone in her hand.

"We should probably go," Caleb said.

"Right, we should go," Mona agreed. Delta stared at the silent phone; she glanced up at Caleb. Mona cleared the dishes.

Caleb quietly turned to Delta, "I'm sorry. I shouldn't have done that," he apologized. Delta nodded, but said nothing.

"Those other interviews, the ones with the other farmers, do you have copies of those that I could look at?" He asked, adding sincerely, "Maybe, I can help."

Delta wasn't ready for his help, not now.

"Really," his eyes were soft-spoken, pleading.

She took another deep breath. "I don't think so."

"I'm pretty good at investigative reporting," he humbly asserted. She knew, based on Mona's recital of his accomplishments, that that was an understatement. He titled his head sheepishly.

"Really, I am sorry. I had no right to …

Something about the way he tilted his head reminded her of the way Karyn had titled her head during the interview and she suddenly realized it was not completely Caleb's fault. He was just being protective. Plus, she knew that she could have demanded the phone from him; she hadn't. Delta recognized that she had used the opportunity to her benefit; if Caleb had the phone, then she wouldn't have to face another threatening message or a possible call from anyone of her distraught interviewees.

"Please," he added, looking for a second chance. This time, she titled her head, looked seriously into his eyes, and reconsidered.

"I have a version with the names blacked out; you know, human subject review and all. I have to protect my subjects," she explained while slipping her phone into her pocket. "Of course, you understand," she added.

"Absolutely, absolutely," he agreed, being a journalist he was always careful to protect his sources. Delta returned to her desk, and began searching through her piles and stacks, but thoughts of the unanswered phone call, the blocked caller id, distracted her. It could have been the anonymous caller with more threats, but it also could have been Karyn. She liked Karyn, of all the women she'd interviewed, Karyn was the most creative, the least needy. Delta began to feel guilty. She had given her phone number to each of them. She should have been willing to answer the call. *Damn.*

Mona said something and Delta turned around, but then realized that Mona was talking to Caleb. Delta continued to rummage through her stacks in search of the interviews.

"Oh, yes, the interviews with the farmers. I put them in a folder," she announced remembering where they were. "Here they are," she said as she pulled a thick manila envelope from under one of the stacks. "Here you go," she said as she walked back toward Caleb and stretched out the envelope toward him.

He nodded and stepped toward the door. Mona joined them and then hugged Delta, as Caleb said, "I'll be in touch. But if there's anything else you can think of, just give me a call. Mona's got my number. And Delta," his tone reassuring, the tenor deep and rich, "Don't worry. We'll figure this out."

After shutting the door, Delta leaned against it and looked at the stained-glass window directly across from the front door—Mary encouraging Jesus to turn the water into wine at the marriage of Cana. She had faith in him.

CHAPTER 9

Saturday, August 14, 2010—Chicago, IL

On his ride back to Chicago, Saturday evening, Caleb wondered about the mysterious messages that Delta had received. He mused over the wording. For instance, the phone caller had said, 'Stop what you're doing,' but not until after several hang up calls. That would indicate hesitation on the caller's part. And the wording was simple enough, straightforward, and yet enigmatic as if she would know exactly what he was referring to, but she didn't. As Delta had suggested, she may be working on a number of projects at any given time. The caller must not be another professor or he'd know that. As for the mysterious computer message, the wording was completely different, 'Cease and desist! Your research is dangerous.' Caleb thought for a moment, *Cease and desist, sounds like legal jargon or at the very least bureaucratic cant. 'Your research is dangerous,' but which research?* As for the car accident, he couldn't be sure if it was related at all. After all, none of the messages included an actual threat on Delta's life. *And who on earth would be stupid enough to steal a yellow Hummer? Or smart enough; those babies are hard to hot wire, most of them have an immobilizer system built into them.*

When Caleb arrived at his apartment in Old Town, Chicago, he lifted a beer from the fridge, sat on the sofa and propped his feet up on the cluttered coffee table, which was not so much a table as a series of four stacks of books which had been placed an equal distance apart, like table legs, to support two wide pine boards. The blond pine planks were covered with graffiti or notes—phone numbers, addresses. He tossed the manila folder and the journal given to him by Delta onto the make-shift coffee table.

Caleb rubbed the stubble on his face, having forgotten to pack his razor earlier and so he simply hadn't bothered to shave while he had stayed at his sister's place. He was in no hurry to shave it now. Traffic had been a bear. He flicked on the TV and scanned channels. Nothing caught his interest. As he set the remote down, he took the journal and manila folder under consideration. He decided he would read the journal article first.

Caleb began reading:

On the hill, before my car swoops downward on the curving valley road, I see a pastoral setting unfold before me—a farm house with barns and chicken coop surrounded by golden fields. The sparkling Wildcat Creek borders the fields and winds its way around the farmland. But as my car approaches the farmhouse, the pastoral beauty disappears into a pungent odor. It's a pig farm. I quickly roll my car window up as I drive through the valley. Covering my nose and mouth with my forearm, I continue driving over the little bridge and up the other side of the hill, finally able to inhale, deeply. On my return trip, after running an errand, I find myself entering the valley from the opposite direction. Now I spy an additional sight. From the top of the hill, I can see the roof top of the barn and on it, the words— *Jim loves Susan*. The pastoral beauty that had disappeared in the smell of the pig stench is restored and revitalized in the words of love—*Jim loves Susan*. For the entire world to see—*Jim loves Susan*.

A sucker for romance I was drawn to this farm. As an academic, I took up this ethno-rhetorical study in order to better understand the cultural identity of small-farm farmers and their families, representatives of traditional America, an iconic yet nonetheless disappearing part of America. This study of one small-farm family led to a follow-up study where I conducted interviews with 30 farmers, the findings from the first study explain what so urgently compelled me to continue.

Caleb read on discovering that after several casual meetings Delta had been granted official interviews with Jim and Susan, the farm couple, and he thought Delta sounded a bit naive when she writes about arriving with her tape recorder in one hand and snickerdoodles in the other—he liked that innocence. As he turned the pages he found that the interview became much more detailed with regard to the life of the farmer and here Caleb took special interest.

At our first meeting, I sensed some resentment on Jim's part. He had no use for professors, it would seem.

"What is it exactly that you do?" Jim asked me.

"*I study stories,* I told him. Lately, I've been collecting stories about what constitutes 'a real job' and sharing them with students in my class." I don't recall if I drew the quotation marks in the air around the expression "real job," but he got my drift.

"A real job?! They want to know what a real job is, I'll tell them what a real job is," Jim launched into a description of the hard work of heaving bales of straw from the lower barn to the loft. The straw is sharp and pointy and pricks him and his wife Susan with unforgiving force. He takes me into the barn to experience the straw, the heat, the weight of it all. I listen, without interrupting him, after all, what do I know about farming? Finally, I ask if I can learn more about their lives. And as I ask, I'm thinking just how embarrassed I am that I don't even know the difference between straw and hay. For me, straw is gathered into bales; hay into stacks which Monet painted in the varying lights of day.

Caleb read Delta's analysis that followed. She surmised that his talking and showing her the bales demonstrated his identity as worthy and compelling through "the suffering" he encounters on a daily basis—this is "a rhetorical strategy, establishing work identity through suffering;" farming is hard work, real work and taking Delta into the barn was a "rhetorical tactic that reinforced the strategy." Delta considered this "dialogic, everyday rhetoric."

Caleb continued to read, singling out one of the stories that Jim told Delta; it felt real in every sense. It captured the daily life of the farmer:

Susan and I came home with the girls one day and discovered one of the chickens mangled and laying right here by the porch. When I realized what had happened, I strode into the house and got my rifle. Then I came out and grabbed our family dog by the collar. And that's when Susan realized what I was going to do. "Jim" she said, "Please, don't." They loved that dog. Susan and the girls, they loved him. But you can't have a dog on the farm that's going to kill and eat your livelihood. So I was carrying my rifle in one hand and dragging the dog with the other and my oldest daughter grabs my leg and wraps her arms around my ankle. And she's pleading with me not to shoot our dog. As a farmer, I should've shot the dog."

Caleb read on. Delta's reflection followed:

I reflected on his words—As a farmer I should've shot the dog. I reflected on what wasn't said—As a father, a husband, a family man, I didn't shoot the dog. Reflecting on what is unspoken is crucial to gathering a complete interpretation. Silence is not only dialectical but also dialogical.

Then Caleb skipped a few pages and stopped when he spotted the words "government" and "stock market":

Jim asserted that the government was writing falsified farm reports that controlled the stock market. Jim told me stories of seed companies selling him bogus seeds on purpose, seeds that they promised would be the best but they seemed to need more water than others and some seeds wouldn't regenerate, others needed special fertilizer to grow. And the price of the seeds, Jim said, has more than quadrupled in the last couple of years. Jim told me that if they don't get the farmer with the exorbitant price for the seeds, then it's the price of the insecticide or the herbicides that'll bankrupt him. More and more, there is nowhere else to turn to buy seed.

Delta's right, Caleb thought. *The farmer blames the government for raising crop prices by printing farm reports that are bogus.* Caleb jotted this down within a file on his smart-phone. Caleb noted another quote from the article, "Middlemen take more than their share of the profit until the small-farm farmer has no recourse but to give up his farm." Caleb added the word, "middlemen," as another major category in addition to "bogus government farm reports." Caleb's third category became, 'seed distributors'. He noticed that the published article had a footnote following the mention of the seed company. He skimmed down to the bottom of the page and read: "A major seed manufacturer and chemical company is mentioned by several farmers in the area as providing dubious seeds. A pseudonym is provided and henceforth the company is simply referred to as Seed & Chemical Company or S&CC." Caleb made farm chemical companies his fourth category.

So far none of this explained why anyone would want to run Delta off the road or send her threatening messages. But someone had done just that. Caleb needed to think. He recharged with another beer, looked through the fridge for food and came up with nothing but mustard. He tried Delta's recipe, found crackers in the cupboard and squirted mustard on them. *It lacks something, like two pieces of bread and a huge stack of deli meat*, he thought.

Hungry or not, Caleb turned his attention back to the farmer's interview as he returned to the living room and continued to read where the article returned to an earlier topic—what is "a real job":

They have emphasized the burdens associated with the small farm, but when I ask again about how they see it as a "real job," their answers flow from the meaning of their work, to the richness of their lives. Jim says, "But you know a real job, a real job, to me, it's a way of life. We milk the cow morning and night ... And that's the milk that we drink. Unpasteurized, which some people cringe at—You're drinking unpasteurized milk?, they might ask. Well, yeah, we are. And yes, I suppose we're taking a chance." They offer me a glass of unpasteurized, non-homogenized milk. I decline on the grounds that I have lactose intolerance. They give me fresh spring water instead, not from a plastic container kept in the refrigerator, but from a ladle that scoops the water straight from a barrel where a pipe sends a constant stream of sparkling spring water from an underground spring to the large metal drum in their house and then sends it splashing on through. I am momentarily lost in thoughts, in memories of the first and only time I ever drank unpasteurized, non-homogenized milk.

Caleb continued to read Delta's words; her memories, aroused from the fresh milk, were written in the following way:

I am a small child, nearly five years old. I am being left at an orphanage in Canada. My father says, "I'll be back for you at dinner time." I see him leaving. I am standing in the middle, holding hands with my younger sister and my younger brother. They are three and two years old, respectively. Later that day, I see images—a wooden table where dinner has been set, a bench to sit on, and adults whom I don't know. There are no other children at the orphanage. It is dinner time and my father hasn't returned. A pewter pitcher sparkles with condensation on this dinner table. The adult pours a glass of milk for each of us. I take a sip. It's a foreign taste, not like the milk we drink at home. I say nothing. I do not eat or drink anything else. Bedtime comes and my father still hasn't returned. My brother and sister cling to me or maybe I am clinging to them. The adult gently takes my brother away explaining that they have a crib in the other room for him. My sister and I curl together in the same bed. My sister cries, it is a soft whimper. I worry about my brother; at home, we sleep in the same bedroom. At home, his crib is in our room. Here on our first night at St. Joseph's Orphanage, he is separated from us. My little sister and I snuggle. We sleep in our clothes. It takes a long time for me to fall asleep. Morning brings a new venture. I'm told to select clean clothes for myself and my sister and brother from a table where clothes have been tossed. I can barely see the edge of the table much less what kind of clothes I am selecting. It becomes a nearly impossible task for a four and half year old, but somehow I find clothes that we can wear which are not so large or so small that we cannot make do. Breakfast brings cereal and more strange milk poured over it. After tasting it, I do not eat more. Where is my father? My brother joins us and I am aware that he seems fine, happy, smiling. By mid-day my sister seems happy. I will have to be on guard for all of us. I search down the dirt road, looking, watching, and waiting for my father to appear in the family station wagon. He doesn't come on the first day or the second day or the third day. The evening of the fourth day I am a different person. Empty somehow. Hollow. I no longer hope. Instead, I drink the strange-tasting milk that is poured for me.

Caleb paused; *Jesus, she's an orphan,* he thought. *God, how does anybody recover from being abandoned?*

Caleb began reading Delta's words again:

Oh my God, I say to myself as I realize that I had been transported in time, reliving a childhood memory, Thank God that I had the tape-recorder going. Oh, my, gosh, what has Jim been saying?

Jim's words then appear on the page that Caleb is reading:

"... And our eggs, our chickens, they're fed absolutely no additives, no drug additives of any kind. The feed is all natural ... corn, oats, alfalfa hay is ground in with their ration of vitamins and minerals. And they free range ... outside in the sunshine. ... and our hogs ... and our cows that we butcher for meat ... and it may not be cheaper ... I don't care ... I want to go out and milk the cow in the morning. I want to go out and take care of the livestock. It is a lifestyle. And I enjoy watching the girls, the girls [his daughters]. To see their expressions when you bring a baby goat into the world, you know, just still wet and how they cuddle it, you know. These girls they take them, hug them, bottle feed them. It's just a precious gift. [Jim has tears in eyes and actually has to leave the room] He returns, and says, "I feel the whole atmosphere. This old house ... it's got so much character.

Susan jumps in saying, "the dumb waiter, the spring, I just wouldn't give it up." Jim adds, "And you look at the buildings out there. Now we have cut down trees on this farm, take them to the saw mill had the lumber sawn and had the newer buildings built." Susan adds, "Finding the right trees that were just perfect." Jim says, "Tremendous." Susan looks at him and adds, "But it was so neat to do that because that's how they were built originally ..." They continue to tell me about the joys of their life "And we have a garden," Susan says. "Susan does a tremendous amount of canning," Jim tells me. Susan continues, "We make jams and jellies." "Peaches and applesauce," Jim adds. Susan says, "We pick strawberries and make our own strawberry jam." They tell me more about milking their cow and the money that can be saved. They've named their cows, Mabel, Miriam, Maggie, ... and [then there is] Crazy Horse. The girls feed the chickens and Susan bakes their bread. There are long hard days when exhaustion sets in, when they work from morning till midnight, when their hands are raw and their backs are sore, but they wouldn't give it up for anything. Sometimes they are so tired they can't eat, they just collapse in bed. But when times are good, they are very good. Jim tells me, "It's pretty easy to sit down and eat. When times are good and at the right time of the season, it's pretty easy to sit down and eat and eat too much. They both agree that whole milk and eggs and pork sausage make a fine meal and that they aren't worried about cholesterol. Jim says, "You take a doggone professor [laughter follows from both of them] who eats a big breakfast and goes over there and sits down. You know, any white collar feller sits down and eats a big breakfast—

Susan finishes Jim's thought, "Just doesn't get enough exercise, basically."

Jim and Susan tell me with great detail about how they have no desire to go on vacation. They love the farm and if one of them goes somewhere without the other, they are heart sick. Jim loves this farm. He takes great "pride in it." And he loves his family. Jim tells me, "I strongly believe that I'm here to do what I'm doing." And Susan adds, "That's always been his dream—to be a farmer number one, and to have a family, number two. And to be happy, number three." Jim modifies the statement, "Well, my family comes first." Susan stands corrected, "Well, as long as we're together ... we're happy." And Jim concludes, "I used to work in a steel mill. A steel mill could break even the best of men, that is, if they don't have a dream. Fortunately, I had a dream. My wife. My kids. My farm. I'm total. I can't think of anything more that I would want. I have everything I've always dreamed about."

Delta's analysis followed, but Caleb skipped ahead to the last paragraph:

The ethnography of the farm became a place for me to exist. I didn't realize it at first, but it gave me the family I dreamt about as a child. Writing about the farm family became a dwelling place for me. I care about this family in ways I cannot articulate as they gave me a glimpse into a life I had only dreamed of, promising that it can be a reality. I now share in the stories that I missed in my own childhood. I have experienced a home filled with love, a place where I could belong. I found this on a small rural farm, in the family that defines themselves according to their life and to each other and to the land.

Caleb stopped reading. He set the journal aside. He had learned more about Delta than he had ever expected. And he was more determined than ever to protect her from harm by finding out why anyone would want to hurt her. *Why*, he wondered, *would anybody try to run Delta off the road, why would anybody send her threatening messages?* The answer is not in this interview, he decided. He stretched, changed the music, used the bathroom and returned to his spot on the couch. After slugging the last sip of beer, he opened the manila envelope that Delta had also given to him and began reading. However, he was only a few sentences into what Delta had given him when he realized this wasn't the folder filled with transcripts of farmers' interviews. *No way in hell does this have anything to do with farmers*, he realized after reading only a few short paragraphs. These were definitely sequestered stories of another kind.

CHAPTER 10

Saturday, August 14, 2010—Lafayette, IN

Karyn woke having slept all night on the deck, two stories up from the ground. She had considered jumping (she foresaw a broken ankle in that future), climbing the water spout (she predicted a broken neck in that scenario), screaming for help (too embarrassing), and calling upon the assistance of a neighbor (female preferably), but no maternal looking woman had come by. Besides, she realized that while she could have feigned sunbathing in the nude and accidentally locked herself out to other neighbors, she still didn't have a key to get in her own front door and that would mean calling the landlord, as well. And yes, she had her phone, but who would she call? Not her mother or friends. She was too ashamed to have anyone find her like this. Hadn't they warned her that he was a selfish bastard who only thought of himself? Immature, at the very least. Later that evening, she thought, telling a stranger, who would never meet her family or friends and who had sworn to keep her stories secret by way of human subject mandate, might not be a bad person to call. She thought of calling Professor Delta Quinn. Professor Quinn could bring her a change of clothes and maybe get the key from the super. Eventually, she dialed the number. It rang. And rang again. No one answered. She left no message. There was no one else that she would call. There was nothing else that she could do.

Sleeping outside became the best solution. But as for the relationship, this couldn't go on. After all, she had now spent the entire night outside and had even had to pee in the coleus pot. She had taken the plant from the railing—the homey touch—and pissed into it. Squatting again over the little clay latrine with coleus leaves brushing her ass and urine spraying off the leaves she peed one more time as the sun broke, still low, through the trees. The tinkling stream sounded cold, she pictured a silver flute. The birds chirped. Chilly morning air brought goose-bumps to her forearms and down her thighs. She teetered, lost her balance and tipped the cold, little, coleus pot over as she squatted over it.

"Damn it. Fuck."

When she was done she pulled up her thong. Even that felt ridiculous under the circumstances. Birds continued to twitter. She went to the glass patio door and pulled on it again with great force, but also without expectation, which left her startled and surprised when the door slid open. She went in. He was nowhere to be seen. After making her way to the bedroom she caught a glimpse of herself in the mirror, red lines marred her left hip and shoulder, an imprint of the wooden slats on the deck. She shivered involuntarily, retrieved a T-shirt from her drawer and a pair of blue jeans and pulled them on before climbing into bed. Curling under the covers and still trembling, Karyn tried to warm her arms and thighs by running her hands up and down them. *Friction. Like rubbing two sticks together. Like making a campfire. Warmth. Warm. War. Raw.* She drifted into dreams filled with unraveling sheets and a blanket that knotted itself into massive spit balls. She tried to find her way out of the tangled mess. The sheets and blanket continued to unravel. *Why?* She searched for the source, only to get more entangled in the stringy sheets and blanket. *I'll have to buy new ones. Oh, my favorite blanket.* She tried to piece the blanket together, but the strands fell through her fingers. She didn't want to give up, but for a moment she considered buying new ones. Then she saw Bola boxes filled with sheets instead of seeds. *I'll make a list for the store. I loved these sheets.* They unraveled more and more. *I'll make a list.* The pencil broke. The paper crumbled. Suddenly she was in a new place in her dream. She saw him. He kept shooting toothpicks from the end of a straw, straight up into a drop-ceiling panel. She was in the high school cafeteria. Professor Delta Quinn appeared as the principal, neither angry nor helpful, just standing there, judgmentally shaking her head.

CHAPTER 11

Saturday night, August 14, 2010—Chicago, IL

With his feet still propped up on his make-shift coffee table, Caleb read the unpublished, strange contents of the manila folder—Delta's other sequestered stories. He read from the beginning to the end. While he liked her academic prose, he couldn't quite describe his feelings regarding the literary story he had found in the manila envelope.

The story at first appeared to him to be an over-the-top revisionist history of the Bible story of the annunciation and birth of Jesus Christ, but as he thought more about it he became intrigued as he began to realize that Delta had switched things up—that is, the miracles became explainable and the everyday became magical.

He picked up his phone and checked the time—too late to call her. He'd have to wait until tomorrow to call Delta. He couldn't believe that she hadn't mentioned this little sequestered story, a bit of sacrilegious blasphemy that might make particular Christians squirm with indignation—Mary raped by a Roman soldier? Joseph was gay? Jesus's whole life engineered on revenge that Mary sought against the invading and colonizing Romans? And Jesus, what of Jesus, not exactly resurrected in the usual way. A magic seed that Mary had been given by a Black Magi allowed Jesus to rise from the dead. Caleb gave Delta an A+ for creativity.

She had taken the miracles and turned them into the probable. That is, she told her reader what probably happened; and then, she had taken the everyday and turned it into the miracles. The piece was filled with magical realism. Caleb turned over the stack of papers and reread the title: *The Probable and the Magical: The Secret Story of the Not-So-Virgin Virgin.** Yes,* Caleb thought, *Delta certainly is creative.* This indeed represented the most unorthodox revisionist take on the bible he had ever read. But of course, it had absolutely nothing to do with the farmers. Nor did it have anything to do with research; it should be categorized as creative writing.

Actually, neither the journal article nor the reinvented gospel story gave Caleb much of a clue as to why anyone would want to hurt Delta, or even scare her. Sure the agricultural reports might have been fudged, but anyone could create excuses to get out of that, simply say they were mistaken. The seed companies might have been gouging prices and overcharging the farmers, but that wasn't enough to make someone send threatening messages. The revisionist gospel story suggesting that Mary was raped by a Roman soldier and that Joseph was gay, would ruffle feathers, but the Catholic Church didn't exactly go after Dan Brown, author of the *da Vinci Code,* with threatening messages or a yellow Hummer. Something didn't add up. But Caleb also reminded himself that Delta had accidentally given him the wrong package; she meant to give him the other interviews with the farmers. *Perhaps, there's something in those interviews that somebody doesn't want the public to know.*

But what Caleb did know from reading the materials is that he found Delta an intriguing individual—intelligent, romantic, naïve, innocent, orphaned and creative—a woman who challenged authority and took chances. He liked that. He began to wonder what other chances Delta was taking in her life.

* Those wishing to read Delta's story, *The Probable and the Magical: The Secret Story of the Not-So-Virgin Virgin* will find it in the Appendix.

PART II

A BRIEF INTERLUDE

Black Magic

The people of Haiti and St. Dominique have always known that Joseph and Mary were too smart to stay in an inn where Herod's men could easily find them. No, as early as 1780 a mambo, a priestess of the island and the slave of a plantation owner, told an adolescent boy who worked in the cane field next to her that Mary and Joseph wisely hid in a cave.

"Caves are good," she told the boy as she dragged a hoe through the dirt. "That is where the young mother safely gave birth. That night, above the cave, a starry message, a brilliant light shone to lead the four magi to the birth place of the holy babe. They came from Persia, India, Yemen, and Ethiopia. They followed the star for many nights, bringing gifts for mother and child. One Magi brought gold, one brought frankincense, one brought myrrh, and one brought the seeds of life, magic seeds."

The boy was listening. He liked this story. The mambo had told him before about the cave where the baby Jesus was born, and about the Black Magi, but this was the first time she had told him about the Black Magi giving Mother Mary the seeds of life.

"Black magic," the mambo said. "The white people are afraid of it."

"Why?" the boy asked as he gathered up the weeds that the mambo had loosened, but before the mambo could answer, screams seared the air, begging screeches that came from several yards away.

"Plait, cease! Plait, cease!" The woman screamed as the overseer dragged her by the hair. She clutched at his hands that were wrenching her scalp, her body flipped like a fish in a net as he dragged her through the dirt. Her body banged against the cane stalks. The slaves stopped their work, but another overseer cracked a whip. The mambo grabbed her hoe; the boy fell forward, clawing at the dirt for fistfuls of dried weeds.

The overseer who had the panicky woman in tow pulled a barrel down from its wooden pedestal outside a tool shack. The woman screamed, "Non, non, non!"

The man threw the lid of the barrel aside and shoved the woman inside, kicking and screaming. He nearly broke her neck squeezing and pushing her into the space of the old wine cask. The mambo hoed harder. The boy looked up. The mambo slapped him upside the head. He looked down, averting his gaze.

The woman's screams were still audible, but muffled from the twisting of her head and squeezing of her lungs as she was crammed inside the barrel. The cries tore at the soul of every slave in the field. They were cries of a terrified animal, desperate beyond description. Eventually, the screams turned into low guttural moans. The mambo cringed and the hair on her arms stood straight up. She knew about the barrel.

The overseer let go of the woman's head that he had been pressing down with one hand and now he shoved her head down with the lid into the oak cask and latched the barrel with metal hooks on either side, sealing her inside. Then he called for the spikes and a man came running with two fistfuls of spikes. Without hesitation the overseer took up a hammer and drove a three inch pointed iron spike through a hole in the side of the barrel and the screams seared the air.

"Mercy!" she cried. He took another spike and hammered it through another hole, no scream followed. It had missed her skin. So he took the third spike and pounded it through the curved wooden slat. A short, screeching scream resounded from inside the barrel even though her lungs were pressed against her knees—it was her soul that screamed and the field of slaves felt the piercing of the woman's flesh and the splitting of her spirit. The boy began to cry; the mambo kicked him. "No crying," she commanded. He stopped and listened as the woman's muffled scream turned into a curdled cry and fell away.

The overseer's rage would not be satisfied. After driving nearly a dozen spikes into various points on the barrel, he flipped the barrel over on its side and began rolling it to the edge of the field. Once again, cries filled the air. The overseer reached the ridge, where he stood back from the barrel, took a running start, and then gave the barrel a hefty kick down the hillside. When the barrel had reached the bottom of the hill, silence swallowed the air.

The adolescent boy could not move, could not speak. The mambo shoved his head into the dirt, "Work!" she shouted at him. "Work!"

As the day lengthened into evening and the sun neared the sea, the wretched and tormented beings in the field knew they had survived another day. The cruelest of the overseers had left the field. Only then did the mambo speak again.

"When you escape, go to the caves. Travel through the jungle. Look for the trail of stones. They are left in a pattern of three, the trinity. They lead the way to a tunnel of caves. Go to the caves. The Maroons will take care of you."

"What about you?"

"I'll slow you down."

"No, mambo."

"Don't let the pictures on the cave walls scare you. They are meant to fend off evil spirits."

"How do you know what is in the caves?"

"I know."

"The way you know about the Magi and the magic seeds?"

"Yes, the way I know many things. I know of the secret places. I have lived a long time. I even know the stories about the Original People. The whites call them the Arawak, the first to hide in the caves. Caves are safe. *Ah Bo Bo!!*"

The mambo's words were curious to the boy, *Maroons? Arawak? Ah Bo Bo! How does she know these things? What do they mean?* The words filled his ears, the ears which had once been filled with the seeds belonging to an elderly, and tortured, Ethiopian priest. The boy remembered the tumultuous waves of the sea, chained to the bunk in the lower deck of the putrid slave ship, nearly eight years ago. He thought of the dying man's struggle to protect and pass on the seeds. The boy knew then that those seeds were important, even if he didn't understand the words, but now after hearing the mambo's story he wondered if the older man had been the African Magi. This he considered with serious interest.

After that long day of toil and terror, the boy returned to his sleeping place. He nourished himself by scraping some raw cane against his teeth; the mambo had given it to him when no one else was looking. As he lay on his banana leaf mat among the other slaves, he sucked on the small, sweet bit of sugarcane, quietly, silently, so that the others wouldn't hear. Once it had melted from his mouth, he ran his tongue across his teeth in hopes of tasting it further, but it was gone. His hunger, unabated, gnawed at his shrinking stomach. He knew that he was barely more than a shell. He lay without sleeping. His mind's eye repeatedly saw the nearly naked woman shoved into a barrel. He heard her screams echo in his memory. He wondered what she had done to raise the ire of the Man. *Did she get caught eating some raw cane? Did she fall asleep in the field? Did she rest for a moment or stand to straighten out her aching back? Or did she try to escape?*

As others dropped into exhausted sleep, the boy remained awake. Once the black bodies had melted into the ground against the green leaves, once everyone had collapsed into coma-like states, the sleep that knows no dreams, he made his way to the mango tree near the edge of the slaves' sleeping quarters. There a family of slaves slept under the tree. The boy moved as slowly and softly as the air between their bodies. He balanced himself cautiously and leaned toward a rock. A child stirred. He jumped back and nearly fell into the sleeping father. The father snorted. The boy regained his balance and moved closer to the rock, which he lifted and set aside. He then dug up a small burlap bag that had been sealed completely with candle wax. He brushed the dirt from the bag and scraped the paraffin free, carefully untied the string from the pouch and unfolded the burlap. Inside the burlap was a folded piece of paper, torn from a slave-wanted poster that had blown across the boy's path. He unfolded the crinkled paper and stared at the contents—the seeds that he had been hiding for seven and half years. He pressed them tightly into his palm. "*Magique*," he whispered. After returning the rock to its place, and knowing what he had to do, the boy summoned his courage. Tiptoeing carefully around the sleeping bodies, so as not to disturb the souls that floated above them, he stole away from the plantation under the light of a full moon—a moon as white as a communion wafer, and planted the seeds of resistance in a secret place.

When the boy finished, he looked up at the bright moon and considered which path to take—toward the caves or back to where the mambo lay.

CHAPTER 12

Saturday morning, August 14, 2010—Lafayette, IN

She lay curled under the covers and awoke with a gasp as if she had been under water. She blinked away her sleepiness and turned to see the clock—9:00 a.m. Rolling over on her back, Karyn put her hand over her forehead and began thinking through the pieces. At 5:30 a.m. she had found the patio door unlocked, her grocery list still on the table, her body marked by the deck slats and she had climbed into bed. All of this was returning to her in staccato-style fragments. She glanced again at the clock—9:07 a.m. and then tossed the sheets aside, abruptly.

Karyn stripped naked in the bathroom, but not before locking the door behind her this time and, prepared, she had taken fresh clothes in with her. A shower, a really hot shower would wash the whole incident away, she decided. Starting at the top, she shampooed, scrubbing every inch of her scalp, lathering a rich suds. She rinsed, letting the warm water melt down her face and neck, shoulders and back. Turning the soap in her hand, bubbles came up from the bar and she lathered it with care around her eyebrow studs and her nose piercing. She scrubbed the back of her neck and systematically made her way down her arms and returning back up them to wash her underarms. She ran the soap over her stomach and around her hips. She gave special attention to her labia, lathering again and washing and rinsing the area twice, as if the coleus leaves were as odious as poison ivy. She continued this cleansing ritual until she had reached her toes and run her lathered fingers between each phalanx. She didn't miss a spot. After stepping out of the shower, she dried with a plain, white towel, ruffled her hair and dressed in clean clothes. Only then did she look in the mirror at her puffy and bluish-colored eye, where the phone had smacked against her face.

She made coffee. Staring at the pot even after it began to drip. Her face displayed no emotion. She simply waited. The rich aroma gave her no pleasure, nor displeasure; to her, it seemed to linger anemically in the air. Once the coffee was ready she poured the cup too full, leaned over and sipped from it carefully as it sat on the counter top, and then she moved it to the kitchen table. There she found the grocery list, again. She stared at it blankly as she drank her coffee, reading the isolated items, reading what might have been. Finally, Karyn stood up, picked up the grocery list and threw it in the wastebasket.

She considered whether to pack a bag or stay. She picked up her phone, planning to call Professor Delta Quinn, but this time there was a message waiting for her, not from the professor but from her boyfriend: *I didn't mean it.*

CHAPTER 13

Sunday, August 15, 2010—Washington D.C.

Midnight in Chicago translated into 1:00 a.m. in Washington D.C., where in a dimly lit office the Assistant Secretary of Agriculture, Tom Bradford spoke in low tones with the Assistant Deputy of the Task Force on Biochemical Weapons (TFBW) for the Department of Defense (DOD), Dr. Ruby Carmichael. The biochemical weapons expert, Dr. Carmichael, stood as tall as the man from the Department of Agriculture (USDA), even while wearing flats. He was therefore pleased that they were sitting—she behind the desk, he sat across from her as visitor to her Pentagon office. They faced each other.

Ruby sported short, curly hair clipped tight around her ears. Her slender figure and narrow shoulders cast a slim shadow on the wall as she leaned forward into the light of her desk lamp. In contrast, Tom Bradford carried extra weight in the form of a pronounced belly that went well with his moon-shaped face and nearly bald head, which reflected the low light of the desk lamp.

"It's late, my friend. Couldn't this have waited until Monday?" She asked him as she glanced at her watch. Actually, she discovered it was much later than she had realized.

"You said that your superiors wanted an update whenever we had it." He liked being right.

"That's true," she sighed, watching as he crossed his leg apparently getting comfortable. His navy blue pant leg slid up revealing a spot of white skin before his matching dark blue sock took over.

"As if you weren't here working anyway."

"True, but I'm working on another project." She sounded mildly annoyed. "What do you have?"

"You did say we could handle it ourselves as long as we kept you updated."

"Yes, yes. Go on," she urged him, her voice deep and impatient.

"We received a package." The white-noise hummed in the background.

"From whom?"

"That's not important."

"Does that mean you don't know who it's from?"

"It means it traveled through several different hands before arriving here."

"Go on."

"It contains transcripts of interviews with farmers, thirty of them in all."

"And…"

"And they seem to suggest a possible awareness of biochemical advances."

"Such as?"

"The zombie seed."

"I thought we were only dealing with backlash about the terminator seed?"

"That's what we thought, too."

"Where are the farmers from—India, Brazil, Bolivia?"

"The U.S.," Tom Bradford announced with significant emphasis. Ruby Carmichael began processing the information. She understood all too well what this might mean; the concern showed in her sudden pause and in the shift of her eyes, a slight lift of the lids, barely perceptible, controlled concern.

"The South?"

"No, it appears to be the Midwest—Ohio, Illinois or Indiana, we think. Maybe, all three. Our experts are going over them now."

"Damn," she said quietly.

Both figures remained silent for a moment. The white noise coupled with the hum of her computer seemed louder at night than in the bustle of her busy day. She paused before asking the Assistant to the Secretary of Agriculture, "What makes you think they know about the zombie seed?"

"A note inserted in the front of the package read: *Is it too improbable to consider the possibility of a zombie seed?*

Ruby Carmichael sighed again and put a hand to her chin, "Okay, that's pretty hard to refute. Of course, knowing about it and knowing how it works are two very different things. It doesn't mean they know anything about the money that has changed hands."

Tom nodded, but this failed to reassure the woman who now pushed the papers on her desk aside. She glared at Bradford. Ruby Carmichael, bio-technology weapons expert then pointedly asked Bradford, "What are you going to do about it?"

"A year or so ago, we hired *free-lancers* to sell the seed to the farmers so that it couldn't be traced to us or to *the corporation*. I've already hired these same two men. One of them currently works for RichField. The other one still freelances. We'll have them find the original interviews and destroy any evidence."

"Is it a coincidence that one of them now works for RichField?"

"No, they hired him after he did the last job."

"I see. RichField must be protected, at all costs." Ruby's chiseled words needed no ultimatum to follow. Bradford understood.

"They will be. Like I said, we'll destroy the transcripts of the interviews and any other paper trail or computer files. It'll be her word against ours."

"Who is she? Who conducted the interviews?" Ruby Carmichael asked.

"She's nobody."

"A nobody who has conducted thirty interviews and suggests the probability of the zombie seed?" Ruby's voice dripped with sarcasm.

"She doesn't have a degree in chemistry or in agronomy."

"What about knowledge of other biochemical weapons?"

"No, no. Really, no need to go there," he assured her. "She appears to be an ethno-rhetorician."

"God, that's a new one—ethno-rhetorician. Inter-disciplinary studies are out of control. What will they think of next? I heard one academic describe himself as a cultural-biologist and another as a geo-videographer. Now what the hell is that?" Ruby didn't dignify her own question with an answer, although she considered doing so; instead, Tom Bradford made the attempt.

"I think geo-videographers map terrain from satellites, but as for—

"Never mind," Ruby interrupted, before adding, "Tom, never underestimate the enemy. This little nobody may know more than you imagine."

"I don't think she's an enemy, Ruby. I think she stumbled onto it, but like I said, I have people watching her. We'll check for backup copies and destroy everything. This time next week, there won't be any evidence of a terminator seed or a zombie seed being used in the U.S. Brown and Slaughtery will take care of it."

"All right then. As long as you trust them?"

"Yes, absolutely. They're not the kind to think on their own, but I've thrown a little work their way every now again over the past few years. Simple jobs. But enough to keep them under my eye and they've done well. They're only interested in the money."

"Are you sure you don't want to use professional agents?"

"No, that can get even messier. Plus, I especially like using freelance associates, so to speak. "

"Why?"

"Who better to throw to lions if something goes wrong?"

"Fine, but let's not let anything go wrong."

"It'll be fine."

"You know, Tom," she rubbed her temple as she spoke, "the zombie seed, whether it's a Savior-seed or a Satan-seed, doesn't matter. It exists and we have to deal with it." She paused. "You'll keep me posted then?"

"Of course," Tom Bradford reassured the biochemical expert from the DOD as he stood to take his leave. His security badge flapped against his pocket as he swung around and walked toward the door.

Ruby Carmichael didn't bother to get up to see the Assistant Secretary of the Department of Agriculture to the door. He knew his way out of her office and out of the Pentagon. Instead, barely glancing away from her computer, the weapons expert said, "Tom, let's do this quietly and quickly. No mess. I don't want the corporation to get involved. I've heard they hire their agents from Blackwater."

Tom Bradford nodded in response; the irony was beyond articulation, deserving of its own category—*twisted reversals*, he considered as he left Ruby Carmichael's office.

CHAPTER 14

Monday, August 16, 2010—West Lafayette, IN

Dr. Walter Steath suddenly appeared in the doorway of Delta's office and announced, "It's lunch time." His upturned wristwatch displayed the time for Delta to see.

"Nice watch," she said.

"Longines," he told her. The brand meant nothing to Delta; his mentioning it meant everything. It had a minute hand, second hand, dial to indicate the days of the week, and even a measure for micro-seconds. At the bottom of the face of the watch appeared to be something like an odometer. "You do have time for lunch, don't you?" He asked with a smile. Delta glanced at the peanut butter and jelly sandwich she had packed.

"Lunch sounds good." Delta opened her desk drawer, dropped the sandwich in it, already saving it for tomorrow, and reached for her purse.

"No, no, not necessary. Lunch is on me," he assured her. Delta grabbed her keys and then locked the office door behind them. "I plan to pick your brain for every bit of knowledge that I can," he said smiling again. "The very least I can do is buy lunch."

They walked down the stairs, out the south-west exit of the building and then headed east across campus. Passing the President's circular fountain where some students lounged and others studied, the pair chatted amiably. At the lilac bushes in front of Recitation Hall, Delta started to turn toward Stone cafeteria, but he gently steered her straight ahead with his words.

"I'm desperate for a Starbuck's coffee," he confessed.

They made their way to the open mall of green grass, where among the returning students, who appeared crisscrossing the pathways, Delta spied the young man who wore white make-up on his face and a sandwich billboard over his body—*Wake up* on the front and *It's not a Game* on the back. He came toward them, but didn't appear to recognize Delta, at least not until the last second, when he briefly looked into her eyes. This time his eyes were less threatening and more compelling, reaching out to her, searching for something. She looked away and kept walking.

"Beautiful campus," Dr. Steath commented, as he took in the view. "Very Ivy League, the brick buildings, the old chestnut tree, and the young people, so bright and energetic and full of hope. Ah, the leaders of tomorrow." He inhaled deeply, apparently not noticing the student dressed as a zombie, wearing a placard. Or else he was politely avoiding comment on the zombie-like student. He continued to spout platitudes about the future of America and reaching the next level. Delta, distracted by the zombie student, let the older academic talk on. She nodded occasionally. He seemed to be saying all the right things, "So, who is currently in possession of the old oaken bucket?" And later, "Well, as the cradle of quarterbacks, who are we sending onto the field this year? Do you have another Drew Brees in the crib?" Moments later, he added, "Ah, I'd love to walk by the new Neil Armstrong statue," and "Do you think Brian Lamb will come from C-Span for a visit this fall? What a treasure he is to have as your alum." Walter Steath had done his homework, Delta thought.

Once seated at Starbuck's coffee shop, a place Delta infrequently visited mainly due to her passion for tea, they ate sandwiches and drank their respective caffeinated beverages.

"So, Delta, tell me about the rhetoric unit?"

"Well,"

"Professor," a student-clerk called from the Starbuck's counter. Delta looked up. Walter didn't.

"Professor." The clerk came from behind the counter and walked toward their table. Still Walter didn't look up. Finally, the student-clerk reached the table. "Sir," she said, "you forgot your change."

"Oh, thank you," Walter told the clerk. "Sorry, Delta, you were saying."

"Well, we're a small unit—each professor with his or her own specialty. For instance, Professor McCor—"

"What's your specialty?" He interrupted.

"Mine? Well, mostly I specialize in narrative theory." Continuing, she explained her focus on sequestered stories and the power of narrative to change lives. She told him a little about studying sexual harassment stories, stories of whistleblowers, domestic violence, and work socialization. She didn't mention the Gnostic Gospels, specifically, but she did sheepishly add, "Well, I do a little creative work when I have the time."

"Tell me, why are you described as an ethno-rhetorician?"

"Where did you hear that?" She asked with a smile.

"I read it in a QJS article by Black; he described you as an ethno-rhetorician. Is he wrong?"

"No, no, it's a good description. It's just that I only recently described myself that way at a conference in New York City a couple of weeks ago. I didn't realize that someone else had described my work as such. I guess it fits well enough. I do a lot of cultural work and then I link culture and rhetoric together."

"For example?"

Delta felt uncomfortable. It was a perfectly legitimate question, but she didn't know if she wanted to talk about any of her research with Walter Steath, or anybody else for that matter, under the current circumstances.

"Why don't you tell me what you're thinking about with regard to building a rhetoric program at Harvard. Or was it Cornell?"

"Yes, yes, well we're wondering how you balance the classics with the postmodern and postcolonial approaches. What courses are required at the undergraduate level and what are the graduate students taking? Where are your research projects headed and can you obtain grants for your work?"

"These days everybody wants a grant. I was under the impression that you were going to teach us how to get the grants," she parried.

"I will, I will. I'm also interested in how, as a land grant institution, you reach out to the local community. How does an ethno-rhetorician incorporate say the local farm community of Indiana?"

She began to give him the barest of bones synopsis of her work with farmers, careful not to mention the farmers' concerns about the government agricultural reports, the complaints about middlemen, or corporate seed giants and their promotion of chemicals. She spoke of how farmers, as a part of a specific culture, create shared identities grounded in the struggles of their work as well as the overwhelming joys of that work. She told him that farmers express this connection with the earth and their families and their communities through rhetorical strategies and tactics. She talked about the phenomenological meaningfulness that farmers experience, well beyond simply producing corn or soy beans. "They birth animals, milk cows, till soil, plant seeds and watch as crops grow. They create pure identities; without metaphor."

"What do you mean, without metaphor?" Walter asked while finishing the last sip of his coffee.

"I mean when we talk about *deadlines*, or the *heart* of a project, or being *buried* under paperwork, we're using metaphors to describe who we are and what we experience, but when a farmer talks about the farm he is literally talking about birthing an animal or burying a dog. The only metaphor I ever heard used during my interviews with the farmers is when they talked about the government or seed companies." Here Delta had gotten carried away; she hadn't meant to mention these issues, nor did she at this point realize that she had opened up to Walter Steath.

"Really? How so?"

"One farmer called the *ag reports* the pitchfork of the devil, tossing his livelihood into the purgatory of Wall Street economics, where he had to wait to see where he would go—heaven or hell. Another farmer called the reports the path to perdition. It's not for me to know if their assessments are right or wrong, but I would like to know if the government reports are being positioned as scapegoats; the way automakers blame the government whenever their profits go down. Other farmers described the seed companies as 'the enemy.' All of these are metaphors," Delta concluded.

"Indeed, they are," Steath agreed with fervor and then checked the time on his watch. "I'm sorry Delta, but I need to get back. I hope we can do this again some time." Steath hadn't taken a single note even though he had a leather bound notebook in his possession. He had laid a legal pad on the table during lunch and now placed the virgin pad back into his portfolio. "I really want to know more. Especially about grants," he added. "You know, what grants have you received? Who can I hook you up with to get more funding? I'm sure that companies like RichField have an abundance of grants and fellowships for work like yours. Just think about it; you could support several research assistants, bring lucrative funding into the university. Maybe if we partnered you with someone from the Agricultural Department it would be even easier."

Dr. Walter Steath seemed excited about his ideas. Delta, on the other hand, was less than thrilled. She liked doing her own interviews; it gave her a first-hand understanding of the issues and the people. She thought of her interview with Jim Hack and some of the other farmers; they had become like family. In addition, Delta hated the bureaucratic paperwork that went with grant applications, deadlines, reporting to the company or agency that funds the project. No, she really didn't want a grant. She had reasoned, if the money didn't come from corporations, it would come from the tax payers. Delta felt that she could do her work without relying any further on the taxpayers. Of course, there are researchers who need the grants. Delta simply didn't consider herself one of them. She didn't need to fly to another country to do her work and she didn't need expensive equipment, a trusty tape recorder and a computer were more than enough.

"Well, I'll look into the possibilities and make suggestions in my report," Steath said as he pushed his chair back from the table.

"Thank you for lunch," Delta told him.

"My pleasure. Now I have a meeting in Stewart Center. I'll walk you part way back."

Delta walked the short distance to Stewart Center with Dr. Steath. She thanked him again and left him at the steps to the building. Once again the crisscrossed paths lay before her. *Christ's cross*, she thought as she considered the origin of the word. Understanding cultural mores are often uncovered by exploring the etymology of a single word, she thought. Farm, for example, can be traced to the Latin words of *firma*—a feast and *firmus*—durable, supportive, and to *feste*—to feast in celebration. Food gives us sustenance and joy, both the means and the ends to celebration. The farm, a place of sustenance and joy, she liked it. It summarized Jim Hack's life perfectly. She scanned the mall area as she continued walking, this time no zombies appeared on the path. She wondered what a search for the origin of the term 'zombie' would reveal. *Haiti? West Africa? People climbing out of graves?*

When she arrived back at her office, Leon Robb, the professor from down the hall, passed her in the hallway. "Well Delta, how's your semester starting?"

"With a bang."

"Oh yeah, I heard you were in a car accident. Hit by a Hummer, right? Wow, how are you feeling?"

"Better, thanks."

"I was just going to lunch with Ralph and Ginny. Do you want to join us?"

"Oh, no thanks, I just had lunch with the Visiting Professor, the Acting-Head of the Department."

"Walter Steath?"

"Yeah."

"Why is he really here?" Leon asked. Delta was only mildly surprised by the question.

"I don't know."

"A professor consultant? I'm dubious. Consultants are usually brought in when they want to lay people off. Or assure accreditation. You're not tenured yet, are you? What did you two talk about?"

"My research."

"Hmmm."

"I know one thing; he's not a teaching professor," Delta pronounced.

"How do you know that?"

"He never looks at the wall clock to see what time it is."

"Hmm," Leon nodded. "Aren't you the observant one, you're right, teaching professors do get in the habit of looking at wall clocks; administrators look at their watches. Be careful, Delta."

"Thanks, Leon."

Leon Robb continued down the hallway on his way to lunch. "Oh Delta, I almost forgot to tell you," he said turning to face her. "The computer tech guy was here. He let himself into your office. He said he needed to fix something on your computer."

CHAPTER 15

Tuesday, August 17, 2010—Chicago, IL

Caleb Barthes had awoken Sunday at noon and realized that by the time he was brushing his oversized smile that he was already thinking of Delta. He had also realized it was much too soon to call her. Even with the excuse that she had clearly given him the wrong package of interviews, it was too soon to call. Caleb knew the three day rule couldn't be broken if a man wanted to appear at all aloof. Any earlier and he'd seem needy; any later and he'd seem remiss. His regular Sunday basketball game with Joe, Ani, and Reuben had kept him busy on Sunday afternoon and he had met some other friends on Sunday night for dinner. Monday he'd spent the day at the *Chicago Tribune* in meetings with his old mentor, Craig "Tracker" Richards. Tracker made it a practice to call Caleb whenever he had a story that he couldn't handle himself. On his sixty-third birthday, Tracker realized that it was time to mentor a younger man, not so much out pure generosity but because Tracker needed a little more help these days. Although he could do the background research on most stories, some required travel to parts of the world that required more stamina than he could muster. Tracker's knees were giving out after an athletic life style, his stomach was giving out after years of alcohol, and his patience was giving out with respect to the tedious details and time-consuming fact checking involved in writing the exposés that he wanted to complete before he officially retired. Other times, he just thought it was a good idea to have a younger man on the team. Tracker felt as if a younger man might blend into a scene better, allowing for investigative reporting to advance more smoothly. For instance, Tracker knew he'd look silly on facebook.

At Monday's meeting Caleb found himself so fascinated with Tracker's latest project that he completely forgot about Delta. It wasn't until later that evening that Caleb called his sister Mona to get Delta's phone number. He then forced himself to wait until Tuesday evening to call her.

"Hey, Delta. It's Caleb, Mona's brother."

"Caleb, hi. Mona told me that you might be calling."

"So, anymore strange messages?"

"No, thank goodness. Did you get a chance to look at the article or the interviews?" Delta asked, without attempting to disguise her anxiousness.

"Well, I did read the article in the journal. By the way, it's great. I love the way you write."

"Thanks."

"But as for the interviews, well there may be a problem there."

"What do you mean?"

"The package didn't contain interviews with farmers. Instead, they appear to be, well, stories, um, alternative gospels."

"Gospels?"

"Gnostic gospels?"

"Oh my God," Delta said suddenly realizing what he was referring to. "Oh no, don't tell me that I gave you the package with the alternative gospel story. Oh, I'm so embarrassed."

"I didn't read them all the way through," Caleb lied, wanting to protect her from embarrassment.

"No, not that. If I gave you the gospel stories, then what did I send to David Gold?"

"Whoa, Whoa. Hold on. Who's David Gold? Maybe you better start at the beginning, okay?"

"Okay, but,...Oh no..." she still sounded a bit flustered. Caleb took control.

"First, tell me, how do these Gnostic gospels fit with the farm interviews?"

"They don't."

"Then why do you have them? What are you doing with them? You did write them, didn't you? "

"Yes, yes, I wrote them. Remember how I told you that I often have more than one project going on at a time?"

"Yes."

"Well, the Gnostic Gospel story is another project."

"How does religion fit with what you do?"

"Like I said before, I study narratives, especially sequestered stories. Well, the Gnostic gospels are the most famous sequestered stories of all time. They're the secret gospels that the Popes didn't want Catholics to see."

"So what I read, well, I mean, read part of, those are the Gnostic gospels?"

"Not exactly, those are stories based on assertions that other people have made, garnered from the Gnostic gospels and other fragments. See, I was trying to test out a theory called narrative theory developed by Walter Fisher that suggests that the story has to meet certain criteria to be accepted and acted upon by a community. Those criteria are—

"Wait, wait let me get a pencil so I can take notes, Professor," he teased her. She sighed before falling silent. "No, no. I'm kidding. Tell me; I really want to know," Caleb promised.

"Okay, well, the theory says that a story has to demonstrate narrative probability and narrative fidelity for a community to incorporate it into its cultural milieu."

"Of course, that makes sense," he said facetiously and with a smile.

"I meant to send them to a scholar who specializes in the Gnostic gospels and to a priest to see if when rewritten with both a probable scenario and one that holds the improbable or magic how they would respond. I know they're not very good, but I wanted to see what religious experts would say. See, in theory, Catholics should find the story improbable, whereas Gnostic scholars should find the rewritten stories of miracles as rational, completely probable. A Gnostic scholar would readily accept the story that what probably happened to Mary is that she was raped. So I told both scholars what I was planning, via an email, and then mailed off the packages. The idea was that I could test the notion in other smaller or more unique cultures, cultures embedded within cultures. For example, the gay community should see the story as completely possible, thoroughly probable; as in, 'this is probably what happened.'"

"Why?"

"Because a single, pregnant girl, at that time, in that culture, would likely have been stoned to death for adultery. For her parents to marry her to a gay man would not only protect her from being stoned, but would protect him as well. The marriage could protect the man from being accused of homosexuality. I mean who else is going to marry a pregnant girl. Joseph had no suitable motive to marry Mary in the original Bible story. In this story he has probable cause. Narrative probability. There is so much to probability. Scholars have been studying it since the time of Aristotle; philosophers and scientists have debated its position in civilization from ancient times to the present day postmodernists."

"Probability?"

"Yes, I mean just think about it. 'Based on what is probable,' is how we determine truth, whether we are addressing narrative probability or statistical probability. Gadamer mentions it in his book—*Truth and Method*. He didn't really care much for statistical probabilities or even qualitative methods that tried to copy quantitative methods. Instead, he felt we needed to recognize that we have a historical grounding, a cultural background, standpoints, and we interpret the world from those standpoints; but unless we stretch, reach out for new horizons, then we will never reach truth, or create truth. It's like Hannah Arendt said, "The more people's standpoints I have present in my mind while I am pondering a given issue, and the better I can imagine how I would feel if I were in their place, the stronger will be my capacity for representative thinking and the more valid my final conclusions, my opinions."

"I'm listening. Go on," Caleb told her.

"I think they were both relying on Heidegger, but I'm not sure. So anyway, I think what is probable depends on more than one perspective and the multiple perspectives contribute to our understanding of truth, at least as we know it. Probability is the ground that we stand on to claim truth and the truth, any truth, calls forth judgment, and judgment, we hope, leads to justice." She paused.

"Ah, I see; so you're exploring a case of social justice," he concluded.

"Exactly," she said with excitement, elated that he understood. "So I wanted to start by sending the story to a couple of experts, to judge its probability. The first expert being—"

"Walter Fisher?"

"No."

"Gadamer?"

"No, Gold. David Gold."

"Now see, if you had let me take notes, I would have gotten that one right."

"David Gold and a friend of mine, who is a priest, were to act as the first experts, each providing different perspectives on the probability of the story. I know my friend the priest received the stories because he emailed saying so, but I never heard from Dr. Gold."

"Okay, so where is David Gold *and* where are the farm interviews?" Caleb asked.

"You're probably right—

"I usually am, but right about what?" Caleb asked. "That David Gold probably has the farm interviews," she concluded.

"Okay, so no problem, we'll just switch them. Where is David Gold?"

"The Newberry Library. He's spending his sabbatical semester there."

"Our Newberry Library? Here in Chicago?"

"Yes, that's the one."

"Oh, excellent! I have a remarkable plan. Why don't you come to Chicago this weekend? We can go see Dr. Gold on Saturday and then I can take you to a Sox game on Sunday."

"One problem with your remarkable plan—I don't have a car, remember?"

"Not a problem. Mona's coming. You can ride with her. What do you say? Will you let me take you to the Sox game?" There was a pause. Caleb tried again, "C'mon I'll buy you a hotdog bun."

At that, Delta laughed. Caleb added, "And they have stadium mustard." She laughed again.

"You know me too well. How could I possibly turn down a hot dog bun with mustard?"

"Hey, Delta, by the way, is there anything else I should know about? Any other research you're doing that you haven't mentioned?"

"Well," she sighed, "I am working on another project. It's a collection of interviews with young women who feel trapped in abusive relationships."

"Just another one of those light-hearted, sequestered narrative projects, eh?"

"I know. That's why I didn't mention it. We were all having such a good time. I didn't want to detail such heart-breaking stuff." But Delta knew there was another reason why she hadn't mentioned it in any detail. She didn't want him to ask why she had picked that topic.

"So what do you do to keep from jumping off of a building ledge?"

"I dance." Delta told Caleb. Caleb smiled.

"To Lady Gaga?" He teased her. "Or Black Eyed Peas?"

"Maybe both," she answered coyly.

"Well, maybe we could go dancing after the baseball game?" He offered more than asked.

"Maybe," she said with a smile.

CHAPTER 16

Wednesday, August 18, 2010—Chicago, IL

Father Langer knelt in the dark confessional. The click of the wooden slat sliding across the opening between himself and the monsignor brought his thoughts into focus. Father Langer swallowed hard.

"Monsignor, forgive me. It has been less than one week since my last confession."

"Well, my son, what brings you back so soon?"

Father Langer paused. His eyes had adjusted to the darkness, aided by the tiny lights that penetrated the confessional's perforated partition with its circular-shaped holes. He could see the monsignor's wrinkled hands folded on his lap and holding a rosary.

"I received a manuscript from an old friend. The friend is exploring the possibilities of the Gnostic gospels and alternative interpretations of other fragments."

The monsignor waited patiently for the young priest to continue his story, but the priest seemed to have lost his tongue.

"Your friend may be misguided, but I don't see how this is a sin for you, my son," the monsignor encouraged.

"I knew after the first chapter that what I was reading is heresy and a sacrilege."

"Go on," the monsignor prodded.

"Even though I knew it was wrong, I continued to read the entire manuscript."

"With what intention?" the monsignor asked.

"Curiosity."

"Curiosity is not a sin, as far as I know. Killed the cat, and all that, but …"

Father Langer sighed. The monsignor's smile dropped from his face when he heard the heavy sigh through the confessional slats; he waited. The monsignor moved his hands onto the next bead, saying the Hail Mary, which gave his sinner time to find the right words or the courage to confess.

"I felt lust," Father Langer blurted out at last.

"How did this manuscript about the Gnostic gospel lead you to lust in your heart?"

"It begins with the rape of Mary, the—

"The Virgin Mother?"

"Yes."

The monsignor of the West-side parish in the Chicago dioceses dropped the beads in his hand. The rosary slipped to the floor. He immediately lunged for the holy artifact. Father Langer leaned forward as if he could pick up the rosary for the monsignor, but was of course thwarted by the partition that separated the two men. Fr. Brandon Langer hit his forehead against the divider. Once upward, the monsignor tightened his grip on the holy rosary, but he couldn't disguise the quiver in his voice as he asked, "You lusted after the Virgin Mary?"

"Oh my God, no!" Father Langer recoiled at the very thought of it. "No, I thought of my friend from high school, Delta Quinn."

The monsignor composed himself. "Don't take the name of the Lord thy God in vain or you'll have another sin to confess," he said as if by rote response to the young priest's use of the phrase, *Oh my God.*" Then the monsignor took a breath and added,

"Delta, eh, that name sounds Greek and Quinn sounds Irish."

"She's mostly Irish," Father Brandon Langer replied, adding "…and part Cherokee. I don't think she's Greek at all."

Relaxing his fears, the monsignor took a deep breath and said, "Oh, those Irish girls, they'll get you every time. So the Virgin Mary is safe from your sexual thoughts; that's good. But now, should we worry about Miss Delta Quinn?"

"I haven't actually seen Delta since high school. But I keep picturing her face in front of me—her dark hair, green eyes and freckled nose."

"You haven't seen her, but it sounds as if you've kept in touch."

"Somewhat. By email. Nothing more than catching up occasionally. But I shouldn't have lusted after her, Monsignor."

"No, you shouldn't have."

"And I shouldn't have continued reading after the rape of the Virgin Mary."

"I have read this accusation, that the Virgin was impregnated by a Roman soldier named Panthera. Reading it isn't a sin. Believing it or promoting it, that's another matter. Papal infallibility tells us that these gospels are forgeries, not to be taken seriously. Others who wrote from these perspectives in ancient days were Greeks with anti-Christian values, making up stories."

"So do you think I should just forget about it? I did promise Delta I would give her my opinion on this and the other issues.

"Other issues?"

"Oh, I'm not sure I should tell you," he hesitated.

"If not your confessor, who can you tell?" the monsignor said in a gentle, coaxing tone, adding again, "Now, what other issues?"

"That Joseph may have been gay ..."

This time, the monsignor tightened his grip on the rosary. His blood pressure rose.

"... and that Mary and Joseph encouraged the rebellious spirit of Jesus to save the people from the Roman oppressors. Oh, and then the zombie seed and the resurrection, that's the most troubling of all, even though it's the most improbable of all the claims."

"Perhaps, you best give me this manuscript to review," the monsignor suggested with a serious authorial voice. His sense of humor had retreated.

"Of course."

"Leave it in my office today. And for your penance, say two novenas to the Blessed Virgin ... without any lusting. Go my son, and sin no more." The monsignor sat quietly finishing the rosary in the confessional cubicle long after the young priest had left. His thoughts, however, were not on his prayers; instead, with each turn of the bead he considered the current dilemma.

CHAPTER 17

Wednesday night, August 18, 2010—West Lafayette, IN

Delta sat across from the young woman at the table in the Stewart Center library on campus. The girl's choppy hair hung thickly to one side, shadowing the right contours of her face. She chewed gum as usual.

"I don't know. It isn't all the time, just sometimes. I don't know why he does it. He starts fights over the smallest things. He's really sorry afterwards. Honest he is," she looked up trying to convince the professor with her words, but the swollen, black and blue eye with the ruptured veins left an entirely different impression on Delta. "And sometimes it is my fault. My eye, it looks worse than it feels. It really happened accidentally, I mean we were arguing, but he didn't mean to hit me. He was tossing my phone to me and I, well, I missed the catch. He didn't mean for it to hit me."

"I'm not here to judge you or him. But I will encourage you to find a way to make this stop. Do you still have the resource materials that I gave you?"

"Yes."

"Will you think about it?"

"Yes. But I have to get going or I'll be late. He gets so upset over the littlest things, you know."

"Yeah, I know," Delta said with a sigh.

"When did he give you the black eye?"

"Friday night."

Delta took a deep breath. She released it slowly.

Karyn repeated, "I have to get to going."

Neither woman shared with the other what they were actually thinking. Karyn packed her books into her backpack in silence and left the library without telling Delta the part about him locking her out on the balcony or how she had tried to call Delta, but got no answer. She was glad now that she hadn't gotten through on the phone. Being out on the balcony, nearly naked was too embarrassing.

Plus, Karyn knew the professor would ask, *Why did you go back after he locked you out?* And Karyn didn't have a good answer. On the other hand, Delta knew there was more to the story of the black eye than what Karyn was sharing, but she neither pressed the girl for more details nor offered further compassion. She was too embarrassed by the fact that she hadn't answered her phone on Friday night. She simply watched as Karyn left the library.

Delta sat for a moment; feeling the pull of gravity more fiercely than other nights. The weight of studying these stories of abuse dragged her down physically and spiritually. She had begun to have bad dreams. She was waking up tired every day.

Delta knew she couldn't stay in the library forever; she took another deep breath and lifted her tape recorder and notebook, which felt like an iron ball with a chain, and put them into her big, black bag. Pushing the chair back, she stood and swung the strap over her shoulder. She stepped back and then leaned in as she pushed the library chair back into its rightful place. That one small gesture felt important to Delta, to return the chair to its place; as if, if she could do nothing else to make the world a better place, at least, she had pushed her chair in tonight.

Delta left the library and walked down the lonely hallway of Stewart Center. The interior of the building appeared desolate under the dim light. She stepped outside into the dark, warm air of August, heading down the steps toward the Memorial Union Building. The darkness was tempered by a street lamp. Delta turned right, toward State Street, planning on taking the bus home tonight as she didn't want to pester Mona for a ride every time she needed to be on campus. Delta began to walk along the sidewalk.

That's when it happened.

So fast, so jarring, so abruptly, that Delta couldn't even scream—the man jumped from the bushes and grabbed her by the shoulders lifting her feet off the ground and knocking her big, black bag to the sidewalk with a crashing noise. He dragged her behind the bushes and pushed her against the brick wall.

"Quit doing your research! You're only making things worse!" Holding her by the shoulders, he shook her twice as he yelled and then shoved her with moderate force against the brick wall again.

As quickly as he'd appeared, he disappeared, running out of the bushes and into the cover of night. She was too stunned to speak. Her heart pounded wildly in her chest. It was over; he was gone, but her hands now drew upward as if to protect herself. It was too late. She let her hands continue their futile upward journey, her palms pressed against her forehead and then her hands swept her hair away from her face. She tried to breathe, she tried to think, to make sense of what had happened, but she was still too overwhelmed. Eventually, she took a deep breath.

After scraping her arm as she made her way out of the bushes, Delta gathered up her black bag from the sidewalk and walked briskly toward the bus stop. She could see the bus coming; she took quicker steps, almost running. Delta boarded the bus, showed her faculty identification card and took a seat. As she attempted to put her identification card back in her wallet, she discovered her own hands quivering uncontrollably. To her dismay, she also discovered that her trusty tape recorder had cracked in half.

CHAPTER 18

Saturday, August 21, 2010—Chicago, IL

On Saturday morning at approximately 10:00 a.m. Mona and Delta had traversed the Dan Ryan expressway in Mona's little Geo and eventually merged into city traffic. By 10:30 they had wrangled their way through the city traffic and arrived at Caleb Barthes' apartment in Old Town. Each woman carried a small overnight bag. In addition, Mona carried her laptop, a backpack filled with readings and a bright red purse. Delta brought her black bag filled with journal articles, as well. None of which she read on the way to Chicago from West Lafayette, as it seemed too rude to read while Mona drove. So she had engaged Mona with small talk most of the way, which Mona continually diverted toward discussions of her dissertation, her job prospects in academe, and her disappearing love life due to the strains of graduate school. It didn't matter what they talked about as far as Delta was concerned as long as it kept her mind off of the attacker who had warned her to quit her research. She hoped a brief stay in Chicago, including a baseball game, would help keep her mind off of the brusque attacker, and of course, she was looking forward to seeing Caleb.

As Caleb opened the door to his apartment and appeared before them, Delta immediately felt better.

"I'm starving," Mona told her brother after their initial greetings. Mona always gave her brother a huge hug and he often lifted her off the ground in return.

"When are you not hungry?" Caleb asked her. "You're as bad as a gremlin." A reference lost on Delta who hadn't seen the movie. Delta bypassed the awkwardness of greeting Caleb—to hug or not to hug, that is the question, by deftly moving past the brother and sister and setting her bags on the couch. She announced, rather than asked,

"How cool is Old Town."

"Isn't it cool?" Mona agreed more than asked and started telling Delta what a "radically artsy" place Old Town is based on its nearness to theaters, galleries, pubs, comedy clubs and dress shops. Caleb let Mona brag about Old Town as if she were the one living in this popular district of Chicago. Caleb had lived in several different ethnic neighborhoods in the 'Windy City.' It was a fluke that he landed this apartment and sometimes complained that the area was too cool for his preferences. Nelson Algren's near northwest neighborhood where the man with the golden arm lived would have pleased the darkly romantic side of Caleb's personality, but as a reporter, instead of a novelist, he needed to be closer to the political action. He had lived in Little Italy, Cicero, South Chicago and now Old Town. He had never failed to find a story no matter where he lived. In addition, when he received an assignment out of state or out of the country, he always found someone to take over his lease. Thus, he found new and exciting places to live each time he returned to Chicago.

"So do you want to get some lunch?" Caleb offered. He was looking at Delta and being as mesmerized by her green eyes as he had been the first time he saw her in her apartment. He had wondered if the magic of that moment might have been explained by the colorful lighting cast upon her face from the magnificent, stained-glass windows in her apartment or by the awe-inspiring subject matter of the windows—angels reaching down from heaven with messages for mere mortals. *No*, he thought *Delta Quinn is just as beautiful standing in the sunlight cast through my filthy, film-covered city window as she was in the light of angels. Yeah, she looks good in the light of city soot*. She appeared a little taller in his apartment. Perhaps, she had been dwarfed by the cathedral ceiling of the transformed church/apartment on the outskirts of Lafayette, Indiana, he thought. He compared her to his sister's height of five feet, seven inches, Delta was probably five feet, four inches tall, slender and perfectly proportioned, he decided. But her eyes seemed sadder, turning down at the corners more than he remembered and the green appeared more hazel, than emerald. Her cheeks weren't as flushed and her skin seemed a paler shade of Irish cream, rather the tanned hue he had noticed the last time.

"Yes," Mona said emphatically.

"Chicago-style pizza?" he asked them. It took little to reach a consensus over Chicago-style pizza and Caleb led the way to a pizzeria that he promised would have some of the thickest crust that they could handle. The streets were filled with people who walked quickly for such a warm day. Delta dodged them astutely. Caleb gave the young women a list of 'what's happening' in the city as they walked several blocks to the pizza pie place, including a rib cook off with bands, volleyball tournament on Lake Michigan beach, practically like being in California, Caleb had quipped, and of course all kinds of sports bars to choose from as well as musical entertainment, he had added. "Dancing is always a possibility," he told Delta, which made her smile.

Delta could smell the stench of fish in the distance as they walked down the street and while the smell was malodorous she knew it would be accompanied by the sound of seagulls and she relished seeing the birds flying above. She had felt somewhat landlocked in greater Lafayette, Indiana, so that when she and Mona had driven in along Lake Shore Ave. Delta had been gripped by the blue of Lake Michigan stretching northward and eastward for miles. She stuck her head out from the rolled down window like a puppy on its first car ride. She would've been happy to walk along the beach, put her toes in the water and feel the breeze in her face.

"So what do you want to do after lunch?" Caleb asked.

Although the option of playing in the city was tempting, Mona begged off. "I think I'll spend the afternoon reading those articles I brought. But I promise, I'll play tonight and all day tomorrow with you."

"I was hoping we might go to the Newberry Library and get the farmer interviews from David Gold."

"Oh, Jeez, I completely forgot. I'm sorry, Delta. Of course, sure, we'll go straight to the Newberry," Caleb promised. After paying for lunch, at his insistence, Caleb walked Mona and Delta back to his apartment building, where they retrieved the manila envelope that contained the story built on the premises of the Gnostic gospels. While Delta placed the envelope in her black bag, Caleb extracted the apartment key from his key chain and gave it to Mona, "In case you decide to go out for coffee or anything." He and Delta then drove by means of his Harley motorcycle to the Newberry Library.

It was a short ride and Caleb pointed out Chicago landmarks on the way. The ride along Lake Shore thrilled Delta. It ended much too soon, but she relinquished the helmet, after they parked on a side street, Clark Ave., in front of the Newberry Library. Caleb paid the meter while Delta took in the surroundings. Across the street and in front of the main entrance to the library's magnificent four story brownstone building with arched windows, pillars and terra cotta roof, sat a park which was alive with the activity of a group of boys playing soccer. Their mothers sat on park benches under elm and oak trees, watching the boys. Another duo of mothers chatted as they strolled around a yellow fountain in the center of the park, babies in strollers. The older boys darted and kicked at the black and white ball, shouting and grunting at each other, calling out in Spanish or English. The boys appeared to be between eleven and thirteen years old. They represented races of all kinds and were dressed in colorful T-shirts, not uniforms. Delta smiled at the ironic liveliness and noise of the scene set outside one of the most famous libraries in the country where one might expect to find a studious if not somber quiet.

She and Caleb approached the entrance, made their way up the stairs, and she started to open the heavy glass door with the vertical brass handles, but was surprised by the weight of it. Caleb grabbed the top of the door and held it open for Delta who then led the way up the marble staircase to the next set of doors. The next set of doors opened into the lobby of the Newberry Library where the marble floors of the hallway gave way to mosaic tiles below their feet and a large modern brass chandelier above their heads. Between the floor and the ceiling, Delta found information kiosks that disguised security people as informational guides. Galleries were situated on either side—the R.R. Donnelly Exhibit Gallery to her left and the Herman Dunlap Smith Gallery to her right. Each gallery entrance displayed a portrait on the wall—huge oil paintings of General Ulysses S. Grant to her left and President Abraham Lincoln to the right. Each painting shimmered from the oil glazes. A baby grand piano took up the corner of the lobby on Grant's side; Lincoln's side allowed one to feel the everyday nature, the public-ness of public libraries with a rickety, wooden book-cart burdened with discarded books from the current day's readers' exploits. The bookstore was tucked in the back corner.

Caleb watched Delta; he didn't rush her as she stood in awe at the history contained within the lobby of the building. Her reverie was nevertheless interrupted within moments as they were greeted by a security guard, who made a phone call on their behalf and within two or three minutes a young woman with a pixie shag haircut stood waiting on the landing of the staircase, nearly dwarfed by the overgrown ficus tree. She introduced herself as Lindsey Polacheck, a docent and assistant-curator intern. "Unpaid," she added, "but it's totally worth it. I love working here. Hey, do you want to see the cage before you leave?"

"Oh, yes, absolutely," Delta said, leaving Caleb in the dark. The docent noticed his quizzical expression just as he asked:

"What's the cage?"

"It's from the book, *The Time Traveler's Wife*," the docent and Delta both said at the same time and then each laughed. Delta was thinking to herself, *jinx*, but didn't say it aloud. Thus, Lindsey Polacheck beat her to it, "Jinx!" and they both laughed again. The docent then told Caleb the story of how the author worked in the library while writing the novel and how the time traveler feared reappearing in the cage, a wired area between floors that protected people from falling from the narrow staircase and which had no access. "If the time traveler re-materialized in the cage and without any clothes on, well you can imagine how embarrassing that would be and how difficult that would be to explain," the docent commented as she led them down the hallway toward David Gold's office.

"Hey, I tell you what, wait here and I'll see if Dr. Gold doesn't mind waiting so I can give you the tour. Not many people come for the tour in the summer time, and it is my job," she beamed. Caleb and Delta waited in the hallway for the young docent while she gained permission for the unscheduled tour. Within moments, she had returned with the permission to proceed, and was leading them down hallways and through book collections. She pointed out books with gold leafing and others that looked like they might crumble into dust if touched by even the most delicate of fingers. They walked through viewing rooms, looked at study rooms and eventually made their way to the sequestered staircase with the infamous "cage." This is where Lindsey Polacheck held out a hand imitating Vanna White and said, "Ta-da."

Without having read the novel, Caleb was less impressed than Delta, but he watched her eyes sparkle and her pupils dilate at the sight of the plain, wire contraption and that made him flash those big white teeth. Following the tour, Lindsey led them back to Dr. Gold's office, where she could place them in the wrinkled but capable hands of the elderly scholar.

David Gold was a mature man, engaging in his fourth sabbatical from his university work, to study a particular archival collection at the Newberry Library. Although Hebrew studies was his specialty, he had decided to explore some of the Ayers Native American Collection for hints as to how early explorers and later philanthropists were able to make the argument that the Cherokee were one of the Lost Tribes of Israel. He didn't believe this claim, but felt that it had been made in an attempt to protect the Cherokee from annihilation. He had spent his previous sabbatical, six years earlier, studying the writings of Elias Boudinot, the philanthropist, at the Henry Ransom Library in Austin, Texas. Boudinot sponsored the education of several young Cherokee in the 1800s.

With an extended hand, the unpaid intern waved them into Dr. Gold's temporary office and left them to their business. "Thanks, Lindsey," Delta said before the interning docent disappeared down the hallway. Dr. David Gold stood to greet them.

"Dr. Gold, I'm Delta Quinn, a professor in the Department of Communication at Purdue University. This is my friend, Caleb Barthes."

"It's nice to meet you," Gold said as he extended his pale hand to each in turn.

"I contacted you via email a few months ago about looking over a narrative construction for its narrative fidelity and probability according to the Gnostic gospels or at least revisionist gospels,"

Delta said with ease. After a moment to recall, Dr. Gold answered her.

"Yes, yes, I don't believe I ever received your narrative. Did you bring it with you?" Dr. Gold asked.

"Well, actually, I believe I mailed the wrong envelope to you. I believe that I mailed you an envelope that contained interviews with farmers, approximately 30 interviews."

He motioned for them to sit down. "You know some days I can't remember what I had for breakfast." He began looking through stacks on his desk to see if he could recover the wrong envelope. Delta provided more information.

"I may have written a quick note, meant for you, but inserted it into the wrong manila envelope. The note might have said something like, *What do you think of the probability of the zombie seed?*"

David Gold pushed his glasses back up his nose and stood abruptly, "Oh yes, now I remember." He went to his office door and called in a stage whisper to Lindsey, and then shrugged and called more loudly down the hallway, "Lindsey!" still no answer. Dr. Gold continued, "The zombie seed and the farmer interviews. Yes, that was quite a mystery."

"I'm still a bit lost myself," Caleb confessed. But Delta directed her answer toward Dr. Gold.

"Several months ago I was working on two different projects, two in particular that I seem to have crossed wires on. One was the narrative based on the Gnostic gospels and revisionist history and one was the stories of struggling farmers. You see Dr. Gold, I study sequestered stories. I was attempting to send the Gnostic gospel story to you and to a friend who is a priest to get two different takes on the story." Dr. Gold listened attentively. Delta continued, "I was also packaging my 30 interviews with the farmers to file, not to mail to anyone. I had been going through them again searching for a particular quote by one of the farmers I had interviewed. Actually, I had recently presented this as a conference paper in NYC and had just extracted quotes for turning the conference paper into an article, but I must have mixed up the packages."

"So you had three manila envelopes on your desk; one with the farmer interviews, and two with the Gnostic gospel story," Dr. Gold summarized, adding, "I can understand how things get confused." He made this comment with a wave of his hand, showing the numerous stacks of folders, envelopes, books, and journals that lay across his desk.

"Anyway, I wrote the note about the zombie seed, which I discuss in the last chapter of the Gnostic gospel story, and must have accidentally put it in the envelope with the farmer interviews that I mailed to you."

At this point, Lindsey was passing by the doorway; Dr. Gold turned his view toward her and called out, "Lindsey."

She spun around with the energy of youthfulness and swung her face, framed by the short, shaggy hair cut, back around the door jamb to see what Dr. Gold needed, "At your service, Sir."

"Lindsey, didn't I assign that mystery to you?"

"Mystery?" the girl asked.

"The farmer interviews and the zombie seed thing?"

"Yes, the zombie seed project, we called it," Lindsey said with a smile. "Indeed, I did my research and found a Danielle Goldman working at the Illinois State Museum and Abraham Lincoln Presidential Library and figured that it must have been meant for her."

"Why?" Caleb asked truly befuddled as to why anyone would make such a leap.

"Because upon further research," Lindsey said with great pride, "I discovered that they house the Oral History of Illinois Agriculture project. They have over 300 hours of interviews with farmers from the last 129 years available for researchers. So, I assumed these were from that collection or intended for that collection and I sent the zombie file to ISM care of Danielle Goldman."

One could sense that the student intern was quite proud of having solved the mystery and indeed proved the point when she added, "Ta-da." But no one was applauding her efforts. Lindsey explained further, "I'm friends with Danielle Goldman's assistant. Her name is Zandi Tan. She confirmed that I had made the right call." At that moment, they heard the phone ring in the distance. Lindsey looked down the hallway and then back to Dr. Gold to see if he needed anything else.

"Thank you, Lindsey," Dr. Gold excused her as he watched the expression of hope drop into disappointment for both Delta and Caleb—their shoulders drooped, their backs slumped.

"Do you want me to call them? Or you could go there?" Dr. Gold recommended.

"To Springfield?" Caleb asked.

"No, not Springfield. To the Illinois State Museum—Chicago Gallery. It's about ten minutes away. But it's 3:30 p.m.," he said looking at the wall clock, "...with Chicago traffic, ten minutes can turn into 30 minutes in no time at all." Dr. Gold made a quizzical face at his own comment. "In other words, you better hurry; they close at 4:00 p.m."

CHAPTER 19

Saturday afternoon, August 21, 2010—Chicago, IL

Following hurried good-bye's, Delta and Caleb rushed to his Harley. Caleb was more than familiar with the city streets and without a second thought pulled out of the parking spot and turned west on West Walton. Delta barely had time to secure the helmet strap, when Caleb saw an opening and turned left again onto North Clark and then after waiting for several cars he took a quick left onto West Chicago Ave., jerking Delta's bag from her side to the middle of her back with the sharpness of the turn. He then turned right at the second cross street onto North State Street, determined to get to the Illinois State Museum-Chicago Gallery before it closed. They drove about a mile with stops here and there, providing Delta with a glimpse of the city street activities. She had never been to Chicago before and the sight of the people walking about and the traffic police waving batons to move cars along gave the city its own unique personality. Somehow the streets felt wider and the sun stronger, maybe the skyscrapers weren't as high as they are in NYC, maybe the people didn't move with the speed and intensity of New Yorkers. This is a completely different city from NYC, she thought, a place where she had lived for a short time, a city that she loved. But most distinct of all was the giant Ferris wheel on navy pier, which Caleb pointed toward, even though it was out of view and told her about it as they passed Grand Ave.

"Did you see the Ferris wheel on your way in with Mona?"

"Yes," she shouted above the traffic and the engine of his Harley.

"Did you know the Ferris wheel was invented by an American engineer? I bet not. Yes, indeed, G. W. G. Ferris invented the Ferris wheel." His encapsulated report was delivered during a brief stop for a red light. Delta smiled.

"I love Ferris wheels," she said with delight and tightened her grip around his waist as they took off again.

"I'll take you to see it later. It's the granddaddy of all Ferris wheels," Caleb shouted into the wind.

"Can we ride it?" She yelled back.

"You've never been to Chicago before, have you?" He asked her.

"No. Can we ride it?"

Caleb smiled at her question, "We'll see. Maybe, if you have all your chores done. And if it's not too windy."

Caleb turned the wheel right and maneuvered the Harley into an illegal parking spot after arriving on West Randolph. He seemed more than familiar with the area.

"This is it," he told Delta. She looked at the building that stood at 100 W. Randolph Street but was distracted by the 30 foot sculpture in the promenade park in front of the building—a curving, organic, cream-colored cave with dark-colored lines painted on its surface; the soft, fluid lines arched and outlined the curvatures of the sculpture. The painted shapes made her feel as if she was looking at a three-dimensional puzzle—the kind with loopy additions to angling squares.

"Okay, then," she said, taking a breath and focusing on the mission at hand.

"Delta, I'm illegally parked," he said pointing to the street sign, which is when Delta noticed that they were directly across from City Hall. "What do you say, you go in and get your package and I'll wait here. If I have to move, then I'll just drive around the block and be back for you." Delta nodded before swinging her leg over the side of the bike.

Delta entered the building, simultaneously pulling the address from her bag. Lindsey Polacheck, the docent, had written the address on a piece of paper for her before they had left the Newberry Library. It read: Illinois State Museum—Chicago Gallery, James R. Thompson Center, Suite 2-100. Now, she held the note in her hand as she stood taking in the grandeur of the building's lobby.

She might as well have been Alice down the rabbit hole, as her world changed with one look at the interior of the J. R. Thompson Center. Delta, literally felt the oxygen rush from her lungs. Breathless, for a moment, her eyes widened and pupils dilated as she took in the immense postmodern structure—a monument to metal and mirrors, girders and glass, where the insides were on the outside of the inside. Girders laid bare but painted salmon and burnt sienna met girders painted turquoise and silver. Their brightness intensified by the reflective windows that circled the inside of the structure. Delta stood in an atrium that reached seventeen floors high and at the top appeared a dome as massive as any she would have expected to see in a cathedral in Paris or Rome. Instead of images of Creation—God's finger reaching out and touching Adam's finger—she saw a crystal dome and she wondered if its glazed appearance was the sky shining through. Girders crisscrossed the apex. The lobby walls were a labyrinth of girders; steel beams sparkled in silver harmony with the reflective office windows that appeared like mirrors. The lobby itself, a wide expanse was circled by stores—the Native American store was directly to her left, she noticed from a quick glance.

After glancing around, she looked straight ahead, still taking in the lobby. A bay of elevators slid up and down in full view, like a constant vertical stream, the elevators continually flowed. They were made of glass and Delta could see a uniformed security guard riding in each elevator. In front of the bay of elevators on the first floor, another security officer remained stationed in front a metal detector—both a full body scanner and a conveyor belt with x-ray machine for tubs to hold visitors' purses, shoes, jackets etcetera to be used before they could enter an elevator.

Delta had expected a boring little bureaucratic building painted in institutional beige. She had expected little boxy offices. She had expected nothing like what she currently witnessed. She squared her shoulders and made her way to her right, toward the up escalator. After all, she needed only to go to the second floor. She could by-pass the security guards and bay of elevators.

Upon reaching the second floor, Delta circled around the open promenade until she reached the Illinois State Museum-Chicago Gallery. The gallery was easy to find; its name printed in large letters, plus, the front of the gallery was all glass and open to view.

She stepped inside the gallery. Two women were at the reception desk. The younger of the two women sat at the desk, appearing to be a receptionist; the other woman stood over her using the desk phone. One under, one over. The younger one waiting submissively, holding her chin in her hands, she remained silent as the older woman talked on the phone. The cord hovering between the younger woman's head and shoulder, occasionally touching her neck. She leaned away from it, ducking or scrunching down, waiting for her superior to finish. Delta implored the younger woman with a look, but the response was a slight shrug, as if to say, *I wish I could help you but as you can see my supervisor has commandeered my desk, my phone, and my meaning for being here.*

Delta decided to look around as she waited for the woman to finish her phone call. Delta relaxed into the gallery space noticing it to be far tamer than the labyrinth of girders she had just come from. In the gallery, oak floors and white walls deliberately allowed for a muted background, so as not to interfere with the artwork. Displays ranged from fabric sculptures overflowing from their pedestals to the floor as well video images of water and stones filtered by lights from the ceiling. On the video screen, a woman's form—nude and sensuous, repeatedly moved within shallow waters. Delta watched as the form curled into a fetal position and back out again like a rose petal opening. She wandered further through the little gallery until she had come full circle and thus, returned to the receptionist desk. The older woman continued to talk, the receptionist continued to be held captive by her lowly bureaucratic status.

Delta wandered back out onto the promenade. Just a few feet from the entrance to the gallery sat a podium with another security guard in front of another bay of elevators. Delta approached the guard at the podium.

Ray Little sat at his post approximately ten feet from the elevator, prepared to stop anyone without the proper credentials—an identification tag hanging from a lanyard around the necks of government workers. Several workers passed Ray, but not without reaching for their badges to show Ray and he nodded them along into the waiting elevator, which in turn was manned by another guard. Delta approached the station; Ray stood from his stool and leaned across the podium.

"Can I help you?" He bore a congenial smile and an energetic voice.

"I'm here to speak with the curator, but she appears to be on the phone," Delta said half turning around to indicate the gallery. Turning back to the security guard she added, "I'm Delta Quinn, Professor from Purdue. Nice to meet you." She extended her hand.

"Ray," he responded, "Ray Little." Delta turned toward the open view of the gallery.

"Oh, actually the curator, Judith, isn't at the reception desk. That's Zandie Tan the intern sitting down. The one hovering, with the phone in her hand," he leaned closer to Delta, "that's Danielle Goldman. She's a big wig from upstairs, a liaison between the department of agricultural and the department of education. Now if it's Judith you want, she should be back soon. She's been working on some photo presentation about farmers from the Great Depression era and I think she may be at the loading dock. So I think that's why Ms. Goldman's been down here lately, the new exhibit. I mean, why she's in the gallery itself, cause that's where they hang artwork." Ray had a full frontal view of the gallery from his post; the elevators that he guarded were behind and to his left.

"Of course, that makes sense. Actually it's Danielle Goldman that I want to see. That is, if Judith handles the gallery and Danielle Goldman handles the archives of agriculture and education—

"Yeah, sure you can see her. If she's too busy today though and you have to make an appointment, then you need to go through security. Here, I'll show you." Ray Little came from behind his podium and walked Delta to the edge of the railing on the second floor overlooking the lobby that she had just walked through. She could see the escalator that she had ridden to the second floor and the down escalator on the opposite side. In the middle, where the bay of elevators ascended and descended, she now had an aerial view of the double guarded entry-way with the full body x-ray scanner and plastic tubs that people were indeed putting their belongings into to be viewed by one of the two guards.

"Wow, this place is like Fort Knox," Delta said.

"Oh not really. Once you get through there, it's all open access. Yeah, that's the way the architect designed it. Above here, where you see all the mirrored glass, those offices are open style, a metaphor for open government," Ray laughed a little and added, "You decide."

119

Delta smiled.

"You know these offices are usually closed on Saturday. But Obama's coming for a visit. So everybody and their brothers are spit polishing the city, from the libraries to the government offices."

"It's a magnificent building," Delta added as they walked back to Ray's podium.

"Oh yeah, it was built in 1985, a testament to postmodernism. I know all about it. A fireman's nightmare though, I'd say. Look at it, 17 floors and all this open atrium. My dad's been on the fire department for years. He wrote books about the fire department." Ray launched into stories about his dad's accomplishments and his friendly demeanor drew Delta in as it made her feel as if she were back in the small town of Lafayette, but she did glance over to see if Danielle Goldman was still talking and she was, so Delta listened amiably to Ray's stories.

"You know, I'm a triplet, well I'm one of a set of triplets." Ray reached into his breast pocket and pulled out a copy of a newspaper clipping. See that," he held the newspaper clipping for Delta to see. A photograph of a mother and her newborn triplets sat under a bold headline, Delta caught a couple of the words—**Birth ... Triple Alarm.**

"Triple alarm. Get it? My dad was on the fire department." Delta smiled again.

"What about you?"

"Me?"

"Got any good stories?"

Delta focused her thoughts on birth stories and didn't recollect anything right away, but within a few more seconds she told him exactly the kind of story he wanted to hear.

"Well, my mother wanted to name me River Delta Quinn, but my father thought River Delta sounded too much like *arrivederci* and that kids would make fun of me, saying things like *arrivederci,* so long, good bye." Ray smiled; Delta continued.

"My father suggested reversing the names; my mother agreed to do so. So my middle name is River." Delta hadn't reflected on this much before, but now the thought crossed her mind that perhaps her father wasn't thrilled by the name because it had a little too much of an old

Native American feel to it. Maybe that's what he thought kids would make the target of teasing.

Ray folded the newspaper clipping of his birth story and placed it back in his pocket. He waved a couple more people through to the elevators. As the elevator door opened he nodded to the guard inside. "He's a friend of mine even though he likes the Yankees. He's originally from New York. Hey, do you know why they call Chicago the windy city?" Delta's thoughts had returned to Ray Little's birth announcement as she had watched him tuck the clipping away; she was still trying to reconcile the fact that this man carried the news clipping of his birth with him; *did he always have it with him*, she wondered. She shifted her thoughts quickly and responded.

"I've heard something about the politics."

"That's right. Most folks don't know that. Yeah, New York City and Chicago were in a rivalry over who would get the World's Fair. Some people said Chicago was blustering and boasting in order to get it—windy city. Get it?"

Delta smiled and turned again to look through the glass window to the Illinois State Museum-Chicago Gallery. Danielle Goldman still stood over Zandie Tan who crouched under the well-dressed administrator, waiting to regain control of her receptionist area.

"Hey, Delta, do you know what's in water that puts out fires?" Ray set her up for a riddle that never failed to trick people. Delta turned to look at him. He repeated the question.

"No," she said getting anxious to enter the gallery and talk with Danielle Goldman.

"Fireboats. They're in the water, like fireboats on the Chicago River. Get it? Most people say H2O. Oh hey, I think Ms. Goldman just hung up." She had finished her conversation and she was walking away from the receptionist's desk.

Delta hurried toward the doors, calling behind her "Nice meeting you, Ray."

"You, too, Delta."

After reentering the gallery, Delta inquired politely, but quickly, of the receptionist, "I'd like to speak with Ms. Goldman, I mean Dr. Danielle Goldman." Once again Zandie Tan's authority was quickly usurped.

"I'm Danielle Goldman," the other woman asserted with a congenial tone as she turned around. Danielle Goldman was a short, plump woman in her fifties with pale skin, but rosy cheeks.

"Dr. Goldman," Delta began. "My name is Delta Quinn. I'm a professor from Purdue University. I have a rather unique and somewhat embarrassing problem," with that said Delta pulled her Purdue University business card from her bag. "And well, it would seem I accidentally mailed some of my research data to Dr. Gold at the Newberry Library." Dr. Goldman titled her head as if to suggest that Delta was in the wrong place, but she didn't interrupt.

"And since it was not the data that I meant to send to Dr. David Gold, his intern presumed it was meant for you."

"Why?" Dr. Danielle Goldman inquired.

"Because the data is a collection of interview transcripts with farmers."

"Oh, I see. So you think your transcripts wound up in our collection?"

"Yes, exactly."

"Can you give me identifiers?"

"Yes, yes. Actually I had placed a note with the interviews asking whether the zombie seed might be a probability." Delta noticed Dr. Danielle Goldman's shoulder stiffen at the phrase *zombie seed*. "I know that sounds crazy, but ..." Delta went on to explain that the zombie seed had nothing to do with the farmers' interviews, hoping to assure the administrator that she is not some whacked out vampire, zombie, Dracula fan. Dr. Goldman held her hand up for Delta to stop.

"We did receive the package. I assure you the zombie seed is not under our administration." Her tone was serious; her face stern.

"No, of course not," Delta said still thinking of the zombie seed as a bit of magic realism that she had invented for her Gnostic gospel story. *What's going on? Why would Dr. Danielle Goldman respond with such an adamant denial of association*, Delta wondered.

"I forwarded your package to the Assistant Secretary of Agriculture. I wish I could give you more information but I'm afraid that's all I know," Danielle Goldman said curtly and flicked her hands as if she had just washed them.

"Well, if you wouldn't mind, you could give me a bit more information. Who is the Assistant Secretary of Illinois Agriculture?" Delta asked her.

"Not the State of Illinois," Dr. Goldman said, pausing, glancing at her secretary and back at Professor Quinn before continuing, "The United States Department of Agriculture. I sent it to Tom Bradford. I'm not happy with anything having to do with the terminator seed. He told me it's just another name for the terminator seed." Dr. Goldman's voice sounded angry, the tone gruff. She continued, "Again, Miss Quinn,"

"Professor," Delta corrected her.

"Yes, Professor Quinn, I'm sorry, but that's all the information I have. Good day," she added dismissively. Dr. Danielle Goldman told her intern Zandie Tan that they would continue their work later and then she turned her back on Delta and headed toward a gallery office, leaving Delta with her own business card still in her hand. Delta watched as the woman quickly pressed security code numbers into a lock on the door and disappeared.

Delta felt as pinned to the floor as the butterflies in a display case nearby. She looked at Zandie Tan, who once again shrugged her impotence. Delta blinked back her confusion, lamely left her business card on the receptionist's countertop, turned and departed the gallery. She strode to the right, past the security guard and toward the down escalator.

Ray called after her, "Hey, joke of the day. Do you know how they make holy water?" Delta was still thinking about what Danielle Goldman had said to her. She stared blankly at Ray Little. "They boil the hell out of it! Get it? They boil the *hell* out of it."

CHAPTER 20

Later Saturday afternoon, August 21, 2010—Chicago, IL

"Nothing," Delta told Caleb Barthes as she hopped back onto his waiting motorcycle.

"Nothing? She didn't have them?"

"No, it was pretty much a dead end."

"Pretty much?" Caleb queried.

"Oh, this is crazy. Let's just put it out of our minds."

"Delta, are you sure? What about the threatening messages?" He asked turning around to look her in the eye.

"They were probably nothing; just a coincidence." She slumped before adding, "Let's go to Navy Pier. Let's ride the Ferris wheel."

"If that's what you want," he acquiesced without an argument and decided not to press her about the missing transcripts.

Caleb drove them to Navy Pier and paid for parking, which normally irked him, but this situation was different. Under usual circumstances, Caleb would've driven around the block more than once to find a street spot rather than pay for a parking garage space, but this time he wanted to change Delta's dark mood as quickly as possible. He sensed her frustration through her silence, as she hadn't spoken a word on their drive to Navy Pier. Even after they had parked, she didn't appear to walk with the same enthusiasm as she had walked to the restaurant earlier or around the Newberry Library or even into the building that housed the Chicago Gallery of the Illinois State Museum of Agriculture. Caleb noticed that she didn't walk as close to him as she had walked before.

He took her to Navy Pier and they moseyed past the ice cream vendor and beyond the rock wall near the auditorium where displays of varying kinds were housed at different times of the year. He told her she might like the art show in May, but Delta only smiled half-heartedly. And when they stood by the Ferris wheel, she said nothing.

"Hey, you know what, if we walk further north we can access the beach and walk along the lake. What do you say?" Caleb suggested. Delta nodded to the proposition. Within a short walk, they had reached the beach.

Late afternoon, in mid-august, Lake Michigan's waves had warmed enough for people to wade into its waters. Seagulls circled above, screeching occasionally. On the cement boardwalk, a few cyclists rode by with headsets on, pedaling to their own electronic tunes. Mostly people were beginning to pack their blankets and Frisbees and stroll to their cars with pink shoulders that would surely blister in a day or two. Teenage boys—Latino, Caucasian, and African-American sat along the cement ledge dangling their sneaker-covered feet, shoelaces half laced; their bandanas the same color but tied to different parts of their bodies—a thigh, a bicep, a forehead. Delta recognized the gang tattoos on their faces and arms, but not their full meaning. "A teardrop doesn't mean that he's sad," Caleb told her. The boys looked harmless enough to Delta, but Caleb steered her away from them and down to the shore line.

She walked near the water, but not so close as to get her shoes wet. The light wind swept her midnight-colored hair around her face. She shook it away. After they had walked for a while, Caleb led her toward the cement ledge, to a vacant and somewhat secluded spot. A tree shaded the area.

"Why so discouraged, Delta?" Caleb finally asked. She sighed.

"I really hoped the Illinois State Museum of Agriculture would have the transcripts."

"Yeah, me, too, but can't you just print another copy?"

"I wish it were that simple."

"It's not?"

"No. That was my only copy."

"Your only copy? You didn't keep a back up?" He seemed disappointed in her.

"I couldn't. The Internal Review Board for Human Subjects Research required that the tapes be erased and the original transcripts, the ones on the computer, be destroyed after one year. I was permitted to keep one copy of the original transcript with the names blacked out. That copy is what I worked from to write the journal article that you read. The one published in *Cultural Studies ← → Critical Methodologies*."

"Are you telling me that there are no copies?"

"That's what I'm telling you. The Review Board said that too many copies can lead to risk of exposing the farmers' identities by way of other information leaking. I had thirty interviews transcribed and copied. Almost three years of work gone. And I've only had time to publish one article. I had plans to publish four or five more articles about the farmers, maybe more. They'd be about the tight-knit community, their loyalty to one another. I had all kinds of farmers— pig farmers, corn farmers. I even interviewed a blueberry farmer who used to be a factory worker, now that would've been an article to read. Then there was the sunflower farmer. That guy was a hoot. He only grew the sunflowers to hide his fallow fields. He was paid to grow nothing. Then he'd use the sunflowers to draw in doves. They shoot doves, you know," she told him with her voice rising with concern over the doves. She paused, slumped sadly envisioning her research and tenure slip away.

Caleb listened with gentle care, beginning to realize how attached she was to the project and how crucial their loss.

"Well, what exactly did they say at the Agricultural Museum? Did you get to see Danielle Goldman?"

"Yes, she said she didn't have them. She said she sent them to Washington D.C. to the Assistant Secretary of Agriculture, Bradford. *And*," Delta placed a good deal of emphasis on the word *and*, "I think there was something funny going on."

"How so?"

"She seemed to squirm when I mentioned the zombie seed note, which at first I took to mean she doesn't like zombies—"

"Understandable" Caleb inserted.

"Yeah, but she said, *the zombie seed is not under our administration and that it's just another name for the terminator seed*. She said it seriously, not sarcastically."

"D.C., hmm?" Caleb mused aloud.

"Yes, she sent them to Washington D.C. Gone forever."

"I do have a few friends in D.C. Let me make a phone call. I'll see what I can do."

"Really?" Delta perked up.

"Delta, there is only one copy, right?"

"Yes," she assured him.

"And you were going to give it to me?" He said suddenly realizing the trust that she had placed in him.

"Yes." She looked into his eyes and said it again, "Yes."

He nodded. "I'll make some phone calls."

"Thank you."

"By the way, speaking of phone calls, my phone has been vibrating on and off for a half an hour and I think I know who it is," Caleb told Delta as he pulled his phone out of his pocket.

"Yep, it's Mona. She's hungry."

Delta smiled and took a giant step upward onto the cement ledge. "Well, we better get going then."

"Just one more stop," he said as he texted to Mona that they'd be back within the hour. Before returning to his motorcycle, Caleb walked Delta uptown and on the way told her he wanted to show her the first place he went to see when he had first come to Chicago.

"It's just a couple of blocks. It's the *Chicago Tribune* tower. It's magnificent. A neo-gothic tower with rocks embedded in the outer façade."

"I love rocks," she said.

"These are very special rocks. In the early days of the paper, reporters brought back a rock from wherever they were investigating a story. Later, different states and countries were asked to send a rock to be embedded in the outer walls of the building. There's a rock from the Parthenon, from St. Peter's Basilica ..." Caleb told Delta about the rocks and how excited he had been to see them when he arrived at Northwestern to study journalism. As they walked over the bridge, Caleb pointed to the *Chicago Tribune* building and then watched as Delta's eyes alit and her mouth dropped open.

"It's practically a cathedral!" She announced.

He loved that she loved the building. "Awe inspiring, isn't it? It's even bigger than your apartment," he quipped. "Wait until we get up close," his tone promised something spectacular.

When they reached the building, Caleb watched Delta's expression as she discovered one rock after another from exotic locales from around the world—the Great Wall of China, the Berlin Wall, the Great Pyramids of Egypt. *A piece of history and each one with a story*, Delta thought, *this is amazing*. She turned to Caleb and simply smiled.

Caleb touched one of the rocks, and told Delta that one day, he planned to read the newspaper stories that went with the earliest rocks that reporters brought back from their investigations. The couple walked around the building, touching the solid pieces of granite and limestone, of brick and sandstone, and slate and marble, rock after rock and looking up wistfully at the ones they couldn't reach, until Caleb's phone rang. He ignored it at first. The number of rocks seemed to have no end and he was enjoying watching Delta. Delta, in a child-like voice, called to Caleb every couple of seconds, "Look at this one." His phone rang again; this time, Caleb answered it.

"It would seem Mona has moved from hungry to famished, and says, starving is next."

CHAPTER 21

Sunday, August 22, 2010—Chicago, IL

The next day, Delta followed Mona and Caleb as they led the way down the stadium steps to their bleacher seats behind home plate. Delta noticed the net above them, the players warming up on the field and the smell of freshly roasted peanuts as they came to a stop waiting for the people in front of them to move into their seats. A couple more steps and they had reached the aisle in which their seats were located. Caleb stepped back allowing his sister and the professor to enter first, but his sister, wanting Caleb to sit next to Delta, said, "No, no, you lead the way." Some people stood and leaned back, while others remained seated but slid their knees sideways, so Caleb, Delta and Mona could reach their seats.

"Those are ours," Caleb said motioning to three empty seats. To Delta's surprise, even after reaching their seats, Mona and Caleb remained standing and turned and faced the row behind them.

"Dude,"

"Dude," Caleb answered and high-fived the guys behind him before introducing them to Delta. Clearly they already knew Mona and she was giving each, in turn, a hug, not easy since they were a level up from her. She seemed to have a special name for each of them, Delta noticed.

"Preacher, ... Joe the Hammer, ... and my sweet, Ani ... How are you?"

A bit of bantering followed and continued until Caleb called for order so that he could introduce Delta.

"Hey guys, this is Delta, Delta Quinn. She's Mona's advisor."

"You're a professor?" The handsome African-American man, whom Mona had called Preacher, asked her with surprise.

"Aren't you too ... short to be a professor?" The second young man, whom Mona had called Joe "Hammer," asked facetiously. Joe meant to diffuse the first man's surprise that Delta could possibly be a professor. The save worked. Delta smiled.

131

"I'm too short to be a lot of things, but professor is not one of them."

Joe 'Hammer' laughed and extended his hand. They shook. "I'm Joe Jaworski," he told her.

"Nice to meet you," Delta said.

"I'm Reuben Alstin," The African-American man said, adding, "I didn't mean to sound surprised about you being a professor. I guess if I can be lawyer, you have every right to be a professor," he added with a smile. Delta tried to hide her own surprise.

"You're a sexist," Mona chided him.

"Mona, Mona, forgive me. I missed my diversity training workshop. Anyway, it wasn't because Delta's a woman; it was because she looks too young to be a professor."

Delta smiled, falling for the compliment.

"Reuben, you're a sexist and an age-ist then. It's still discrimination. I suggest you stop before you dig yourself into a deeper hole," Mona scolded. The announcer's voice blared from the intercom, interrupting the banter, announcing the national anthem.

"And this is Ani Kapur," Mona said more quickly, turning Delta's attention to the third man, a tall slender man of Indian descent, according to his accent.

"It's very nice to meet you," he told Delta as the singer's voice began to ring through the stadium. The group turned to face the American flag. When the song had finished, the announcer yelled into the microphone, "Play ball."

"This is the first time I've been to a professional baseball game," Delta announced.

"Me, too," said Joe who then let out a laugh. "Just kidding, of course," he told her. With a big brotherly overture, he mentored Delta on appropriate baseball behavior. "Here's all you need to know: Beer, hotdogs, beer, peanuts, beer, ice cream. In that order," he added. "And don't ask for ketchup on your dog. Put mustard, cucumbers and onions on it; then you'll fit in just fine."

"She's a vegetarian," Caleb told him.

"K.B. you're killin' me. How can you bring another vegetarian into our midst? Wasn't Ani enough?" Joe feigned frustration and posed the question to Caleb, but Ani said, "Good woman. We need more vegetarians to counteract the gluttonous carnivores." A vendor came down the steps shouting, "Dogs! Fresh dogs, hot dogs. Get your fresh hot dogs!"

"Beer!" Mona shouted back at the vendor.

"Exactly," Joe approved. "The guy's getting everything out of order."

Suddenly a roar came from the crowd; someone nearby yelled, "That's the way to do it!" The game had begun and Delta hadn't even noticed as there was so much to see around the stadium.

"What happened?" She asked Caleb.

"He's out at first," he answered. Delta watched as the pitcher threw the ball to the first baseman, who threw it to the second baseman, who threw it to the short stop who threw it to the third baseman. He in turn threw it back to the pitcher. "I like that," Delta said. "Like high five, only with a ball. It acknowledges each of them; a ritual of care or camaraderie."

"Yep, she's a professor," Reuben said. Delta smiled, not sure what she'd said to warrant the academic description.

"It also keeps them warmed up, ready for action," Caleb told her. "It's called *around the horn*." A second vendor came through the stands yelling, "Beer! Get your ice cold beer. That's why you idiots are here. Don't be shy about it. Buy a beer!"

Caleb shouted to the vendor and raised his hand showing all five fingers plus one more. His sleeve slid down and Delta almost caught the ending of his tattoo—*never quit searching for t...*

"Six beers coming up," the vendor started passing the large plastic cups filled with hops down the row and Caleb's money was passed back to the vendor.

"K.B., you really must bring Delta more often," Joe told him with a wry smile. As the beer reached Delta, she said, "I'm sorry, Caleb. I didn't realize that you were getting one for me. I don't drink beer."

"No worries," Mona told her taking the extra beer.

Reuben turned to Joe, "Delta doesn't drink beer, that's the last round K.B.'s going to buy."

Delta leaned over to Caleb and softly asked, "Why K.B.? Do you spell your name with a K?"

"No, but Ani thought I did. He started it. We all met at Northwestern at a pick-up basketball game. Reuben went on to become a lawyer. He works with his father in a firm in downtown Chicago. Joe started at Northwestern and then told us college is for sissies. He quit and started working in construction."

"I didn't quit," Joe corrected Caleb, smacking him on the back of the head. "I took up different options."

"He's right," Caleb admitted. "Joe never quits, he just changes direction. Plus, he's the smartest of us all. He was majoring in engineering when he realized he could teach himself everything they were teaching him and he could get paid at the same time."

"That's right," Joe concluded.

"As for Ani, he graduated in political science. Nobody knows what he does for a living," Caleb told her. Ani only smiled in response.

"So, Delta," Joe asked. "You don't drink beer and you don't eat hotdogs, what are you doing here?"

"I came to see the men of summer, specifically, the boys in black. Sadly, they're not wearing black." Delta seemed genuinely disappointed. Everybody laughed.

"It's a home game. They wear black when they're on the road," Caleb told her. "And the expressions are 'the boys of summer' and 'good guys wear black.'"

Mona finished her first beer and crunched the cup and tossed it on the cement step in front of her. She burped. By now the White Sox were up to bat and a player hit the ball and ran for first—"Out," the umpire signaled.

"My grandmother can run faster than you!" Mona shouted at him. The second batter struck out. "Put your glasses on," Mona yelled. "C'mon, make your mother proud!" The third batter swung hard and spun around missing the first pitch. "This isn't ballet; this is baseball!" Mona yelled and threw her arms up in the air like a frustrated coach. "I should give you guys up for the Cubbies!"

"Leave the Cubbies out of this," Caleb told his sister.

"As long as it's not the Yankees," Joe told her.

"The Evil Empire," Mona blurted. "The Yankees suck!" she chanted even though the Sox were not playing the Yankees that day.

"Is she always like this?" Delta asked Caleb, referring to Mona's antics.

"Oh yeah, this is nothing wait until she's had her third or fourth beer."

"Plus, I like New York," Delta added.

"Oh, you can like New York, you can even love New York, you just can't like the Yankees," Joe told Delta.

"Don't let Joe tell who to like or not like," Caleb asserted, giving Joe a glance. "Let *me* tell you who to like," Caleb joked. Delta smiled, even verged on laughing.

"We play the Yankees soon," Joe told them, adding, "We should try to get tickets."

By the seventh inning stretch Mona had had four giant beers and was singing "Take me out to the ball game" with flourish, if not on key. Delta's cheeks hurt from smiling so much; she had until then forgotten about the loss of her data, and her concerns about tenure. But as she thought about driving back to West Lafayette, Indiana her world of work returned.

"I think I know who's driving us home," Delta said to Caleb. Caleb looked at his raucously drunken sister, who was tossing peanuts into the air and trying in vain to catch them in her mouth.

"Why don't you spend the night? You can go back tomorrow," he suggested.

"Oh, I wish I could, but I have a meeting in the morning and classes to teach. Mona has to teach, too."

Caleb bought Delta an ice cream cone and they watched as the White Sox tied the score 1-1. He asked her for her cell phone and she handed it to him. He programmed his phone number into it and then set up speed dial. And then handed it back to her saying, "Not to brag or anything, but I'm number one." Delta smiled and put her phone back in her purse.

Mona stood up, yelling and slurring her words, "Okay, finish it, already. I've got *shome sherious* drinkin' to do before the bars close!" And although everybody laughed at Mona, the next player up hit a home run.

CHAPTER 22

Sunday evening, August 21, 2010—from Chicago, IL to Lafayette, IN

Delta drove Mona's car back to Lafayette after Caleb guided her to the freeway. He took the lead with his motorcycle, taking his time, eventually leaving her at I90/94 entrance. Delta was nervous about getting lost; she had always suffered from anxiety over the fear of taking a wrong turn, a phobia she had had for as long as she could remember. Mona had, of course, asked to drive, but Delta had squelched her request with the comment, "I have my rules: no talking and texting; no drinking and driving."

"What *can* we do?" Mona had whined with child-like exasperation.

"Car dancing," Delta told her. "You can car dance all the way to West Lafayette." Delta had danced the rest of the way to the car, which put a smile on Caleb's face, but Mona wasn't satisfied.

"What else have you got?" Mona demanded.

"How about dashboard drumming?" Delta offered.

"Really?"

"Yeah, really." Delta dug deep into her black bag and pulled out two drum sticks. She turned them over to Mona who attempted to twirl them, but one went flying through the air and the other fell to the ground. Caleb caught the one that went high.

"She might poke somebody's eye out. Better stick to dancing," he had said, but he handed the sticks to Mona nonetheless. This satisfied Mona, although she didn't take advantage of the offer. Instead, Mona mostly snored on the ride back home, occasionally switching positions, opening her eyes for a moment and asking Delta if she was okay. Each time, Delta smiled and assured Mona that she was fine.

Two and a half hours later, when they reached Lafayette, Delta made an executive decision. She pulled into the parking lot of Mona's apartment building, turned off the car and took Mona's apartment key from the keychain. After helping Mona from the car, who vomited alongside of the 99 Geo Metro, Delta rolled her eyes and tried not to breathe in the smell.

"Oh, I'm so sorry, really, I'm so embarrassed. Oh, what you must think of me," she said looking down at her shoes. "Look at my shoes. I mean who wears red ballet shoes to a baseball game? What was I thinking?" Mona apologized profusely for her fashion faux pas as Delta shook her head and walked her inebriated advisee up the steps to the door. Delta inserted the key and unlocked the door, while asking Mona, "Would it be okay if I use your car to drive myself home? I can pick you up in the morning, say around 8:30?"

"8:30. aaawwgg," Mona groaned in anticipation of a hangover. "Yes, sure, but don't drink and drive."

"I know, I know. No talking or texting, either. I promise." Delta pushed Mona's door open for her and then handed Mona her apartment key, before heading back to the car.

Delta drove across town and just beyond the city limits to the old remodeled church where she was already picturing her bed and pillow. She pulled into the parking lot. The church had easily been converted into six apartments, but the developer had built nothing else on the massive parking lot adjacent the building. So there were rarely more than ten cars at any one time in the lot, leaving not only many empty spaces, but making the place look like a school parking lot on a Saturday morning—all but empty. Delta pulled up and parked close to her apartment door. Lifting her cell phone from the cup holder where she had placed it earlier, she checked the time— almost midnight. She slipped her phone into her jacket pocket, remembering that Caleb had told her to call when they made it back. She'd call before climbing into bed she decided. She pulled her big, black bag filled with papers plus her purse and overnight bag from the back seat. Noticing that Mona's bag was still in the car, she took care to lock the doors.

Exhausted from a day of baseball and the two and a half hour drive home, Delta looked forward to curling up in bed, pulling the sheet up over her shoulders and drifting off to sleep. She was thinking about that very thought as she fumbled through her purse for her key in the dark. She found it. A great yawn came over her as she turned the key in the lock. Using her foot, she softly kicked the door open and reached for the wall switch. When the light came on, Delta's body went stiff.

If Delta could have forced any air into her lungs, she would have screamed or yelled, "Oh my god," but instead she found herself caught motionless and voiceless as if her whole body were paralyzed. As the light flashed on in the apartment, revealing the form of a man under the choir loft, standing in Delta's office, she froze from fright to her spot, unable to move. The man also froze to his place in the shadows. The seconds between them seemed like an eternity. Delta couldn't breathe. She stared in disbelief at the man standing over her computer with a flashlight in his hand. She took in the sight of her home office—papers strewn about, books on the floor, file drawers opened and overturned. She was still trying to make her feet move, her lungs contract, when the shadowed figure, dressed in black suddenly jumped from his spot at the computer and took a running leap through the stained-glass window of Delta's apartment.

The crash of the glass and the sight of the fragments—azure and cream-colored, turquoise and wine-colored pieces—flying through the air broke Delta's catatonic condition. She, too, flew into action. Dropping her bags, she turned and ran for Mona's car. She watched as the intruder dove through the passenger window of a waiting car. *Why hadn't I noticed it when I came home*, she thought. She watched as the accomplice screeched out of the parking lot. Delta unlocked the little green Geo, started the motor and took off after the burglars.

They tore down a back road and turned left at the first opportunity. Delta saw the car lights in the distance; she sped up to catch up with them, careening out of the parking lot and down the road. Once on the same back road she shifted gears, getting the little Geo nearly to its top speed. If nothing else, she planned to get their license plate number. Street lamps were growing fewer and farther apart. The road curved. The intruders took the curve well but had to slow a bit. Delta knew these back roads. These were the roads that led to the farms of Indiana; she didn't slow to take the curve. Speeding around it with agility, she was closing in on them. As the road straightened again she reached for her phone and hit number 1 from the speed dial, and then she pressed the button for the speaker phone. It rang, and rang again.

"Delta, are you home already?" Caleb said answering on the second ring.

"Caleb, somebody broke into my apartment," she told him with urgency in her voice.

"Are you all right? Did you call the police?"

"No. I mean, yes I'm okay and no, I didn't call the police."

"Why not?"

"Because it all happened so fast. I just jumped in Mona's car and started chasing them."

"Where are you?"

"I'm on the back roads."

"Is Mona with you?"

"No, I'm alone. Listen, I've almost caught up to these guys. I just want to read the license plate to you. Okay?"

"Hell yes, but be careful. Did you say them? As in two or more guys?"

"Yeah," Delta said maneuvering a gentle curve and then bouncing over a bridge.

The road straightened again. A street lamp came into view. A million moths fluttered under its ray of light. Delta knew the street lamp indicated an intersection. No street lights, only stop signs were used this far out in the county with a street lamp to light the intersection. She slowed a little, unable to predict which way the burglars would go. It was a natural reaction, but then she realized she just needed to get close enough to read the license plate and then she would back off. She accelerated.

The car in front of her hesitated for moment before careening sharply, making a right turn. Delta knew where that road led. It would take them back toward a main state route, once there the intruders would be able to pick up I-65 within about ten miles. She pressed the gas pedal harder. "Hang on," she said as if Caleb were in the car with her.

"Why, what's going on?" He responded via the speaker phone. The little Geo made the turn, but swung too far to the right.

"Shit," Delta said, as she veered the wheel the other way, compensating. The car swerved and then straightened out again.

"Delta, you okay?"

"Yeah, intense curve. Everything's cool." She stepped on the pedal, gaining velocity; the Geo would overtake the car in front of her within moments. Suddenly, to her surprise the car in front of her came to a stop, spun around and headed straight for her.

"Oh my god, Oh my god!"

"Delta? Delta, what's happening?"

"They turned around. They're headed straight for me!"

"Delta, turn the wheel, turn the wheel. Don't let them hit you straight on."

"How hard?"

"Turn it as hard as you can, now!"

Delta turned the wheel just as she felt the crashing impact and Caleb heard the sickening sound.

"Delta?!" His voiced yelled with desperation from a phone that had sailed through the car, bounced off the dash and landed under the seat.

"Delta?! Delta?!"

PART III

ANOTHER BRIEF INTERLUDE

Graveyard Dirt

In 1791, a mambo lay dying on a banana leaf mat even though she could smell freedom in the air. The French peasants had achieved it, then so could the Blacks of St. Dominigue on the island of Hispaniola. All had agreed and all had worked toward its possibility, including the boy who had grown into a man, a priest of the people— a *houngan*.

He had learned his art from the white-haired woman whose calloused hand lay in his at this very moment. He thought back on all she had taught him, beginning with the language of the people, Creole. She told him of the loa, the African gods—the good gods, like Damballah as well as the volatile gods, the petro gods, like Baron Cemeterre. Damballah is the Moses of the Black people. He is a benevolent god who deserves white chickens, bananas and perfumed flowers, she had told the boy. Damballah works slowly to answer the prayers of the people, in turn the people must be patient and of good heart. Damballah is the *Great source.*

As the boy grew into manhood he served Damballah first and Erzulie second. Married to the goddess, the man took no earthly wife. But Erzulie gave him great pleasure, so much so that he never regretted his decision. But today he prayed to Damballah and presented him with two white pigeons and a cup of sweet white wine. Despite all the cures he had learned under his apprenticeship to the mambo, he couldn't find the right combination of herbs to cure her. Now, as she lay dying before his eyes, he beseeched Damballah for a magic that would keep his mambo from the grave.

The mambo had taught him that religion was born in Afrique from the spirits of two black doves. He remembered how she had told the tale, rocking her form under a moonlit sky, stroking the silence with her words and her soft hum:

Mhhmm, mhhmm.

Captured in the desert, two black doves were carried across the seas.

O' they couldn't talk, but they could sing.

On the ship, strange men clipped each wing,

Ignoring their cries and begging pleas,

Forcing shackled spirits to bended knees.

Mhhmm, mhhmm,

Far closer than sisters, the hugging pair was wrenched apart;

As ships hoisted sails; the bows set forth,

Sending cries to the east and tears to the north.

Exhausted screams lingered long after their depart—

Echoes then that pierced the heart.

Mhhmm, mhhmmm,

Black sisters grew silent,

Bereft of their homeland, their songs did cease.

Without each other, their voices failed;

And in the hull of the ship, their futures paled.

For coins, captors delivered one to Persia and the other to Greece—

Foreign lands, threatening no release.

Mhhmm, mhhmmm,

In these harsh, godless places, a solemn task helped the loneliness ease.

They built altars of slate and shale,

Or so it is told in my grandmother's tale.

Each, unbeknownst to the other, prayed for peace—

One prayed in Persia and one in Greece.

Mhhmmm, mhhmm

To the heavens, voices rose; they sang of Zeus and of Anahita.

They gave the people Mithra and they gave them Athena.

They prayed for power and they prayed for peace;

They sang to Persia and they sang to Greece.

And they begged the gods for their own release.

They gave the people Damballah, who became Allah

and they gave them Erzulie

who became Arethusa.

Two black doves longing each,

Stretched out their voices, but they couldn't reach.

And not a single god, whom they beseeched, answered the cries

Heard only on each distant beach.

They couldn't talk, but they could sing;

They couldn't fly on damaged wing.

One stayed in Persia and one in Greece,

Where they prayed for each other ....

... And they prayed for peace.

Mhhmmm, mhhmmm

He remembered her words. She made sorrow sing like wind through the tree branches. He didn't want her spirit to end. She had been Afrique to him—home and mother. She had told him of the origin of song and dance in Guinea, the meaning of the plants, how to cook without fire and ways to resist the overseer; she lighted his dark life.

He fanned smoke and lit more candles. He sang to Damballah.

In spite of his efforts, the worn, wise woman took her last breath. It wheezed out of her lungs with a small whistle. Then her body fell limp; her hand toppled over. The houngan made one last desperate plea, "No, don't go, mamba. Don't go." Gently, the people in attendance told the houngan, "We must bury her quickly so that evil spirits don't do an injustice to her." But the houngan pushed them away, refusing to let them bury his mambo; instead, he left to make one last formula. "You do this in vain, Monsieur," the people told him. He closed his ears to their moral contradictions and their medical contraindications.

He slipped away to his secret place and plucked the leaves that had grown from the plant, from the seed that had been sewn into an Ethiopian magi's heel, a seed he had carried, and protected by secreting it away under a rock for so many years, before allowing it to grow. He remembered the night that he had planted the seed. It followed the day in which the cruelest of overseers had forced a terrified woman into a barrel of spikes and rolled her to her death. A death he could not prevent. The houngan steadied himself, *now*, he decided, *is the time to save a life.*

He returned to the lean-to, crumbled the leaves into a small container of water and waited for it to boil. Together, the water and the leaves, eventually, turned into an infusion. By now, the woman had been dead for nearly an hour.

The houngan dipped his fingers into the medicine bowl, and then applied the herbal concoction from his fingers to her lips. Opening her mouth, he poured medicine onto her tongue. All the while the villagers shook their heads, saying, "This is not good. We must bury her."

"O' Legba, you god of the crossroads. You must not let her crossover. O' Damballah. Oeuo ou ce' gran moun la k'lle ou, you must give her the source to live."

"Monsieur, si vous plait, cease," the crowd pleaded.

Suddenly, the mambo sat up. Straight up. The crowd jumped back. People gasped. They watched in disbelief as her arms lifted. A collective breath held still. They all waited, awestruck and speechless, to see what would happen next. But as they waited they began to realize, one by one, that the mambo could not speak.

They watched along with the houngan as the mambo stood, and then walked past her adopted son, as if he were a stranger. Taking up a hoe, she headed for the fields. The crowd followed her, watching the unfathomable unfold. The houngan followed her, pleading with her to recognize him, but she did not. "Mamma Afrique," he cried repeatedly. "It's me, your son." She walked, undeterred, to the field, without a word, and began to work the earth under her hoe. She labored all day that way and long into the night. Word spread of the enigma; a larger crowd gathered around the houngan at the edge of the field, expressing their concerns and giving their suggestions:

"Pour salt on her; it will release the spirits."

"No, no salt will make it worse."

"No, you are both wrong. Salt will let her speak again."

As the people bickered, the houngan could stand it no more. He could not bear to watch his mambo in such a state, half dead, half alive. Taking up the salt pouch, he marched out into the field. The crowd followed. There, he threw salt on the zombie mambo and uttered the words, "Regardez moi, maman Afrique. Tu est morte." *You are dead.*

The mambo at once dropped the hoe. She said, "Enfin, mon travail est fini." *At last, my travails, my work, it is done, finished.* She walked back to her banana leaf mat, lay down and folded her hands over her stomach and slept as peacefully as Cilla, the sleeping wife of Damballah. The houngan lay his head on her breast, listening for the rhythm of Afrique in the beat of her heart, but all that lingered was silence and a slight hissing of air as it left her lungs once again; he, thus, pronounced the mambo dead.

This time the mambo was quickly buried by the people; a following service to Damaballah was completed. Stories of the strange event—the waking of the dead mambo—spread far and wide. Everyone agreed that the houngan was very powerful. For in the end, it was he, through the gods, who brought her back to life and he who laid her back again.

***

Subsequently, young men bent on becoming houngans and young women with talents toward being mambos arrived at his hut in the late evenings after their work was done in the field. Each seeker of wisdom arrived exhausted but refused to sleep when there was knowledge of the spirit world to be learned. He took these applicants under his tutelage, in the darkness of night.

They had so many questions:

"May we beseech Damballah without first calling upon Legba?"

"No, always call upon Papa Legba before praying to Damballah. Papa Legba will prepare the way."

"Is there a way for a wife to reclaim her husband from Erzulie?"

"No, it can't be done. She must learn to live without him or share him completely with Erzulie."

"What is the best way to poison an evil man?"

"Graveyard dirt. Dig down, elbow deep and scoop up a handful of dirt. It may be slow, but it always works."

"How do we save a good man who has been poisoned?"

"If he has been poisoned with night shade, then save him with the kola nut. If he has been poisoned with bitter cassava, then try mixing wholesome clay with water and have him drink it."

"What of the graveyard dirt?"

The houngan only shook his head. There was no antidote.

"What of zinc?"

In similar fashion, the questions went on through the night, night after night, some nights longer than others; until, someone dared to ask *the question* concerning the knowledge they all desired.

"Tell us the secret; how do we bring the dead to life?"

The houngan took a deep breath, before speaking. He gently rocked as his mambo had rocked when she sang her lyrical stories to him, but his words were not poetic; they were prophetic.

"The zombie is someone's selfish desire. The greedier the intention, the worse it is for the zombie. I brought back my mambo but her eyes were dead and all her body could do was labor like a slave who had gone crazy under the intense blaze of a summer's sun and from the monotony of the toil and the brutality of slavery. Her arms lifted and her body worked, but she wasn't there. She had no soul. She would have worked into eternity."

His justification laid the matter to rest; the houngan wouldn't teach them how to raise the dead. "If the dead are raised, nothing good will come of it." He had spoken his final words on the matter.

One applicant though became determined to find out the secret. He stalked the houngan night after night; he skulked in the shadows until he found the patch of herbs that had come from Afrique. He interviewed those who had been present when the mambo came back to life, asking them, *what did the drink smell like and would you know it if you smelled it again.* He experimented on animals, killing them and trying to bring them back to life, corpses of little dun-colored rodents discarded in frustration until following a few minor successes, he finally thought he was ready, and so he stole a little girl, Marie, from the plantation. A little rum candy enticed the child to follow him into the bushes where he killed her, strangling the last breath in her throat into a knot that made her eyes bulge from their sockets. Then, he brought her back to life—his first zombie, the first of many yet to come.

His plan was more evil than the houngan could have imagined. The young applicant knew a white man through a mulatto. He promised this plantation owner that even if the revolution came to be he wouldn't have to worry because, he, the applicant, could supply him with willing workers, workers who would labor all day and night, without rest, and for only a little water to quench their parched lips and tiny amounts of food. The plantation owner challenged the applicant to prove it, telling him to bring him willing workers now and he would pay him handsomely.

The applicant took to offering to bury the dead in order to reclaim their bodies. After burying the corpses, he would return to the graveyard at night, dig up the body and turn it into a zombie. He delivered the resurrected dead to the plantation owner. But one day the plantation owner said, *these laborers are old and work very slowly. I want workers who are lithe, agile and strong. Find younger workers; I'll pay you even more money.* Thus, the applicant filled the order in whatever way he could, until a field of zombies worked day and night with only short breaks for food and water.

A slave woman chanced upon the fiendish field while delivering a load of cane to market for the new master. She recognized her husband who had died only a few weeks ago. Shocked by the discovery, this woman ran to tell the houngan. Together, that evening, they went to the field, there the stark evidence supported her claim, the houngan stared at the field of zombies. At first stymied by the situation he stood quite still, but within moments he recognized the exigency. One by one, the houngan broke the spell and returned them to their graves, to Baron Cimaterre.

The plantation owner told the applicant that he would no longer pay him for zombies, since the last group of zombies had disappeared. The greedy, malicious applicant was enraged by the news. He knew who had the power to raise the dead and put them back again; he knew who had done this—the houngan. The applicant hatched a ruthless plot in response; immediately, he went to the graveyard where he dug deep into an old grave of a man whom he had known. The man had died of scarletina a couple of years earlier, too long dead to be brought back to life. The applicant took up a handful of the moist dirt from the man's grave.

The applicant, pretending to care for the houngan, drew closer to him each day. Every morning he brought the houngan a small cup of thick coffee flavored with nutmeg and sugar cane. The houngan drank it each morning for fourteen days, always thanking the applicant. But on the fifteenth day he told the applicant that he felt queasy and feverish. A rash appeared on his belly. A fever made him sweat. Within a week the houngan died.

The applicant was afraid of the power of the houngan, so he buried him in a coffin and nailed the houngan's shirt sleeves to the wood. The people mourned the loss of their houngan priest.

Within a few days zombies began to appear again—one here; one there. Stories of warning surfaced and were passed from mother to child, from friend to friend in the fields, to beware. Without the houngan there was no one to protect them.

The woman who had accompanied the houngan to the field of zombies went to the houngan's grave every night after he had been buried. She slept beside his grave. The people worried about her and one night, they gathered around the houngan's grave to speak with her, but as the crowd formed, the woman appeared to be mounting an invisible horse. Someone in the crowd yelled, "It is Guedé! Guedé pas drah—Guedé wears not a sheet—he covers up nothing. He is the god of the wretched, poor people. He will tell us the truth."

So the people listened to the woman who had been possessed by the god and now seemed for all intents and deserved, righteous purposes to be galloping an invisible horse, holding its invisible reins.

She pointed to the evil applicant who had murdered the houngan, "He has a small penis, but big dreams. He wants money so much that he would turn his own mother into a zombie. He killed the houngan. The houngan has spoken to me from the grave. The houngan's soul hovers above the grave. He has told me these things." Then the woman spoke directly to the murderer, "I know how to raise the dead and I know how to put them back again. The houngan taught me. Be gone or I will have this crowd kill you and then I will raise you up again to be a zombie, forever!"

The frightened man ran off as the crowd hurled profanities and rocks at him. And he was never heard from or seen again. The people praised the woman, and she became known as the successor, protector, healer—their new Mamma Afrique. And this mambo would lead the people to revolution.

CHAPTER 23

Sunday night, August 22, 2010—outskirts of Lafayette, IN

Delta's head continued to spin long after the car had come to a stop. The blow to the rear side of the vehicle had spun it 180 degrees. The little green Geo now faced the opposite direction from which it had been headed, causing Delta a bit of confusion; she couldn't quite get her bearings. Compelled to move, she unsnapped her seatbelt and then opened the door of the Geo. Out of habit, after getting out, she shut the door behind her. Delta walked to the rear of the car, which had taken the brunt of the impact since the front had been turned away from the on-coming car. Crunched metal reached the edge of the gas tank. Delta didn't seem aware of how close to an explosion she'd come; instead, she touched the ruptured metal, sliding her hand along the paint-stripped dent as if it would speak to her. Ouch!

Delta continued assessing the damage until she reached the front of the car, which was pointed in the direction from which she had come, but the scene didn't look familiar to her. The headlights shone down a long, lonely road. An ocean of shoulder-high corn stalks stood to her left, a sea of low, green, leafy soybean plants lay to her right, and so it went until the crops disappeared into the deep-green darkness of the night. Delta could see an occasional silhouette of a pine tree or sycamore or craggy brush that sprouted along the edge of the farmer's field next to the road. But there were no houses within view. She could see the crossroads from which she had so recently turned, but even there she saw no signs of people, only trace evidence of their existence in the street lamp and the cultivated fields.

The stars above repeated the loneliness of the road. Distant. Silent. Delta began to feel an overwhelming sense of solitary existence. She felt lost; she felt alone. Empty and hollow. With the car behind her and the headlights shining a path forward, Delta began walking, without any purpose beyond the shear fact that the light shone in that direction. But then her brain, which seemed to have a mind of its own, gave a vague, dream-like purpose to her direction. This road would somehow take her home, she determined. Delta felt a memory unfolding in her mind. Each step forward took her deeper into the past. Before reaching the crossroads, she remembered being a child; she remembered having an adult lift her and take her back inside the orphanage. It was St. Joseph's orphanage where her father had left her as a little girl, promising to come back, but he never returned. Delta imagined the voice of a woman saying; *Listen to me, little one. Everything will be all right.* But Delta knew nothing would ever be the same. She recalled the adult trying to soothe her with a story, something about the sun and moon promising each other that they would find one another in the early hours of the morning or if not, then surely they would find each other in the dusk of the evening because the light of day and the light of night are celestial partners, reflecting each other. Delta stopped, looked up and searched the sky for the moon.

Delta now felt as alone as she had on the fourth night at the orphanage, the night when her father still hadn't returned and she knew he never would. It was a moment that left her filled with emptiness. An ineffable emptiness. Later, as a five year old child, she had struggled to explain it, but she couldn't find the right words to express her feelings. She sometimes thought of it as a sheet of white paper, emptiness, but adults don't understand that sort of thing, so when Delta would say she felt like white paper, they thought she wanted to color. With crayon in hand, Delta usually became motionless; there was no way to color emptiness. Emptiness cannot express itself. Sometimes, she did apply crayon to paper, always the same thing, the colors couldn't quite take shape, but if asked, she would tell people it was the night sky, the moon and the stars, the fourth night. It was all she had; everything else had vanished.

Yet, as she turned and looked, finding the moon in the ebony sky brought a slender sense of calm to her moment of nothingness, where all is lost, there is also no anxiety, no concern, no fears, no regrets. There is motion without action, walking like a zombie, going nowhere. It was the moon though that turned her around. She found it in the night sky. At least she had the moon, a point of departure from which to get her bearings; she stood still under the glow of the moon, reorienting. Delta inhaled the redolence of the rich soil, the dry corn, the pine scent from the trees ahead. She breathed in August, the earthy heartland, the fragrance continued to remind her of that cool summer night, long ago, in Canada at an orphanage called St. Joe's. She exhaled the past slowly before she inhaled more vigorously as if she were emerging from a dream and only now opening her eyes.

An owl hooted in the distance from somewhere behind her. She turned and found herself facing the car. As bright as two suns, the blinding headlights jarred her mind back to the present, here and now, incinerating her memories—the story of the sun and the moon disappeared like a final spark, a tiny, dying ember from a fire. Poof. In one quick movement Delta squinted and pulled her hand toward her eyes, shielding them from the brightness of the beams.

"Oh my god! Mona's car!" she exclaimed in full control of her senses if not her situation.

Delta now realized where she stood and what had happened. She jogged back to the car, now able to reassess the damages with a clearer head. "Oh, no!" she reasserted the sentiment, adding, "Mona's going to kill me." At this point, she suddenly remembered that she had been talking to Caleb, Mona's brother, at the time of the crash. "Caleb, oh my gosh," she repeated as she opened the door and began searching the car for her cell phone—back seat, front seat, she ran her hand across the rough rug fibers of the carpeted-floor mats, reached over and under Mona's overnight bag—nothing. *They need an app for this*, she thought. Just then, her hand expeditiously came to rest on something smooth and hard—her phone. She found it under the passenger's seat. She quickly pressed number one.

"Cale—," she said, but before she had a chance to say more than the first syllable of his name, he interrupted her.

"Are you okay? Jesus, Delta, what's going on?"

"They broke into my house."

"Who were those guys?!"

"I don't know, but one man broke into my house; there was another one waiting in the car. And then the two of them crashed their car into me. Oh, good call on the advice for me to turn the wheel, by the way. Oh my god, Caleb, they smashed the back end of the car and sent it spinning into a circle facing the other direction. If they had hit the Geo head on, I'd have been headlines on the front page. But, Caleb, Mona's going to be so upset about her car. She loves this little Geo."

"Who cares about the car? Are you sure you're all right? Who are these guys and why are they after you? What do they want?" Caleb shot more questions at her, "This is more than fudged figures on the morning farm report. Do you see their car? Are they anywhere in sight?"

"You don't think they'll come back, do you?" Delta began looking, anxiously scanning in both directions, as far as she could see down the crossroads.

"No, no. I'm sorry; I didn't mean to say that. Really, Delta, it's been over five minutes since the crash, if they didn't come back by now they've headed for the hills. Why didn't you call sooner? I was about to call the police. Are you sure you're okay?"

Delta sidestepped the question. "It's dark. It's really dark," she said, her voice beginning to quiver, "There's nobody around."

"Okay, it's going to be okay. Listen to me, Delta." But Delta didn't listen. Instead, as the adrenaline ran down so did the tears, big tears, that flowed down her cheeks.

"Oh my window," she told Caleb as she inhaled a small sob. "They crashed through my stained-glass window. It's broken into a hundred pieces. It was my favorite—The Annunciation. The angel takes Mary away from her troubles."

"Delta, listen to me. It's going to be okay. Everything is going to be fine. But you need to get home."

"Home," Delta repeated. "Yes, you're right; I need to go home."

Delta turned the key in the ignition of Mona's green Geo. Miraculously, it started immediately. She told Caleb the car sounded good to go and that she'd call him again when she got back to her apartment.

"Maybe you should stay on the phone with me," he told her.

"No, no. I'll be fine now, honest. I'll call you as soon as I get back to my place."

"Promise?"

"Yes."

CHAPTER 24

August, 1986—New York City to Combermere, Ontario

The Baroness learned of the children being *deposited* at the orphanage via courier. The courier had been sent from the Bishop of the Archdiocese of New York, whom the Baroness answered to when she ministered to the needy who lived within the crumbling infrastructure of Harlem. Harlem, it seemed to The Baroness, could well be described as an orphan itself. Neglected. Abandoned. Surviving on a dare to exist. *God bless the child that's got his own.* Her long history of work in Harlem had been met with nothing but stinging criticism; it was one thing to help the "poor colored folk," but another matter entirely to attempt integration programs. In the late 1930s, The Baroness had reached out with one hand to the white community and she had reached out with the other hand to the residents of Harlem. Both hands got slapped. It took another thirty years and a civil rights movement to change the hearts and minds of the people, some of the people. The tumultuous sixties gave way to a tentative decade—the seventies—in which integration still sparked debates, if not physical violence. But by the eighties, barriers were being broken down in education, in law, and in media; at last, The Baroness' integration programs were being accepted. *Who would have thought we could reach this point*, The Baroness had mused to herself with a small smile resting on her wrinkled lips; she reminded herself of the Russian saying, *Live for a century—learn for a century.* Indeed, The Baroness, had lived nearly a century, just a decade or so to go, long enough to see her work finally accepted. She was on a speaking tour that summer, in 1986, promoting her simple spiritual message of acceptance when the courier arrived with the message.

"Baroness," the young man had said as he handed her the envelope. Everyone still called her Baroness when addressing her, and when they spoke about her, they called her 'The Baroness,' as if one could hear the capital letters of the title. She accepted the message with a shaky hand. *Old hands do shake a little*, The

159

Baroness told herself. The tiny tremors come with the territory when one is nearly ninety; she imagined herself like a fragile autumn leaf on a windy day, waiting, quivering, not with fear or trepidation, rather as testament to life's fragility. The Baroness acknowledged her age, and with it, her impending death; facing its inevitability she consoled and comforted herself by imagining death like an autumn leaf, falling into the hands of God. She fell asleep each night with this image, but so far she had awakened every day. "Well, well," she often said, surprised to be alive, "What is it that God has planned for me today?" On this day, The Baroness had gone to check on matters at the Friendship House in Harlem where she now stood with shaky hands opening the envelope and then reading the message that it contained:

Three orphans have been deposited at your facility in Combermere. Your services are needed.

"Orphans," The Baroness said, ignoring the verb that followed, not much caring for the term *deposited,* she then continued, "Orphans have found their way to Madonna House. They are being cared for at St. Joseph's orphanage."

"Yes, Baroness," the messenger agreed with the woman's declaration. The Baroness looked sturdier than what would be expected of someone her age. In part, this was due to the fact that she kept enough weight on her bones to assist gravity in its job. *Meat on the bones—keeps them from the grave.* Somehow the saying rhymed when you said it in Russian.

"Orphans, well, well," she repeated. The messenger gave a startled look as a small smile appeared on The Baroness' face and a sparkle came to her milky eyes. It is always awkward to experience joy over a sad prospect, but The Baroness was indeed suddenly filled with renewed purpose and an energy, and yes, all right a sense of joy. She didn't try to hide it from the messenger. *The Holy Spirit has filled my soul,* she thought. *And why shouldn't it be so?* After all, the orphanage had been one of her first acts of service devoted to those most in need when she first arrived in Combermere, Canada. *Ah, such a long time ago.*

Born Ekaterina Fydodorovna Kolyschkine in Nizhny Novgorod, Russia, in 1896, she lived the life of a minor aristocrat. Her parents' home had a glass chandelier in the dining room and finely-crafted furniture in the living room, velvet draperies hung from Victorian style hooks to keep howling winter winds at bay and the Persian rug kept the floors from cracking under January's cold. The lace tablecloth had been imported from Ireland and acted as backdrop for the silver and china on the table. Ekaterina warmed her hands at a fireplace that never wanted for wood. Indeed, her bed was warmed with hot stones before she and her sister climbed into it at night, where they faithfully repeated their Byzantine Catholic prayers before they fell asleep, giving over their adolescent innocence to the Church. But genuine warmth of the spirit and refinement came from the leather bound books in the library, which the parents encouraged the children to read.

Educated during her early adolescent years at the prestigious Princess Obolensky Academy in St. Petersburg, Ekaterina grew into a mature girl who held such poise and grace that her father had to make matrimonial decisions on her behalf before she even reached the age of fourteen. At that time, he chose to marry his daughter to her own first cousin, Boris de Heuck. Boris was charming, albeit a bit of a sycophant, who would do well in sophisticated social circles, the father decided. Boris would certainly be able to carry on the family business and make additional connections for the Kolyschkine family. More importantly to Ekaterina's father, marriage to Boris would assure that the blood line would be preserved, purity undisturbed, keeping the wealth and reputation of and in the family. At the age of fifteen, the girl entered marriage.

The First World War interrupted the newlyweds, separating them as each took on their duties for mother Russia. Ekaterina became a nurse with the Red Cross; she was sent to the front line where she witnessed the blood soaked horrors of war. She hoped to put the smell of rotting entrails and gangrene limbs behind her at the end of the war when she and Boris returned to St. Petersburg. But when they arrived on the edge of the city they heard the news and found themselves in the midst of a revolution. They made their way to her parents' home only to find it being ransacked—velvet draperies being dragged through the streets. They watched from the alley across the narrow lane until someone spotted them, a past servant of Boris's family. The mob turned on them. Boris grabbed his wife by the hand and flew through the back alleys of St. Petersburg. Their lives in jeopardy, they found a priest in a darkened corner of a cathedral who helped to secret them out of the country.

The pair arrived penniless in Finland. The cold and hunger nearly ended their lives, but the kindness of strangers plus their own ingenuity allowed them to survive. With Russia behind them, they made their way to England, where Ekaterina, once again sought help from the Church. Eventually she accepted baptism into the Roman Catholic Church, but she continued to hold a decided preference for the Greek traditions. This new baptism took place on November 27, 1919, a time of turmoil in Europe.

While Russia was no place for nobility, England was no place for Catholics. Three years later the couple immigrated to Canada. Calling herself Catherine, she began telling her story of survival— her words were eloquent, her stories filled with danger and drama, close calls, and humble heroics. Audiences begged for more; they paid money to hear her lecture; soon, she and Boris found themselves, once again, quite capable of buying velvet curtains. Boris had longed for his comfortable life to return and he spent their money on strong drink, red meat, and gifts for other women.

Catherine, to the contrary, sought solace in the Church. She spoke with the Bishop of Toronto and with his guidance she used her money to open a place for the poor, an interracial house of friendship, one in Toronto and one in Harlem. Ahead of her time, her work on racial integration was questioned, but she refused to give up. She dedicated herself to social activism as passionately as Boris dedicated himself to debauchery. Eventually, Catherine, unable to stomach Boris's infidelity and gluttonous ways, had their marriage annulled.

She began writing books, which allowed her to extend her lecture series. Dozens of Friendship Houses opened and Catherine became a minor celebrity. Not only was she telling stories on the speaker's circuit, but now stories were being written about her, most notably by Eddy Doherty, an award-winning reporter, who found the Russian-born Baroness mesmerizing. A rascal and an adventurer himself, the charming Irishman won the heart of The Baroness. He called her

"Katie" and she couldn't help but smile at his American brashness and sense of humor. She was as taken with him as he with her.

Divorce, an ugly word for Catholics, turned Catherine from famous to infamous, as she made the split from Boris official in civil terms and married Eddy Doherty. Disgust hung on the final syllable of the word divorcée as gossips gathered to drop judgmental comments. Tsk, tsk. Her reputation sullied and her work tarnished, The Baroness and Eddy went north to Combermere, Ontario. There they opened the Madonna House and the St. Joseph's orphanage in 1947, as well as a place where families could come on retreat, staying in simple cabins, enjoying the kinship, building bonds with each other without the distractions of the everyday. Loyal followers staffed the orphanage and ran the retreat. The Madonna House became headquarters for training the multiple missionaries that the notable couple supported and sent around the world, from Harlem to Haiti.

It was there in Harlem, in 1986, that The Baroness read the message, which reported that orphans had been *deposited* at St. Joseph's and her services were once again needed with respect to caring for the lost, little ones. The Canadian orphanage had not cared for children in nearly twenty years. The news came as a surprise, and carried a mixed message for The Baroness—meaningful work dressed in someone else's loss. The nearly-ninety-year-old Baroness folded the note and replaced it in the envelope. Her silver hair, swept up in a chignon, fluttered slightly as she elegantly threw her thick knit shawl over her shoulder, saying, "Duty of the moment calls." The Baroness thanked the messenger and promptly took leave from Harlem in order to meet the latest orphans.

CHAPTER 25

August, 1986—Combermere, Ontario

Immediately upon her return to Combermere, The Baroness called a meeting with her staff. With her husband Eddy at her side, the group sat around the long, pine wood dining table, the same table where Delta had received fresh un-homogenized, non-pasteurized milk and discovered that it tasted very different from the store bought milk she had been used to drinking at home. The adults who were now convening at the table drank warm tea, while the children slept.

"When did they arrive?" The Baroness asked.

"About a week ago," Marie told her.

"What do we know about them?" Eddy asked.

"Very little," Teresa added. "We don't even know their names."

"The father appeared at the door with them, holding the two youngest in his arms and the girl by his side. He explained that his wife had taken ill and he just needed to leave the children until dinner time, adding that he'd be back," Tom reported.

"And it's been seven days?"

"Yes."

"Did you call the authorities?" The Baroness questioned the staff members.

"Yes, we called you and Eddy," Tom said with a smile. The Baroness smiled in return.

"B, we're concerned about the eldest child," Teresa told The Baroness, addressing her in the informal endearment sometimes used around Madonna House and St. Joseph's orphanage.

"Not the other two?" The Baroness queried.

"Apparently it's easier to distract younger children," Tom surmised.

"How so?" Eddy asked for details.

"The little ones like imaginative games. They play hide and seek. They pretend to ride horses, galloping about. They'll listen to stories and climb up in your lap."

"How old do you think they are?"

"The little ones? Two and three," Teresa guessed. Tom and Marie nodded agreement.

"And the older one?" Eddy asked, taking a sip of tea.

"Four or five, I'd say," Tom looked to Marie and Teresa for confirmation. All agreed at the assessment. "Marie has been taking care of her, for the most part," Tom added. The Baroness looked to Marie, a First Nations woman, a Winnebago and Fox woman, a Catholic woman.

"How is the child adjusting?" The Baroness asked. Marie, who usually begins her conversations with silence, gave thoughtful pause before answering. The Baroness waited. But Teresa, a New Yorker by birth, always found the silence a bit too long and unsettling, she jumped in.

"It's been so long since children stayed at the orphanage, well, we really didn't know how to take care of them at first," Teresa pleaded her case. "The father did say he was coming back at dinner time the first day." The Baroness listened to Teresa's sentences laden with disclaimers, building a defense, exacting an apologia. The Baroness concluded that Teresa felt as though she or they had done something wrong, and needed to confess. Teresa continued to explain. "I should have done more. I put a pile of old clothes from the donations' collection on the table," she explained, tapping the very table at which they were all sitting. "I just expected them to be able to pick out what they wanted to wear. The four year old ended up dressing her siblings."

The Baroness nodded. "Perhaps, you offered her purpose," The Baroness said gently.

"Perhaps, but more likely I handed her a nearly insurmountable task," Teresa berated herself. The Baroness smiled softly at the staff member, absolution offered. Then she turned her gaze toward Marie again. The First Nations woman spoke:

"Every day the little girl went to the end of the drive and watched one way and then the other way, down the road, waiting for her father to return. But on the fourth day, she gave up. I saw it in her eyes. I tried to console her by telling her that parents and children are like the sun and the moon, once they were one light in the sky and somehow they became separated, but the sun and moon follow each other, looking for each other, sometimes they meet in the morning and sometimes they meet at night, they see each other and then they're happy again."

"Did the story help?" The Baroness wondered.

"I'm not sure, I doubt it," Marie shrugged. "But maybe she'll carry it with her. For now, I think the child's spirit has left her. She's like a zombie. Today, I told her that you were coming. I said, 'The Baroness is coming; she'll help.' She seemed interested, maybe even hopeful." The Baroness' body appeared conflicted, first rising to the challenge, then slumping slightly under the weight of the responsibility.

"It's late," The Baroness announced at last. "I'll meet the children in the morning." With that said the meeting was adjourned. Reality had arrived, slapping romanticism in the face. The Baroness now secretly berated herself for a sin for which she had no name, described in her own mind as embracing joy at the expense of someone else's pain. *The poor child.*

CHAPTER 26

September, 1986—Combermere, Ontario

"I am The Baroness Ekaterina Fydodorovna Kolyschkine from Russia." The Baroness' title and rich Russian accent mesmerized the child. The Baroness appeared stately, regal, like a fairy godmother or an older version of the Good Witch of the North. Her staff—Tom, Marie, and Teresa—and her husband, Eddy, waited in the wings, so to speak, listening in and watching from the kitchen. They cleaned the breakfast dishes ever so quietly so that they could hear the exchange between The Baroness and the child.

"What is your title?" The Baroness asked the child.

"Title?"

"You do have a title, don't you?"

"I don't think so," Delta responded a little worried.

"Well, at least you have a name, yes?"

"Yes, Delta. Delta Quinn."

"That's a good name," The Baroness told the child. "Why wouldn't you tell my staff your name?"

"We're not supposed to talk to strangers."

"Of course, but then why are you willing to talk to me?"

"The lady, who looks a little like my mother, said that you were coming to help us. Can you?"

"You're asking me if I can help," The Baroness repeated. The child looked up with wide hope-filled eyes. The Baroness hesitated.

"My father is important," the child offered as if it would persuade The Baroness to help find him or at least be helpful.

"How do know he is he important?"

"He wears a cape—black with red trim—and carries a sword at his side in the parade."

"The Knights of Columbus?" The Baroness considered.

"Yes!" the child responded quickly.

"Where was your father going when he dropped you off here?"

This question had a dismaying effect on the child. She envisioned her father driving, driving, driving.

"Nowhere. He was just driving."

"How long had you been driving before arriving here?"

The child thought before answering the question, "Three days, I think." She paused again adding, "I think my father is at the North Pole by now. I think the van is stuck on the ice. The tires are spinning, but he keeps driving."

"What makes you think he is still driving?"

"His eyes. His eyes were filled with emptiness."

"Emptiness?"

"Yes, his eyes said he would drive and drive and drive and drive. I think he's in our van driving across an icy land, maybe his wheels are spinning, maybe he needs our help, or else he's going to drive forever, maybe all the way around the world," the child became quiet, pensive. She looked far away, and simultaneously, deep inside herself, before adding sadly with a slight shake of her little head, "He's not coming back."

"I believe you," The Baroness offered, nearly overwhelmed by the honest assessment coming from a four year old, nodding in sympathy and extending her arms wide so that the child could climb up onto her lap and into a waiting hug. Delta, exhausted by grief and fear, homesickness and longing, climbed into that hug with great relief, but also with a realistic conviction that hope had disintegrated; they would never find her father. Delta's moist eyes expressed dried up dreams. The Baroness, who had known so much loss in her own life, wrapped her thick knit shawl around Delta and rocked her gently. As she rocked backward, The Baroness noticed the child's hand was still curled into a fist. She touched her fingers gently, eventually loosening Delta's grip.

"What have we here?"

"My stones," Delta told her. The child uncurled her fingers; she held two small stones—one, a tiny, dusky rose-colored piece of granite with shades of pink and grey swirled through it, the other, a small flat rock with the impression of a fossilized fern. Addressing The Baroness, she added, "My mother said they have a soul. Everything has a soul. The stones keep me safe."

"Where did you find them?" The Baroness questioned.

"This one is from my grandmother's home. We visited there a long time ago," Delta said of the pink granite. "This one is from my home. It's a fern from the time of dinosaurs," she told The Baroness.

"They're quite beautiful, quite beautiful."

The Baroness sat quietly for a while with the child before calling Marie and the others into the parlor. "Marie, would you take the children for a walk by the lake?"

"Delta, would you show Eddy your special stones?"

Delta nodded. Eddy Doherty took each stone in turn, rolled it through his fingers, flipping each over, studying them carefully before returning them to the little girl. There was nothing Eddy Doherty, the investigative reporter, liked better than a good mystery to solve. The few answers that Delta had given, along with the stones were not much to go on, but as a journalistic sleuth, he had used far fewer clues than this to discover people's identities or their secrets. Once Marie took the children for a walk by the lake, Eddy set The Baroness' mind at ease.

"Katie, I promise you, I'll find out what happened to her family."

CHAPTER 27

Sunday night, August 22, 2010—outskirts of Lafayette, IN

On the drive back to her apartment Delta tried to steer her emotions away from the burglary, the loss of her majestic-stained-glass window and the brutalization of Mona's car. She also tried to put the image of the lonely, dark road behind her as she drove home to her apartment in the converted church. But the attempt failed; her thoughts moved from one disaster to the other repeatedly, until it had landed on the memory of St. Joseph's orphanage.

After a long stretch of country road and memories emerging from the past, after she had turned left and crossed the bridge, gone around the curve and finally driven down the side street and into the parking lot of the remodeled church, Delta parked the mangled Geo. Two sheriffs' cars were sitting in front of the building, emergency lights on and spinning—red and blue. Now her mind re-entered the moment where memories disappear and the nearness of now threatens the endorphins that had been flitting about the neuron-receptors, landing like butterflies that deposit pleasant feelings over sad memories. In this moment, with police flashers spinning, Delta began to regret not having told Sheriff Turner about the threatening phone calls she had received before being hit by someone driving a Hummer. Delta wiped away the tears that had smudged her mascara, inhaled a great breath of oxygen, steeled her nerves, and exited the car.

Within moments, she stood in the archway of her apartment. Her overnight bag, purse, and black, canvas bag filled with papers lay exactly where she had dropped them previously–when having come face-to-face with a burglar in her apartment. Sheriff Turner along with another deputy stood in the center of the living room, shaking their heads at the broken glass and ransacked office area.

But it was her neighbor, Mrs. Rushka who took a step toward Delta and spoke first. Mrs. Rushka had been standing next to the sheriff and deputy, dressed in her flower-print housecoat and fuzzy slippers; she held the front of her robe together, modestly at the neckline, with one hand. Her henna-colored hair seemed less abrasive in the soft illumination. Delta was used to seeing Mrs. Rushka in the unforgiving light of day, where her hair appeared like a tawny, copper-colored covering, with dried, thinning strands of dyed grey, but now under these circumstances and the calming glow of the stained-glass lighting, Mrs. Rushka's hair looked warm, framing her aging face in a kind, forgiving manner. Her Russian accent seemed protective; her words maternal.

"I was so worried about you, my dear. When I heard the window crash and then saw you chase after that car, I called 911."

"Oh, thank you, Mrs. Rushka," Delta expressed genuine indebtedness. "I really appreciate your help, but it's so late, I shouldn't keep you up any longer. I promise I'll talk with you tomorrow," Delta politely assured her, thinking it would be easier to explain everything after a good night's sleep.

"Nonsense," Mrs. Rushka told the young professor. "I'll go fix you a nice cup of sage and rooibus tea while you talk to the sheriff. The tea will help you sleep. Poor girl, what you've been through," Mrs. Rushka added while lightly squeezing Delta's arm before taking her leave.

However, a good night's sleep was not in Delta's immediate future. The sheriff had questions to ask and a report to write; he needed a statement. "Of course," Delta agreed to answer his questions, right after she called Caleb so that she could tell him that she had arrived safely at home. Then Delta gave her full attention to Sheriff Turner.

Unlike her first conversation with Sheriff Turner, following her original car accident—the hit and run that totaled her coup—Delta told Sheriff Turner the entire story this time, beginning with the threatening emails and phone calls. Sheriff Turner was respectful, polite and professional, but exhausting; he had a dozen or more questions:

"Was it the same vehicle? The yellow Hummer?"

"No."

"Can you describe the car?"

"This one was a mid-sized car, tan, light beige."

"But what make and model?"

"I really don't know cars very well," Delta apologized. The sheriff sighed.

"Two doors or four doors?"

Delta shrugged.

"Did you get close enough to see the plates to get the numbers?"

"No, but they were an ice blue, you know, kind of a white background with light blue around the edges with red numbers. But I couldn't make out the numbers."

"That's Illinois, I'll betcha," Sheriff Turner said to his deputy. The deputy nodded before walking to the hallway while speaking on his walkie-talkie. The rest of the sheriff's questions related to the "Breaking and entering," as he put it.

"More like 'breaking and exiting,'" Delta corrected him with a sigh. The broken stained-glass fragments covered the floor, she realized that more glass must have landed outside.

"Did you get a good look at the burglars?"

"The one in the apartment was standing in the shadows. He had a stocking cap over his head, like a ski mask, only rolled up. I think I caught a glimpse of blond hair, but it's hard to say for sure. He did have a medium build, but that's about it."

"What about the other one?"

Delta shook her head as if to say she hadn't gotten a good enough look at the driver. The sheriff had a few more questions.

Delta finished answering Sheriff Turner's questions, after which the sheriff and his deputy helped her to hang a blanket over the fractured window. The men stood on chairs, which were insufficient as they were still unable to reach the very top of the window; they tacked a blanket as high as they could, leaving a good couple of feet exposed. The radiant glow of the angel's halo remained uncovered and intact at the pinnacle of the arch, but the angel's wing was broken leaving a crescent-shaped opening against the dark sky where the parking lot light burst through—giving the appearance of sun and moon, together. For a moment she felt hopeful, but then her eyes rested on the image of the broken wing, which meant that the angel couldn't fly.

"Take care of that as soon as you can, you hear," the sheriff said with a paternal concern in his tone. "You don't want to leave an easy access for burglars."

Delta nodded, "I will."

"We'll keep cruising your neighborhood tonight," the sheriff reassured her.

"Thanks."

Mrs. Rushka returned with a calming cup of tea for each of them. Steam billowed lightly from the surface. "I added a splash of vodka," she confessed. At that Delta smiled. They each took a sip.

"Would you like to stay with me tonight, dear?"

"Oh, that's very thoughtful of you Mrs. Rushka, but I think I'll sort through some of the mess. You know, try to figure out what the burglars took."

"Yes, of course. Oh, your beautiful window, such a shame," Mrs. Rushka said looking at the shattered glass fragments scattered across the wooden floor. "Do you want me to help you clean it up?"

"Not tonight, thanks." Delta heaved a sigh.

"Well, I'll let you get some rest. But you remember, you're more than welcome at my place. Give a call or just come knocking; I'm a light sleeper."

By the time Mrs. Rushka left it was so close to morning that Delta decided to stay up. She spent the next hour circling, pacing and pseudo-sorting through some of the mess in her office. After showering, she dressed and made hot tea, this time using three black tea bags for more caffeine, but even 270 mg of caffeine couldn't keep her from feeling as if she were one of the walking dead. She swallowed an allergy pill with pseudo-ephedrine. She used the pills to self-medicate whenever she felt distraught. They took her mind off her concerns; instead, she simply worked. She cleaned; she wrote; she read; she did anything but think of what depressed her. The pseudo-speed kicked in pretty quickly. Nevertheless, by the time she picked up Mona at 8:30 a.m. her mind and body felt as fractured as the stained-glass window of the Annunciation. Her body felt as racked with pain as the Geo looked. She knocked on Mona's door, not looking forward to having to show her the damaged car.

"God, you look like a zombie," Mona told her advisor when she opened the door, "And to think, I'm the one with the hangover."

"Speaking of the walking dead, I need to tell you something about your Geo…"

CHAPTER 28

Bobby Brown stopped the car on a dark road in rural Indiana, a good five miles across the county line. He wasn't lost. His GPS on the dashboard informed him as to his exact coordinates; he knew how to get back to the freeway. He hadn't stopped because he'd lost his way; he stopped because he'd lost control; he needed to think.

"Well, that didn't exactly go as planned," Jason Slaughtery quipped with a sarcastic edge to his voice.

"Shut up. This is your fault."

"My fault? My fault! I'm not the one who crashed a perfectly good rental car into her GEO."

"No, but you're the one who crashed your body through her window."

"A broken window. Big deal. But the car, how are we going to return it?"

Brown didn't answer. He got out of the car to assess the damage.

"Plus, you could have hurt her," Slaughtery shouted after him.

Brown had had no intention of hurting the professor, scaring her, yes, hurting her, no. His plan had been to play chicken with her, just come close and then swerve and miss. But she swung her car at the last second, surprising him and he ended up scraping the back side and clipping the corner which spun her vehicle in a 180 degree pirouette. He looked down at the corner of the rental car, the fender—barely dented—and the front head light—burned out, but not broken. Her car must have taken the brunt of the crash. He began to coordinate a plan in his head, once satisfied he returned to the driver's seat to ask Slaughtery a few pertinent questions.

"Did she get a good look at you?

"You mean in the apartment? No."

"Are you absolutely sure?"

"Yes, I had the stocking cap over my hair, or over most of it, plus I was working in her office area, under a loft, my face was shadowed."

"Then we finish the job."

"You mean go to her office?"

"Yes."

"Now?!"

"No, of course not. Tomorrow. We'll go in the morning, just as planned." Brown felt slightly better about things. He turned the key, started the car, and headed down the road. The original plan had been slightly disrupted, which disturbed him, but he could straighten this out. Neither he nor Jason were common criminals; however, they weren't above engaging in white collar crime—investigating people, phishing their computers for information, hacking their phones, maybe planting evidence from time to time to frame someone else. All of this, he felt, was a natural part of doing business, of playing the game, everybody plays the game. Downtown Bobby Brown, the man who loved to play the stocks, considered all adults fair game; anyone with a brain should know that there are unscrupulous people like himself in the world. It's their fault if they don't take precautions. But he drew the line at being a common thug. He began driving faster. He didn't like finding himself in this position. He needed to finish this job, professionally. And then, get out of town. He lost track of the car's speed.

Just then, he noticed the lights in his rearview mirror. He turned around verifying that the lights were coming from a county sheriff's car coming up behind him, cruiser lights on, swirling, no siren.

"Damn."

Brown pulled to the side of the road. "Let me do the talking," he told Slaughtery as he watched the county deputy, from his rearview mirror, head toward him. Slaughtery shoved the black stocking cap under his thigh.

"You were going kind of fast, fellas," the deputy indicated, while holding the flashlight up to see inside the car. Nothing out of the ordinary stood out to the deputy—a briefcase on the back seat and dark sweater or jacket. "License and registration," he added. Brown handed over his license adding, "It's a rental." The officer looked at the license and back at Robert Cornelius Brown (a.k.a. Downtown Bobby Brown). Brown spoke again, "I think I took a wrong turn, officer."

The deputy sheriff looked at the driver's license again. "I'd say that's an understatement. You're a long way from home, fellas. What are you doing out here?"

"We had a business meeting in St. Louis. Flew there from New York City and decided to drive back."

"Now why would you do a thing like that?" he asked Brown as he turned his gaze toward Jason Slaughtery, adding, "Check the glove compartment for the rental information, son." Jason found the paperwork and passed it over. Brown didn't answer right away.

"Well?" the sheriff said, "Why would a couple of young businessmen like yourselves decide to drive back to New York City?"

"Oh, well, we, uh, you see, my friend here is an alum of Purdue University. We just thought it would be fun to visit his old stomping grounds."

"What year did you graduate?" the deputy inquired.

"2002."

"Uh, huh. What was your major?"

"Business."

"Well, how 'bout that, my nephew went to Krannert. Yeah, about the same time you did. Did you know Tyler Camden?"

"Oh, gosh, no Sir, I don't think I did."

"Well, you boys sit tight for me, while I run this registration."

The deputy returned to his cruiser. Jason started to ask Bobby Brown a question, but Bobby cut him off. They sat in silence until Jason couldn't take it anymore. "Do you have any priors?"

"About a hundred parking tickets."

"Don't tell me we're going to get arrested for parking tickets!"

"They're not going to take us in for parking tickets. You worry too much."

"What's he worrying about?" the deputy queried as he suddenly appeared at the window, startling both men.

"He's worried about my parking tickets."

"Yeah, you do have a few outstanding tickets in the Big Apple. I guess we can let New York's finest handle those tickets. I'll just give you one ticket for the speeding issue, but I noticed your headlight is out, too. I'll let that one slide since it's a rental. You can pay the ticket by mail. But you boys sure did take a wrong turn. You need to go back about five miles and turn right on States Route 26. That'll put you back in Tippecanoe County—home of the Boilermakers— and then you can go romping around your old turf. So, are you planning to stop in at Harry's Chocolate Shop?"

"Harry's? Oh absolutely, we can't leave town without Harry's chocolates," Jason added with a smile. At that, the sheriff ever so slightly cocked his head, a barely visible, micro-movement, clearly something had given him pause, but he decided in that moment what to say next and what to do.

"Okay, then, well you, fellas, have a nice stay."

CHAPTER 29

Monday, August 23, 2010—West Lafayette, IN

The campus was alive with the activity of approximately 40,000 students starting the fall semester. Parking spots were at a premium; fortunately, Delta had remembered to remove her parking pass from her little compact before it had been towed to the body shop and she now placed the parking decal on the dash of Mona's crippled Geo. They parked in a lot on North University Street near Beering Hall. As they walked to the building Delta felt as if she were moving in slow motion and everyone else was hurtling past her at warp speed. The only person moving slow enough for Delta to register was a bald man with copper-colored skin crouching at the rear of his tan car, adjusting his license plate. Everyone else rushed to cross streets, traverse pathways, hustle from one side of campus to the other. Orientation week was over; the semester had begun; classes were in session.

"I'm really sorry about your car, Mona," Delta told her advisee again. "I'll call my insurance agent this morning to see what we can do. I think he's supposed to get back to me today about my car."

"No worries. One of the reasons that I love this little Geo is because it has character."

I suppose, every dent is another story, Delta thought, but she knew better than to say that aloud. It didn't hold much sympathy for Mona or her car. "Maybe I should get that tattooed on *my* forehead," she thought instead.

"Get what tattooed on your forehead?"

"Oh jeez, did I say that aloud?"

"Yeah."

"Nothing."

"No, not nothing, do tell."

"I was just thinking that every dent is another story," she sighed.

"On your forehead, eh? I don't know Delta, I don't think of you as the tattoo type."

Delta smiled in response, realizing that Mona had yet to notice the tattoo on the top of her foot, a turtle to symbolize mother earth, on the back of the turtle was a geometric design of Gaelic origin—in memory of her Cherokee mother and Irish father, respectively. Tattoos say so much, Delta thought, remembering the tattoo on Caleb's arm—*Never quit searching*; she wondered what the rest of it said.

"Speaking of dents, how are *you* feeling?" Mona added, interrupting Delta's thoughts.

"Like I've been in two car accidents within two weeks. Oh wait, I have been." She tried to laugh before adding, "Forgive me, I didn't sleep at all last night."

"How are you going to make it through classes today?" Mona asked while holding the door to the building for Delta.

"Thank goodness, it's the first day. I'll pass out syllabi, go over the particulars, give them their assignments and dismiss them early, so they can go buy their books," she said as the two entered the smaller atrium and moved toward the lobby of the building.

"Sounds like a plan," Mona told her, adding, "Just let me know when you're ready to go home. I'll give you a ride." After nodding, Delta went to the right; Mona turned left. Their offices were at opposite ends of the building on the second floor; each used a different staircase.

As Delta turned the corner of the hallway on the second floor, she could see a figure standing by her office door. *Jeez, students already*, she thought as she peered down the long hallway. But as she moved closer, she could see that the man didn't appear to be a student—no backpack—and he paced back and forth instead of sitting on the hallway floor, waiting with a copy of *The Exponent*—the campus newspaper—in hand, like most students would've done. Instead, he had a clipboard in his hand. As Delta took a few more steps, she could see that his blond hair was combed forward, to the side, slicked with gel. His black framed glasses were slightly crooked. He wore a short sleeve, plaid shirt and Dockers-style pants. His shirt pocket held an array of pens. As Delta came even closer she could see that he appeared to have a massive outbreak of acne on his face. Delta averted her gaze, trying not to stare. She spoke first:

"Are you Jim Sherman?"

"Jim Sherman?" the man inquired.

"The insurance agent?"

"No, no I'm the computer tech rep. I was told to check computers on this side of the hallway for internet problems. I know it's early, but could I start with your office?" He pushed his glasses up the bridge of his nose.

Delta unlocked her office door, entered and set her bag on the visitor's chair. She glanced at the clock. "I have a meeting in a few minutes and then two classes, back to back," she added.

"Oh, if you can just log on, I can check the connections," he told her.

Delta sat down at her computer. The CT representative turned his back so as to offer Delta privacy as she put in her ID and password.

"Where's Gina? Doesn't she usually do this sort of thing?" Delta inquired as she began typing.

He turned back around to answer, "Oh yeah, Gina's here. She's doing the same process in the other wing."

Delta scooted out of the way after logging onto her computer. She packed the folder that she needed for her meeting and the stacks of syllabi that she needed for her classes. The blond technician began typing at electric speed into her computer.

"Okay, then, would you shut the door when you leave. It's on automatic lock," she told the computer technician.

"Will do; roger that," he said with a clip to his voice.

By the time Delta returned to her office in the early afternoon, she felt beyond exhausted. While answering emails, she ate her packed lunch at her desk, barely tasting the banana, yogurt or peanut butter and crackers. She made herself one cup of tea after another which led to several bathroom trips. She checked administrative details for an upcoming conference and emailed several colleagues about their roles in the future panel discussion. She answered several students' requests to be added to her already oversubscribed class. She typed a handout for Wednesday's class and prepared it for the projector by simply emailing it to herself. Emails could be called up on the classroom computers with ease and then projected onto a large screen for all the students to see. Delta often prepared her lectures this way.

Occasionally, she still used handouts allowing the students to have a copy to write on as she went over the points. Finally, Delta walked to the main office in order to make copies.

When she returned, she logged onto her computer again and emailed Mona to let her know that she was ready to go home anytime Mona was ready. Delta missed having an office telephone; they were removed the previous year due to budget constraints. *Oh well*, she thought, *Mona is really more of text person anyway.* Delta preferred to hear a human voice and had never really jumped on the texting band wagon. But she placed email second to phones in terms of warmth and friendliness, better than texts which are so abbreviated. Subsequently, she was still in the habit of sending emails.

In character, Mona replied to Delta's email by text. Delta's cell-phone vibrated—*C U at the Car.*

The ride home was uneventful, which Delta appreciated. Mona chatted about her classes and a number of graduate student concerns, but Delta was too tired to do much other than listen with polite disinterest. So much so that when Mona got out of the car at the remodeled Church of the Annunciation, instead of simply dropping her off, Delta felt a bit surprised. In addition, Mona, without an invitation, walked toward the door of the building with Delta, further raising Delta's curiosity.

"Did you want to see the window?" Delta asked. "It breaks my heart that that thug smashed my favorite stained-glass window." She clenched her teeth with the thought of it.

Mona didn't answer; instead she turned her head in the direction of the other end of the parking lot. Delta's gaze followed Mona's lead, and seeing what Mona saw, her jaw dropped in surprise.

CHAPTER 30

Monday afternoon, August 23, 2010—outskirts of Lafayette, IN

Joe 'The Hammer' Jaworski exited from the driver's side door of the truck, while Caleb Barthes jumped down from the passenger side, followed by Reuben Alstin who had been sitting in the middle. Delta couldn't believe they had driven all the way from Chicago; her hands spontaneously flew up to cover her mouth, which had formed into a little round o shape. Her lungs sucked in the surprise before letting out a little cry of delight. Now, with a livelier step and smile pushing her cheeks upward, Delta let everyone into her apartment.

Joe immediately went to work assessing the damage to the window. He kept muttering phrases, like "damn shame, damn shame" under his breath, not to anyone in particular. "Wow, this guy was in some kind of a hurry," Joe added as he walked carefully around the shards of glass. "Give me a hand here, will ya, Caleb?"

Reuben began telling Delta about victim's compensation, "I can help you with the paperwork," he offered, setting his briefcase on the island countertop between the kitchen and living room. Delta peered into the professional case filled with 8 ½ by 17 inch legal pads and documents of the same size, always a little longer than what the rest of world needed.

After helping Joe upright the file cabinet that lay on its side, Caleb and Mona offered to go to the store in order to get any supplies that Joe might need and to stock Delta's fridge.

"Are you low on mustard?" Caleb asked her.

"Mustard supply is good," she smiled.

"What else do vegetarians eat?" he added.

"Probably vegetables," Joe said as he put another one of Delta's desk drawers back into its slot.

"Where's Ani?" Mona asked.

"He couldn't make it. That's what he gets for working a 9-5 job," Reuben remarked.

"And lawyers don't have to work 9-5?" Mona questioned Reuben.

"Only when they have paying clients," he said facetiously.

"I can pay you," Delta added quickly.

"No, no that's the whole point of victim's comp. If they can't find who did this or who wrecked the car, then we can file for victim's comp. No, no I'd never take your money. I was being facetious, Delta. Honestly, I have too many clients."

"Beautiful desk," Joe interrupted as he admired the smoothly veneered mahogany surface. "A shame about the scratches," he remarked as he ran his hand along the gouged scar.

"It had a few dings, but," she said sadly, "that's a new one. That one's from the robbery," Delta shook her head at the marred surface. A long, deep scratch followed the path of where the burglar had shoved a ceramic vase to the floor. The vase pieces intermingled with the stained glass.

"I can fix all of these scratches for you," Joe said as if it were practically done.

"Really?"

"Oh yeah, piece of cake. I do a lot of staining. I know how to touch up a beauty like this," he told her. Delta smiled.

Caleb called out to her, "Okay, how about bread, and—

"Avocadoes and crackers and organic yogurt," Delta requested, adding to Caleb's list.

"And get some organic beer," Joe added, his head popping up momentarily.

"You know I got that covered," Mona told him, laughing.

"Sugar," Delta added as if partly requesting and partly stating a fact.

"Sugar? Plain sugar?" Caleb asked.

"No, no, she means SUGAR. You know, donuts, cookies, brownies," Mona translated.

"Which?" Caleb sought confirmation. Mona interrupted.

"—No worries, Delta. I've got your addictions covered."

Caleb and Mona left the front door open. The summer breeze felt full of sunshine and hope to Delta. A smile emerged on her face as she listened to Joe 'The Hammer' Jaworski whistle as he went back and forth unloading the equipment from his truck. First, Joe carried his tool box in one hand and a blanket under his other arm. The next trip he brought in a ladder, followed by a third trip with a second ladder. Then he and Reuben carried in three long sheets of plywood.

"I've got it from here," Joe told Reuben as they leaned the plywood against the wall. Delta and Reuben left Joe to his work. They sat on stools at the kitchen counter, where Reuben talked with her about insurance, victim's compensation, how to order the police reports, insurance reports, and a number of other details, until Joe called for his help with the window.

"You guys are great, really great," Delta told them with sincerity.

"Don't thank us yet. At least don't thank us until I see if we can get the remains of this window out without breaking anymore of it," Joe told her from across the room.

Joe was carefully loosening the wooden frame that held the window in place. After having leveraged the plywood sheet against the bottom of the windowsill, he pushed its length upward toward the apex of the archangel. Once it covered the entire window, he used small nails to attach the window frame to the plywood board. Now Reuben helped to hold the plywood in place while standing on one of the ladders that Joe had brought inside from the truck. Balancing on a second ladder, Joe secured the panel lightly all the way around. Gentle taps. Delta watched with curiosity as Joe went outside, carrying the ladder he had been standing on. He returned quickly.

"Okay, Delta, you stand inside and take the low end; Reuben, you reach above her and steady the top part of the window as I release it." After giving instructions, Joe went back outside.

"Ready?" he called through the openings between cream-colored and azure-tinted glass that were now blocked, for the most part, by the plywood. Joe climbed the ladder and gave a gentle push to the top of the window frame. Standing on the ladder inside the apartment, Reuben braced it from his side as it began to fall slowly forward, toward him. Joe inched his way downward, until, at last, the bottom of the framed stained-glass window, supported by the ply-wood sheet fell gently downward, first into Reuben's hands and then it eased into Delta's waiting hands at the lower end. Reuben had inched his way down the ladder, step by step, gently lowering the plywood, moving back while carefully sidestepping the shards that remained on the floor, although an occasional crunching could be heard, which made

189

all three of them—Reuben, Joe and Delta, cringe. Delta and Reuben laid it carefully on the floor away from any broken pieces of glass and awaited Joe's reentry into the apartment. Joe climbed through the massive opening, a gaping hole left behind in the shape of a steeple. "Voilá!" he said.

"Good word choice," Delta commended him.

"Why?" Reuben asked.

"Because, *Voilá* means By God. Well actually most etymologists say it is descended from the Arabic word *Wallah*—A combination of Allah, meaning *God* and wa, meaning *by. Voilá* —By God. You know, kind of a pun under the circumstances." She nodded toward the stained-glass window.

"I don't think so," Reuben interrupted, dismissing Delta's assessment, but Delta missed the indignation in Reuben's tone. So she continued to explain.

"Oh you're right, some people think it's related to *voyeur* meaning *to behold*. Either way it's an annunciation of praise, in this case, for a job well done, I'd say. It's fitting because this window is an annunciation of—"

"Okay, Professor," Joe interrupted her, "I get it."

"I don't think *Voilá* has anything to do with Islam," Reuben said sternly. "If anything, it would've been the other way around, Aramaic influencing Arabic. *Behold, an angel said to Mary*—"

Delta shrugged politely, not wanting to offend her new friends, but added, "All I'm saying is that there's a story behind every word. I suppose," she added considering it further, "a story behind every story. Anyway, Joe's choice—"

Joe stepped between the two of them, "Behold. The mess is still on the floor; let's get back to work." He began placing the scattered fragments of glass that had shattered and dropped to the floor the night before onto the plywood in approximate places where they might go. Reuben helped. It would most certainly be incomplete until they collected the rest of the glass fragments from outside, as well.

"Be careful; it's sharp," Delta warned in a maternal manner as Joe and Reuben picked up the shards.

"Isn't that just like a girl," Joe said shaking his head.

But before Delta could defend herself, she was startled by the sound of a knock at the open door.

CHAPTER 31

Monday afternoon, August 23, 2010—outskirts of Lafayette, IN

Delta looked up at the sound of Sheriff Turner's rapping on the door jamb of the open doorway.

"Professor Quinn, are you okay?" he inquired, giving Joe and Reuben a suspicious glare.

"Yes, I'm fine. Please, come in, Sheriff."

As the sheriff entered the apartment he sized up Joe and Reuben, and he clearly didn't like what he saw—strangers. The shorter man—Caucasian, husky, with medium brown-to-blondish hair, about 5'7'' and 170 lbs. wearing jeans and a White Sox, black T-shirt—stooped over the glass fragments. The other man—African-American male, 6'2'' 190-200 lbs., wearing khaki pants and short sleeved button-down shirt—appeared to be about 30 years old. Delta quickly introduced Joe and Reuben to Sheriff Turner.

The sheriff didn't move toward them, neither did he stretch out his hand in a welcoming shake. Instead, he remained close to the door, with his hand on his holster. He barely nodded.

"Professor Quinn," he said without taking a step toward them, "May I have a word?" His request along with the stationary stance compelled Delta to move toward the sheriff. Once she stood close to him, in a low tone, he whispered, "I have a bit more information." As he spoke, he never took his eyes off of Joe and Reuben. He kept his voice low, out of eavesdropping range.

"What is it?"

"I received a phone call from the deputy in White county. Last night he gave a speeding ticket to a couple of *supposed* businessmen. They said they were on their way to New York City after leaving a meeting in St. Louis, but planned to make a short stop at Purdue University. Tan car, Illinois plates."

"Do you think it's them?"

"It's certainly possible."

"Why would they have Illinois plates, if they were coming from Missouri?" Delta asked.

"It was a rental. Sometimes that happens; they rent one that somebody else has driven from another state. That's not the suspicious part."

"What is?"

"The sheriff in White County just thought it was strange that they decided to visit their old stomping grounds when there's no football game, no alumni events, nothing really to draw them to the university this weekend, no good reason to give up a round trip ticket and drive all the way back to New York City. That's a long drive for businessmen who probably need to get back to work on Monday. Even more suspicious, they didn't seem familiar with Harry's Chocolate Shop—that's got to be the most famous watering hole by campus."

"So you think those were the guys that broke in and later crashed into my car? Well, I mean Mona's car," Delta corrected herself. The sheriff delayed his response to that particular question; instead, he seemed very interested in the two men helping Delta.

"Professor Quinn, Delta, if I may, who are these guys?" Sheriff Turner asked under his breath, nodding in Joe and Reuben's direction.

"Like I said, that's Joe Jaworski and Reuben Alstin."

"And you know them from where?"

At that moment, Caleb and Mona arrived. They stood behind the Sheriff.

"She knows them through me," Caleb said with authority, handing off a bag of groceries to his sister.

"Who are you?" the sheriff demanded in a no nonsense tone. To which Mona stepped forward.

"I'm Mona Barthes. Professor Quinn is my advisor and this is my brother. And these are our friends, Joe and Reuben. What seems to be the problem?" Mona's voice was tinged with anger. She didn't like the accusatory tone with which Sheriff Turner was asking questions.

Sheriff Turner ignored her. He took Delta gently by the arm, "Let's talk outside for just a minute." Caleb started to object, but

Delta assured him it was fine, calling off his concern with a raised palm. She stepped outside with the sheriff.

"Those two guys in your apartment, how long have you known them?

"A few days. Why?"

"They fit the description of the two fellas that the White County deputy stopped last night. One was blond, Caucasian, about thirty years old; the other was dark, maybe African-American or Mediterranean or a blend of both."

"No, oh no, it couldn't be. These are friends of Mona and her brother Caleb and I've known Mona for over a year. Plus, it was Mona's car that got hit."

"But you've only known these two men for a few days? I just want you to be careful. Somebody wanted something that you have and they were willing to break in here to get it." Then he added, turning back toward the apartment door, "If they're innocent, they won't mind answering a few questions."

"That's really not necess—

The sheriff ignored Delta's plea as he stepped back into the apartment.

"So you two fellas mind telling me where you were last night?"

Joe and Reuben looked up from their work. Cocking his head to left, Joe appeared confused; he glanced from the sheriff to Caleb with a questioning look. Caleb squared his shoulders and stared straight at the sheriff. Reuben looked offended; his jaw dropped with surprise at first, and then quickly clenched with indignation. Caleb saw Reuben's response; he shot a stabbing look of anger at Delta, before he answered the sheriff's question.

"They were with me last night, in Chicago," Caleb asserted with directness and finitude, but he feared it wouldn't be enough.

"Is this because I'm African-American?" Reuben asked, carefully placing the stained-glass fragment down on the plywood and standing to his full height of 6"2". He took a step toward the sheriff. "I'm a practicing attorney from a reputable firm in Chicago. I'm also an assistant to the pastor at the Church of the Nazarene and I do volunteer work in the community. I might add that the police officers' widows' and orphans' fund gets a donation from me every year. I'm talking about the legitimate fund. And I tell you, Sheriff, I do not like your tone of voice or what you are implying. We came here to help Delta not to hurt her." Reuben's controlled anger filled the converted church like a minister warming up to the moment of rectification, where he extols the word of God condemning sinners to hell. Reuben took another step toward the sheriff; each step felt like the silent wrath of God against sinners, and each word by carefully selected word hit the rafters of the cathedral and echoed throughout the apartment—"By the way, Sheriff, profiling is a dangerous habit to get into." The tenacious tone of his voice and the pedantic punctuation of his words caused everyone to stand still, paying close attention and waiting to see what Reuben would say next as the words accusing the sheriff of racism could easily erupt into a fiery confrontation. The sheriff partially diffused the situation by taking one step backwards toward the door before commenting.

"As for your *where-abouts* last night, I'll take your word for it," the sheriff said. Reuben relaxed his shoulders, but stiffened his back and his resolve again when the sheriff added, "for now." Then the sheriff turned to leave, but before doing so he addressed Delta.

"Call me if you need anything."

"She won't," Caleb blurted.

CHAPTER 32

Monday to Wednesday, August 25, 2010—outskirts of Lafayette, IN

Delta was clearly aware of the shift in everybody's mood, especially Caleb's. After the incident with the sheriff, she felt a visceral coolness in the air from the distance that Caleb kept during the rest of the evening. He directed his comments toward his friends or his sister, unless he had to ask Delta something in particular. And then he didn't look at her when he spoke. Mona, as well as the Chicago trio, left without eating dinner, even though Delta had offered. Delta had been in no mood to defend herself. *Caleb shouldn't have assumed it was my fault that the sheriff asked such pointed questions of Joe and Reuben.* She ate two brownies for dinner and drank a glass of red wine. *It wasn't my fault*, she decided, repeating the phrase like a mantra, but the mantra hadn't helped her to fall asleep.

After a restless Monday night, she spent Tuesday morning questioning herself, wondering if she should have been more adamant in her response to the sheriff, that the sheriff needn't question Joe and Reuben. *Maybe, I was wrong.* She took a slow, hot shower, but with the August heat the shower wasn't relaxing, instead it intensified her feelings of frustration. She needed to cool down. She stood naked in front of her bedroom fan, allowing her wet hair to drip down her bare back. Once Delta began to feel better, she slipped into a long T-shirt and then curled up on the couch. She read in an attempt to distract herself. Then got up and checked her email, wrote a few notes for her upcoming classroom lecture and later tried transcribing some of the interview data from the abusive relationship study. After several hours of the tedious work of transcribing, she considered talking with Walter Steath, the Acting-Head of the Department about writing a grant to get funding for more sophisticated transcription equipment. In addition to the tedium, Delta couldn't look another sad sentence in the face; her concentration crumbled under the weight of the insults laid on some of the women. Delta closed her eyes remembering her mother's face, her dark hair, her dark eyes, her sweet smile.

Amber and rose-colored sunbeams cast a dusky glow over the room. Delta set the transcripts aside and went to her bedroom. On top of the tall set of dresser drawers sat a small collection of stones. She picked up two of them—a piece of pink granite and a flat fossilized fern. She turned each over in her palm. She felt the smoothness, the coldness. She listened to the click when they hit against each other. And then she opened the top drawer and pulled out a manila envelope.

Delta returned to the couch to sit in the glow of the setting sun as she read and reread the contents of the envelope. There were four items—two newspaper articles, one copy of a police report, and a letter from The Baroness.

Shooting Ends with Good Samaritan Dead

August 12, 1986—Akron, Ohio

An Akron woman was shot to death on Friday evening after attempting to intervene in an incident of domestic abuse. Angela Quinn was rushed to Methodist Hospital after being shot by Connery Dade, a neighbor who had twice prior been arrested and convicted of domestic abuse. A restraining order had been put in place by Judge Raimer, restricting Dade access to the neighborhood where his wife, Gloria Dade resides. Mrs. Quinn's children reported that they all heard screams coming from the neighbor's house and their mother ran to help Mrs. Dade. The sheriff reported that according to Mrs. Dade her estranged husband was waving a gun around and threatening to kill her when Angela Quinn entered through the back door. Connery Dade claims that is when the gun went off accidentally, shooting Mrs. Quinn. Although Mrs. Quinn was rushed to the hospital; she was pronounced dead on arrival.

No matter how many times Delta read it, the last line always caught in her throat—*she was pronounced dead on arrival*. Delta folded the yellowing piece of newsprint. She set it down as though it was a holy relic before lifting the next newspaper article.

Funeral for a Brave Woman

August 15, 1986   The funeral for Angela (Beauvoir) Quinn was
held at 10:00 a.m. in St. Thomas Catholic Church where she and
her husband were members. Angela Quinn was of Cherokee and
French descent. She is survived by her mother, Emma Walks-the-
Ridge Beauvoir who lives in Tennessee and a grandmother who
lives on the Qualla Boundary. Angela is also survived by her
husband Daniel Quinn of Akron, Ohio. The couple met in Ohio
when Angela's father, Mr. Beauvoir brought the family north so
that he could work in the Goodyear rubber factory. Angela was
killed trying to protect her neighbor from a violent attack of
domestic abuse. Angela (Walks-the-Ridge Beauvoir) Quinn, a
brave woman, leaves behind five children; Jacqueline, 9, Nathan,
7, Delta, 4 ½, Carrie Ann, 3, and Tommy, 2.

Delta refolded the funeral notice and set it down on top of the first
article. She lifted the copy of the police report. Bureaucratic boxes of
fading ink appeared on the paper. Her eyes moved to the line that
read: *Connery Dade charged with involuntary manslaughter.* There
was nothing else of importance to see on the sheet as far as Delta was
concerned. She set the paper aside and then unfolded the letter from
The Baroness.

Dearest Delta,

I cannot give you what I am sure you most want—your mother and
your father.

I can only give you the story. Beyond what you see in these
documents, Eddy found out that following your mother's funeral,
your father took you, Carrie Ann and Tommy to the car. He got in
and drove away, never to be heard of again. No one knows for sure
why he didn't take the other two children, but some neighbors
have said that Jacqueline and Nathan were holding hands with
your grandmother at the time and that your father had Tommy on
his hip, Carrie Ann by the hand, and you by his side.

I know that you must wonder why he came north and left you at
an orphanage. I believe he was trying to take himself and you three

children as far away from the pain as he possibly could. He drove north, until he could drive no more. I believe it is God's providence that brought him to our door step. And I believe that God will lead him back home again when he is ready.

May God Bless and Mary Keep You

The Baroness

Delta folded the letter and carefully collected the stack of documents along with the stones. She returned the pebble and the fossil to the top of the dresser and the envelope to the top drawer.

Tired and depressed, she fixed herself a cup of African red bush tea and curled up on the couch again. She took a sip of the tea and watched the steam rise from the dark brew, before setting the mug on the coffee table. She rested her eyes from time to time. Sipped her tea and stared into space.

There were no lights on and the apartment grew dark with the exception of a lamppost light streaming through one of the remaining intact, stained-glass windows. Archangels with massive wings and golden halos harkened her gaze toward the opposite side of the room, across from the fractured and boarded up Annunciation window. She suddenly sat up. *What was that?* She heard a noise outside the window. From her place on the couch, she could see a shadowy form outside the window. Lurking. The figure passed by the window.

Delta held her breath, rose and tiptoed toward the window where she stood at the edge of the gothic stained-glass masterpiece, peering out through the most lightly-colored pieces of glass. A kaleidoscope effect fragmented the image; she turned her head to get a better view. The dangerous form of the figure seemed fractured but looked like Reuben. *Reuben, it is Reuben.* She left the apartment, circling around to the patio that was laden with herbs and flowers, broccoli and lettuce, ripe tomatoes and tall garlic plants with curving stems that looked like swans' necks. She could smell the rich soil and the fragrant foliage even if she couldn't see it very well. She brushed the edge of the tomato plant. *What's Reuben doing back*, she wondered. *He must have forgotten something.*

200

The outside of the stone and brick church seemed so cold to the touch that Delta imagined an empty castle housing ghosts of yesteryear. Nevertheless, she made her way by touching the side of the church, not quite ready to leave it behind entirely. *Where had Reuben gone?* Then a sinking feeling invaded her thoughts, *What if it isn't Reuben?* She seized solid momentarily.

Now she was outside in the dark with a possible stranger, she took another step with great caution. A twig snapped in the dark, not from under her foot, but from something or someone else. She froze. Her eyes darted back and forth, but in the darkness all she knew was that she was between the church and the unknown.

"Delta."

She heard a woman's voice call her name. She turned. Susan Hack stood in the dark next to her husband Jim. Susan's golden hair matched that of the angel. "Delta, it's the seed *and* the soil. Look at the roots."

Jim Hack, the farmer, knelt in the dark, a small seed in his hand. He dug at the dirt with his free hand. She could barely make out what he was doing under the light of the stars and the moon, but he appeared to be planting a seedling that had already taken shape from the seed; she watched it take root. It sprouted shoots through the moist earth and then to her dismay, she watched as it shriveled and died.

That's not right, she thought. Jim looked at her imploring an explanation as well. Delta turned around, as if she could find the answer, but there was nothing behind her, it was all darkness. When she turned back around she found Reuben kneeling next to Jim. Reuben put his hand on the soil before raising it high into the air. His fist pumped the starlit sky and then opened, revealing within it something small, a tiny particle resting in his palm—a seed. Delta reached for the seed, but it curled and dried before her eyes. Then she looked Reuben in the eye and she saw a tear, but worse yet she now studied him more carefully and found that his wrists were locked into metal shackles with heavy chains. Now she felt a tear in her own eye.

"Delta!"

She looked again at Susan whose voice was filled with urgency. Susan wanted Delta to help Jim and Reuben. But Delta didn't know where to turn or what to do. Her feet were suddenly mired in mud. None of them were free to move.

The mud of Africa, Reuben told her. In front of her the Serengeti, she turned, behind her she saw St. Joseph's Orphanage. Her younger brother, Tommy and sister, Carrie Ann stood motionless not knowing whether to enter the orphanage or not. They looked toward Delta. She turned back around. Reuben was a child, Joe was there and he was a child, as well. She reached out to take their hands, intending to bring all the children together. But the grip failed to take form; instead, her hand passed through each of them as if they were ghosts. The Baroness reached out to her. Again her hand met nothing but air. If she could just touch them, then she knew they would be real again, substance and matter, flesh and blood. She had to protect the children. She spun around, spying the red bushes of Africa and she heard the drums, not the drums of Haiti or the Caribbean, or even of her Cherokee heritage, but the drums of Africa. A resounding African beat. A call to action.

"DELTA!"

CHAPTER 33

Wednesday morning, August 25, 2010—outskirts of Lafayette to West Lafayette, IN

"DELTA!"

The persistent knocking, like the sound of an African tribal drum beat, continued at the door rousing Delta from the deepest sleep she had ever experienced, one laden with the weight of colorful and intense dreams, so real and yet so bizarre. Delta was still in the thick of it. She stirred. A nearly empty mug, which had been filled with rooibus tea, had gone cold and lifeless, an oily film rested languidly on its surface. She reached out, not sure what she was reaching for, and accidentally knocked the cup to the floor. The handle broke away from the mug; tea spread out in dark streams like the tears that had fallen down Reuben's cheeks in her dream.

"DELTA!" This time, she heard her name. Wrapping the blanket around herself, she stood, realizing that someone was knocking on her apartment door. But she could only get one eyelid to lift as she unlocked the chain and opened the door to find Mona waiting for her.

"C'mon, c'mon get ready or you're going to be late!" Mona shoved past her advisor.

"What time is it?"

"Time to get ready," Mona said turning her advisor by the shoulders toward the bathroom, toward the shower. "I'll make some coffee for you," Mona added.

"No, no I don't drink coffee, only tea."

"Okay fine, I'll make some coffee for me."

Delta showered and dressed quickly. When she returned to the living room, Mona handed her a thermal-carrying cup brimming with hot tea and as the two headed for Mona's car she chastised Delta for not having coffee in the house. "You're un-American, you know. A regular communist. Really, Delta, who doesn't drink coffee?" Delta swept her hair up into a messy ponytail after buckling the seat belt and mumbled an apology for the oversight. She'd rather have a Diet

203

Pepsi for breakfast than coffee, and had actually lived on that for fuel throughout her graduate school years, at least until Carri Ann had talked her into a more professional morning form of caffeine. Carri Ann had wanted her older sister to look the part of a professor and she didn't believe that professors drank soda pop for breakfast. "*Image is important,*" Carrie Ann had told her; "*But substance is everything*" Delta had countered. Delta wondered why she was thinking of her sister.

"Do you want to stop at Starbuck's or somewhere? I'll buy," Delta offered, apologetic over her failure to provide Mona with coffee, and simultaneously fumbling through her bag to see what she'd remembered and what she'd forgotten for class while searching for her wallet.

"No, don't worry about it," Mona told her. "You'll be late. Don't you have a curriculum meeting before class?" Delta nodded, sipped the tea and continued to fumble through her black canvas bag.

"Yeah, it'll be all right if I'm late for that meeting. But class ..." Delta's voice trailed off. Mona knew what she meant. Students are the top priority; research is second even at a 'research one' university, like Purdue University.

The pair traveled with little to no conversation for the next few blocks on their way to campus. Eventually, Mona broached the awkward subject of how Caleb had stopped speaking to Delta after the sheriff practically accused Joe and Reuben of being the burglars.

"My brother was just concerned about his friends."

"What does that make me?"

"He's known them longer."

"He will always have known them longer, always," Delta pointed out.

"The sheriff was rude. Racist."

"He was only doing his job. The men who broke into my apartment fit Joe and Reuben's description. I told him that Joe and Reuben are innocent. Caleb had no right to assume I had anything to do with the sheriff's comments. But he did. He assumed I had said something negative about Joe and Reuben. I didn't! Case closed."

But Mona refused to allow the folder to be filed, so to speak. "He wanted you to stand up for them."

"I know what he wanted; he didn't give me a chance to explain. I know he's your brother, but he was glaring at me."

"He didn't want you to explain. He wanted you to help Reuben. They came all the way from Chicago because they care about you."

"They don't even know me."

"Fine. They came to help you because they care about Caleb. And he cares about you."

"You couldn't tell it by the way he acted. I don't want to talk about it." Delta's harsh words belied her real feelings; she was pleased to hear Mona say that Caleb cared about her.

Mona bit her lip to keep from saying anything else. They arrived at the university with only minutes to spare. Delta grabbed her bag of notes and quickly thanked Mona before rushing to her office and then to class.

Once in the classroom, Delta read the roster, buying herself a few minutes more to shake the grogginess of sleep from her mind. She glanced at each student as they lazily raised an arm in response to attendance call that interrupted their chatting, texting, or reading of the campus newspaper. *They all look so young,* she thought as she looked into each student's face after calling his or her name. *How long had it been since she'd been an undergrad, a senior,* she wondered without answering. It hadn't been that long; it just felt like a lifetime ago. She checked their names off as they raised their hands or said, "Here."

"Anybody miss the first class? Need a syllabus?" she offered. One student raised her hand. Delta passed the syllabus back.

"Okay, I gave you your first assignment on Monday, to bring in a press release from a company that is listed on the New York Stock Exchange. Our goal is to learn how to do a systematic rhetorical analysis of press releases, as a way of learning how companies speak to their publics—internal and external. First, we'll define rhetoric. Second, we'll go over the rhetorical elements—purpose, audience, persona, tone, etcetera. Finally, we'll try analyzing a few of these press releases accordingly."

Delta questioned the students, asking them to supply Aristotle's definition of rhetoric and after affirming that, "Yes, Aristotle considered rhetoric all the available means of persuasion," she noted that "from Isocrates to Quintilian rhetoricians agree that the purpose of studying rhetoric is to prepare people to be discerning citizens who can contribute to society." The students stared at her. "Write that down," she told them. They scrambled for their notebooks, a few typed on their laptops, some used their phones.

A student raised his hand. "Yes?" Delta said.

"Professor, is it persuasion if you hold a gun to somebody's head."

"Good question. No, it's not persuasion; that's coercion. Sometimes there is a fine line between coercion, persuasion and hegemony, but we'll talk more about that later in the course."

Delta passed handouts to the first student seated in each row to pass back and then provided an overview of the rhetorical elements necessary to a solid analysis of any rhetorical artifact. After this she asked the students to volunteer to share their press releases. One young man was quick to raise his hand.

At Delta's request, he came to the front of the room and told her that his press release could be pulled up on screen. Delta logged into the computer and then turned it over to the student.

"What's your name?" she asked.

"Drew," he told her. She pulled the master screen down and then took a seat near the front of the room. The young man typed, *google*, and then in the drop down box he typed *Richfield Corporation press release.*

A number of choices appeared.

The student kept scanning; eventually he found the specific source he wanted to share. "This one, Professor Quinn," the student said and with that the press release about the press release appeared:

RichField and Terminator Technology

From Concerned Citizens

RichField Corporation came under serious scrutiny recently with concern over the development of their "Terminator Technology," known technically as V-GURTs (Varietal Genetic Use Restriction Technologies). The terminator technology allows a plant to grow and produce seeds as usual, but when farmers attempt to plant the next year using the seeds from the crop they find the seeds are sterile. This compels farmers to buy more seed every year, and RichField continues to raise the prices of those seeds in an exorbitant manner.

Ecologists fear that terminator seeds may cross pollinate with crops causing unintended consequence. Under pressure from the public and the United Nations which called for a moratorium on the seed, RichField promised to end their use of terminator technology. But in a recent press release, the company espoused a new stand, saying that they plan to look into a new kind of technology which is an offshoot from the V-GURT. They suggest that the derivative technology is a more advanced form of V-GURT. One must ask what is hiding behind this statement; does the derivative terminator technology simply do a better job of sterilizing the seed? The RichField Company needs to stop hiding behind ambiguous language and keep its promise to stop advocating for terminator technology.

"So Professor," the student said, "What I think is really cool is that this is a press release about a press release. I mean, it critiques a press release. That's exactly what you wanted us to do, right?" Delta could barely believe what she was seeing. *Is this what had happened to Jim and Susan,* she wondered. *Had a company like RichField led them into a dependent relationship that was bankrupting them? Were they planting terminator seeds?*

"Look what happens when you try to open the RichField press release that this one is talking about," the student added. He clicked on the link; an error page popped up on the screen. Drew clicked back to the press release of the press release. He repeated this several times, making his point that the company must have pulled the original press release.

"Do you think we can analyze this issue, Professor Quinn?"

"Absolutely, Drew, absolutely. As a matter of fact," she said to the whole class, "I think it's our duty as citizens to explore the issue—both sides of the issue. But I'd rather have you explore the original press release from the corporation in question so that you find out their side of the story and so that you learn to do the critique yourself."

"So why can't we find the original press release from RichField?" another student asked.

"Corporations control their communiqués carefully. It appears they removed the original one from public view."

"Professor Quinn?"

"Yes?"

"Is that normal? To a hide a press release, I mean?"

"Let's hope it's not the norm," she paused, gaining their attention, "but let's not be naïve either."

"So what should we do?"

"Time to investigate, my young friends; it would seem we have a mystery to solve."

CHAPTER 34

They sat in Stone Hall cafeteria, meeting for the first time. Delta had asked Ralph Goodman, a colleague in the Department of Communication, if he knew anyone with agricultural expertise who might explain a problem concerning genetically-modified seeds. Indeed, he did, and recommended that Delta meet with Professor Devika Sharma from the Agronomy Department at Purdue University.

"Professor Sharma, thank—

"Please, please, let's not be so formal. Call me Devika."

"Thanks, Devika. I really do appreciate you agreeing to meet with me."

"Not a problem. I rather enjoy getting out and meeting new colleagues. I haven't had much time for that during the school year and I spend the summers in India, New Delhi, mostly," she explained, sounding more British than the British-as the saying goes, with her Indian accent. They sat at a table for two by the window that overlooked the leafy, lilac bushes.

"Do you go back to see family?" Delta inquired out of politeness.

"Yes, family and India. I miss India very much. It's so colorful. The people have character to match in India, very lively, dramatic, as I said, quite colorful. Even a walk through the markets can make me smile. The vendors, the baubles," she smiled as she spoke, lifting her wrist to show an armful of copper and silver bracelets. "My family, on the other hand, pressures me," Devika dropped the comment along with her wrist in a casual manner. The bracelets jingled to a halt.

"Pressure you?"

"Every time I go home it's the same lament from my parents: Devika, have you found a husband yet? Do you want us to arrange a marriage for you? At least let us bring you a few prospects to meet,

209

and so on and so forth." Devika shared this information with gleaming eyes and a gay tone, adding, "I'm almost 29, an old hag."

To the contrary, Devika Sharma's beauty could bring men to their knees. She had likely already turned down several marriage proposals, Delta thought. The Indian professor had large brown eyes that glistened like morning dew drops on burgundy rose petals. She had a small nose and full lips. Her skin appeared smooth, unblemished. Her hands were like those of a ballerina, as she spoke they danced, polished nails fluttered gracefully in perfect pirouettes, which were accompanied by the sight and sound of her sparkling, tinkling bracelets. She moved a strand of hair away from her eye. Her long, dark hair reflected the fluorescent cafeteria lights.

"I didn't realize that arranged marriages still take place," Delta shared her ignorance on the matter.

"Oh, my yes. But it's not the law or anything. There's nothing wrong with it really, but I hate that some men make decisions based on superficial traits. You know, they look at a picture of a girl and read the description, and decide, this one is too short or that one's skin is a shade too dark." Devika Sharma's light-colored skin looked like a mid-summer tan to Delta. The preference for a light hue—a trait still praised by many postcolonial Indians—according to Devika Sharma, existed much to her dismay.

With respect to stature, Delta had noticed, while they had waited in the cafeteria line, that the young woman stood quite a bit shorter than Delta herself; Professor Sharma, may have reached four feet, eleven inches when stretching in yoga sun pose. The petite agronomy professor continued, "I want to meet a man and get to know him first, not later. Or I would like to see someone across a crowded room and fall madly in love, like in the movies." She smiled brightly. "But enough about my problems. What can I do for you?" Devika asked before she slid a forkful of rice into her mouth.

"Well, I really need a primer. I know nothing. I need lessons in Agronomy 101."

"Do you know what agronomy is?" Devika asked assessing where to begin.

"Alphabetically, it falls somewhere between agriculture and astronomy. I'm guessing it is closer to agriculture, literally and figuratively," Delta answered.

Devika laughed, "I like that. Yes, it falls closer to agriculture." Devika continued, "Agronomy is the study of soil and seeds. Okay, that is Agronomy 101. Now, what can I really help you with?" Delta smiled in appreciation of Devika's directness.

"One of my students brought in a press release." Delta extracted it from her bag as she spoke. "It's an assignment that I give in the Rhetoric and Public Relations class. The students have to critique a press release. This one is about RichField; it talks about a genetically-modified seed. At one point they seem to suggest that RichField promised to stop research on the seed but in another sentence they say that if they come across related bioengineering they may look into that in the future." Before Delta could continue, Devika put her fork down, took a deep breath, and then began to tell the story of the terminator seed.

"Okay, in the 1970s RichField developed an herbicide called Parched. You may have seen commercials on television from time to time. You spray a little Parch and the weed shrivels to nothing, dries right up. Glyphosate. That's the chemical we're talking about here. Of course a farmer shouldn't use too much herbicide or they will also kill their crop. This is where it starts to get tricky. RichField engineered a seed that was resistant to the herbicide. It's called Parch Prepped."

"Catchy," Delta appraised the product name.

"It's actually a genetically-modified seed, known technically as Varietal Genetic Use Restriction Technologies V-GURT. Anyway," Devika moved on, not belaboring the technical terminology, "the farmers can spray all the glyphosate or Parch they want as long as they also buy RichField seeds and it won't kill the cotton, corn or soybeans or whatever crop as long as they're planting RichField's genetically-modified seeds." Devika looked to see if Delta was still following.

"And?"

"And RichField gets the farmers hooked so to speak on the Parch Prepped seeds and on the Parch Prep herbicide. Pretty soon they raise

211

the prices as high as they like. Some estimates suggest they have raised the price one hundred forty-six percent over the last ten years for the Parch Prep seeds and sixty-four percent for the herbicide that goes with it."

"Wow, that's some mark up," Delta agreed.

"One hundred and forty-six percent! Not twice as much or ten times as much or even one hundred times as much. No, they raised the prices 146 times as much."

"Yes, the amount is hard to grasp; it's staggering," Delta agreed.

"And that's nothing, compared to what else they've done," Devika told her. "So RichField cornered the market, but they didn't stop there. They found out that a company in Louisiana had created a seed whose offspring seed wouldn't germinate. RichField became very interested."

"Why, would a seed company want a seed that won't germinate?" Delta asked worried that she might be losing the essentials of Agronomy 101.

"Exactly, it's insane, isn't it?" Devika continued, "The seed was nicknamed the terminator seed. The seed company planned to sell it to the farmer who plants it; usually, it grows the first season, but the seed it generates or produces won't germinate the next season."

"I don't get it," Delta told her.

"You're not alone. Thousands of farmers didn't get it either. But think about it this way. What if a company told you it had the hardiest seed and the best herbicide, but also told you, you are not allowed to replant the seeds that come from the plants next year and they write that into the sales contract? They affix a label to the seed bag or box that legally binds the buyer to never plant or resell the seeds or anything that comes from the seed other than its initial crop. What does it mean? It means that the farmer has to buy new seeds every year. Well, you've got to guess some farmers aren't going to pay attention to a contract like that because they've been saving their seeds for generations. Everybody saves seeds, in the U.S., in India, in Turkey, everywhere. The farmers think of it as part of their yield. Farmers save seeds and they share them, exchange the best seeds with each other, but let's say a company puts it in the contract that you can't save or share. Then they raise the prices. They are dictating changes to culture. Because then the farmer can't share and can barely afford to buy new seeds because the prices keep going up. Well, then, the farmers, like the ones in Canada, might just save their seeds and claim that they blew onto their property from somebody else's farm," Devika told her. Delta's eyes narrowed as she listened to Devika narrate the story of the terminator seed. "The farmers claimed the seeds had blown into their fields."

"What happened to the farmers in Canada?"

"RichField took them to court."

"And?"

"And RichField won."

"But couldn't the seeds have blown into their fields?"

"Yes, but no one knew that at the time. Some say the farmers were telling the truth; others say that RichField just had the superior legal team."

"Wow! How did RichField find out about the farmers using the seed? I mean how would they know what is growing in the farmers' fields? "

"Inspectors."

"Inspectors? No kidding?"

"Yeah, exactly. RichField hired people to be inspectors, to inspect the farms. Sometimes they called them Public Relations Investigators." Devika raised her eyebrows at her own comment, "Yes, their version of relating to their publics." Delta shook her head; Devika continued. "So if RichField wanted to keep from having to inspect farm fields and going to court every year, they had to find a way to keep the farmers from replanting the seeds. So, instead of a contract, they created a seed that wouldn't grow again."

"The terminator seed," Delta concluded.

"Exactly. They bought the Louisiana company, which had developed V-GURT—the terminator seed. Then they added it to Parch Prepped, solidified the patents, and planned to sell the terminator seed to farmers around the world. But they needed to test it first—so now we come to my homeland—India."

"What happened in India?" Delta asked.

"The farmers didn't understand or blatantly ignored the contract. As usual, they collected their seeds at the end of the season and when they sowed the seed later, during the next season, nothing grew; the crop failed. The cycle had been terminated. Shortly thereafter, the seed companies demanded even more money to replace the seeds. Not twice as much or fifty times as much, but as I told you, one hundred forty times as much money. The farmers borrowed from money lenders who charged outrageous interest, four hundred times the original amount. Worst yet, the farmers found that the seeds were not as healthy or strong as promised. Many crops failed. The farmers gave up. They are very poor to begin with and this only added to their poverty and misery. In the last ten years, approximately one thousand four hundred farmers have committed suicide in India. Their despair is too deep. One source tells us his estimates are that forty-six farmers a day kill themselves in India, the poverty, the droughts, the high price of seeds, it's all too much. In India, the terminator seed is called ... *the suicide seed.*

"I know of this first hand," the agronomy professor continued, nodding sadly. "My father is a wealthy and generous man. Sometimes in India the businessperson who has reaped a small bounty will hire a family in need. The hired family will take on roles such as chauffeur, cook, and such. The wealthy man will send the hired family's children to school. It is less a form of servitude and more along the lines of adopting a whole family."

Delta listened with interest as Devika continued.

"So my father was approached by a local vendor who told the story of his brother's debt and asked if my father might consider taking his brother and his brother's family as his household domestics. He agreed and we drove to the rural district to pick up the family and bring them back, but it was too late."

"Too late?" Delta asked.

"That morning, the farmer told his wife that the cotton seed had failed again even though he had bought this seed fresh from the American salesman. It had failed because the V-GURT seeds need twice the amount of water as traditional seeds and even the mild drought had destroyed it. The farmer had to borrow money in the past and already owed so much money to the money lender that it would be impossible to ever pay it back. The man told his wife that

214

they would be beggars in the streets. He told her that he had chosen another course of action.

"He kissed his wife and his baby son before drinking a cupful of herbicide, glyphosate, and then he lay down in his field to die. Parch running through his veins. Burning him from the inside out. The wife ran for help. The villagers came, but there was nothing they could do for him. We were told that he wretched and moaned in agony, begged his wife's forgiveness for leaving her in such a wretched situation, and then he died. It took less than an hour.

"The villagers knew that an agricultural specialist from the U.S. was in the area. They went to him in outrage over their friend's death. They blamed RichField. In answer to this travesty," here Devika leaned forward toward Delta, "... the man from RichField suggested that maybe the farmer drank the poison because he was an alcoholic."

"Oh my god," Delta said, covering her mouth with her hand. "Who thinks that way?"

"Yes, yes. The villagers were horrified that such an evil and insulting thought could be expressed about their friend. Yes, I'm telling you the truth. You can read about him or others like him in *World News*, if you don't believe me. One article by Malone is quite interesting, absolutely like the one I mention. But in the story I tell you the tragedy is not over, for the wife felt only despair, defeat, depression. She returned home and drank the same poison—the glyphosate."

Delta's face fell into her hands.

"The man's brother found the baby wrapped in cotton swaddling, crying, yes, the child is from the new crying fields. He, of course, adopted his nephew. We had arrived the very day after all this had happened. We turned around, went home that same day, the back seat of the car as empty as our hearts. That was just two years ago. His story is one of more than a thousand. Sadly, that number is growing steadily. Yes, this is very common in India today." Devika turned back to her rice, "Very sad, but very common."

Delta didn't know what to say. The story was beyond tragic. The death toll was astronomical. Farmers around the world were struggling far beyond what she had realized. *Are U.S. farmers facing the same or similar practices,* she wondered. And to think her most recent studies were about farm life. Delta felt woefully inadequate. She had been an outsider, someone with little understanding of the magnitude of the problem. She thought of Jim and Susan, the farm couple whom she had interviewed. *Have they been subjected to this seed nightmare, to the intense corporate greed that Devika Sharma has described,* she questioned. She tried to remember everything Jim Hack had told her in the interview. Then she wondered, *will they fare any better now that they've planted an organic crop? What if their harvest gets contaminated?*

"This," Devika Sharma said reaching for the press release on Delta's tray, "This is the kind of pressure—from activists, farmers, and finally the local government in India—that got RichField to end its terminator seed project. Yes, this activism led to their saying they would stop using the terminator seed. But as you can see their promise is ambiguous at best. In one sentence they promised not to use their terminator seed anymore, but yes, as you can see, they do suggest that if related technologies appear in the future, they will explore those potentials."

"Do you know of any *related technologies?*"

"Like what?"

"Like maybe a seed that seems to be dead but can come back to life."

Devika looked both intrigued and concerned simultaneously. She shook her head. "No, I haven't heard of anything that diabolical; the most pernicious thing I have heard of is the terminator seed."

"What would the advantages be, I mean, of a seed that could return to life?" Delta queried the agronomy expert.

"You could control the entire market. If you could turn germination genes on and off at will; you could decide whose crop will yield and whose crop will fail. But there's nothing out there like that."

Delta remained pensively silent.

Devika queried, "Do you know something I don't know? Tell me what's going on."

Delta Quinn then told Devika Sharma the story of how her car was run off the road by a yellow Hummer, how she had received ominous telephone messages and even a computer message to 'cease and desist' her research. She told her how she and Caleb had tried to track down her original farm interviews. How Danielle Goldman had mentioned that she didn't want to have anything to do with the zombie seed. And finally, she told her how her apartment had been ransacked and her graduate advisee's car had been struck.

"Well, you've had quite a week. To think I've only written and passed out syllabi. So what do you think you'll do now?"

"I think I'll begin re-interviewing the farmers, the same ones, to see if I can figure out what's going on here in the Midwest."

"May I help?" Devika asked with eager, wide eyes.

"Are you free Saturday?" Delta offered. Devika smiled and nodded in affirmation.

Following lunch Delta returned to her office. There she sent Mona an email summarizing the lunch conversation and inviting her to come with Professor Sharma and herself to Jim and Susan Hack's farm on Saturday. She gave her the address and added a P.S.—You were right; I should've done more to keep the sheriff from accusing Joe and Reuben. I'm sorry.

D—

She also knew that Mona was not the one to whom she most needed to apologize. But that would have to wait.

CHAPTER 35

At 10:00 a.m. on Saturday morning, Mona turned her little green Geo into the dirt driveway of Susan and Jim Hack's farm. Delta directed Mona to park between the house and the barn, immediately in front of what had been the pig pen on Delta's last visit. The barn, to the west of them, was a stately blend of stone and wood with a rooftop that Delta remembered as being painted with the words—*Jim loves Susan.* An old tractor and spare parts sat idle on the grounds outside the barn where wild daisies and Queen Anne's lace sprouted from the edges of the barn, between the machinery parts. To the east, stood the simple mail order Sears, Roebuck and Company house, a classic from the twentieth century which the local museum had documented as 'historic.' Historic or not, the place was not for sale according to Jim who had turned away more than one offer even though the house failed to keep them warm in the winter or cool in the summer. No need for the vultures to know that Jim only rented the property. He acted as if he was the owner, authoritatively turning down their requests. Ownership had a great deal to do with possession and care, and as far as he was concerned his twenty years of steadfastly nurturing this farm—land and house—made it his baby. Jim also had an opinion on the Sears catalogue homes.

Early 1900s Sears, Roebuck and Company catalogue homes had reduced the need for carpenters and bricklayers by supplying the factory made materials, which Jim didn't approve. This is why any remodeling improvements he made to the house or barn were done by him or local tradesmen. On the positive side, the Sears homes did incorporate asphalt shingles in place of wood or tin roofs. This reduced the chance of fire and reduced noise from storms. Jim thought that was an invention worthy of respect. *Six of one, half a dozen of the other,* he had thought. In keeping with these pros and cons, the Sears catalogue homes hadn't been designed with insulation in mind, leaving Jim and his family to freeze in the winter and swelter in the summer. Consequently, the porch became the extended living room during the dog days of August. But Jim did love those summer evenings on the front porch. *Six of one, ...*

Mona exited from the driver's side and slammed the door shut. A startled rooster with ruffled feathers settled down and then strutted away. The rooster had been an accident from the first time Jim and Susan had ordered baby chicks, but they kept him just the same for the girls' sake. They had laughed at themselves when they realized at least half of their purchase failed to be 'layers.' Jim didn't tell the girls about the other five roosters; he simply traded them to Thomas Gustasfon for a tractor part, apple-butter and pumpkin bread. In the end, those roosters became his neighbor's dinner. Delta opened the passenger door and after getting out she pulled the seatback forward for Devika, who had been riding in the back seat.

At the sound of the car doors closing, Jim Hack opened his screen door. Dressed in blue jeans and a white T-shirt, he stepped out onto the porch, allowing the screened door to bang behind him. He liked the sound of it—the bang; it reminded him of his childhood. Jim squinted against the morning sun; his weathered hand above his eyebrows shielded a handsome and tanned face.

"Hey there," he called out to Delta.

"What happened to the pigs?" Delta greeted him with the inquiry as she gave a quick glance toward the empty pig sty.

"Susan was tired of the stench; we doubled up on the chickens instead. The pigs that we did keep we took to market already," he said as he took a jaunty step from the porch to the driveway. Susan and their two girls came out onto the porch and waved to Delta. Susan wiped her hands on a dish towel and then threw it over her shoulder. The girls jumped down the porch steps to hug Delta.

After months of getting to know each other, first through interviews, which came complete with snickerdoodles, and later through friendly bartering—Delta traded the *Chicago Tribune,* a newspaper one would have to drive to town to get, for fresh eggs from Jim and Susan on Sunday mornings—the Hack family had agreed that Delta could be described as "genuine."

"Who are your friends?" Jim asked with a hearty smile and an earthy and friendly stance. Delta introduced Mona Barthes and Professor Devika Sharma.

"Now, Delta, you know how I feel about professors," Jim said with a half a smile and a wink, which he followed with a welcoming hug.

"I know, Jim, but this professor knows all about the seed industry—the good, the bad and the genetically modified."

"Well, you know the saying, you can't live with 'em and you can't live without 'em." He led the way back to the front porch.

"Professors or genetically-modified seeds?" Susan asked facetiously with a smile and then gave Delta a hug. "Good to see you, Hon."

"The seeds," Jim said with a serious tone. "Farmers have to play the game to compete. If somebody else is goin' to buy GMs, then you got to buy GMs. You can't live with 'em; you can't live without 'em. That's my opinion of the seed companies."

"But you got out of that game," Susan added with reference to the *seed game* that Jim had mentioned.

"That's true. I suppose I did." Jim shook hands with Devika and then pulled her in for a hug. Devika Sharma's big, round, brown eyes popped with surprise.

"Since when do you hug professors?" Susan half-teased, half-chided her husband.

"I know, but I've never seen a professor in such a little package."

"Forgive him. He doesn't get off the farm often," Susan apologized.

"No harm," Devika assured Susan. "It's nice to meet you."

"He's just in an unusually good mood. We sold the pigs for a good profit this year, for a change. And we just got the check in the mail this morning."

"Anyway," Jim said. "Any friend of Delta's is welcome here. Right, Susan?" Susan agreed by smiling warmly, and adding, "Absolutely, absolutely."

And Jim gave Mona a hug as well. "She's not a professor, right?" he checked with his wife instead of Delta. She gave him a scolding smile. After greeting Delta, the girls—Cody Lynn and Lacey—ran back up the porch steps and settled into oversized, wicker chairs on the front porch to have a game of cards, leaving the adults to talk.

"Delta, we missed you last week," Susan said brushing strands of blonde hair from her face as she stepped onto the porch.

"Yeah, I had a little car trouble," Delta summarized in understated fashion.

"You didn't tell us much on the phone the other day. So what's this all about?" Jim asked.

"Look, Mom," Lacy, the youngest daughter, cried out, as she tugged at Susan's pale turquoise blouse with one hand and pointed with the other hand toward the road. Delta and Susan turned around and looked as well. Having already heard and recognized the familiar sound of a Harley motor, Jim had spotted the motorcycle before his daughter had called out.

Caleb Barthes pulled into the driveway on his Harley Davidson.

"Is this another friend of yours, Delta?" Jim queried before taking steps toward the cyclist. Delta nodded, realizing immediately who was on the bike. Caleb turned off the engine and swung his leg over the bike seat as he unhooked his helmet. He left his helmet on the seat of the bike and walked toward the porch.

"Well, he's just full of surprises, isn't he? How did Caleb know we were going to be here?" Delta commented, looking pointedly at Mona.

"I may have mentioned something along that line," Mona confessed coyly.

"Mona's brother," Delta explained to Jim as they walked toward Caleb.

Caleb approached the group, stretching out his hand to Jim, saying, "Caleb Barthes," and then he nodded to Susan.

"Jim Hack," the farmer returned, adding, "I used to ride one of those, didn't I Susan?"

"And you looked good on your bike," his wife added.

"Had to do it before summer ends," Caleb told him.

"No, I don't blame you. How far did you ride?"

"From Chicago."

"Chicago? Long ride."

"Where, by the way, we don't have anything like this," Caleb said taking in the pastoral beauty of the farm. "Better than the Ponderosa." Caleb had seen reruns.

Jim smiled. "We like it. Come on, I'll show you around."

Delta began retelling her story of how she had been run off the road, received mysterious messages, and had her farm interviews sent to Washington D.C. Delta assured Jim that his last name had been deleted and his first name had been changed to a pseudonym. She added that besides trying to figure out what's going on she wanted to recover her lost work as much as possible. She also wanted to know if Jim thought she might be able to get local farmers to come together for a meeting, so that she and her friends could reconstruct the earlier interviews. Of course not all of the interviews came from this area of Indiana, or just from Indiana for that matter, but Delta explained that recovering even some of the interviews would help. Delta had a lot of work ahead of her collecting interviews from several different locations across the Midwest.

"That's feasible. Maybe at the Annual Fish Fry Dinner," Jim suggested. Susan agreed, adding, "Yeah, we could probably get folks to come early so you could do that."

They walked as they talked. Jim showed Mona, Devika, and Caleb the restored barn and chicken coop. He walked them out to see his fields which were bordered by the Wildcat Creek. Their talk soon turned to the terminator seed and the numerous lawsuits that RichField had filed against farmers, and had won. During the tour Devika asked Jim more pointed questions about the seed companies. Jim told her he was familiar with the stories, he'd read about them in the local *Ag Rag*. Jim added, "Some of those Canadian farmers might have come by that seed fair and square. It may have blown into their fields, highly likely, with the prairie winds they have up there, who's to say?"

"The judge ruled against them," Devika Sharma curtly reported but then quickly added sympathetically, "Not that I agree with his ruling." Jim gave her a sharp look. His loyalty to the small-holdings farmer was intense.

"The problem with the herbicides, pesticides etcetera is that some species can build up a tolerance, and then you'll wind up with a super weed or a super bug. Plus, nobody wants contamination from seeds blowing in from somebody else's field. Believe me; the government knows what's happening. It's hardest on the smallholder farmer because the way the government wants to control for it is by leaving fields fallow next to fields that are planted with GM seeds. See, they know those GM seeds are floating into neighboring fields or they wouldn't have made that law. Well, that's all well and good if you've got a lot of land, like those corporate farmers, but me, a guy like me; I rent small plots from other people or I farm small plots for other people who can't farm it themselves. There's no way to leave a field fallow and still make money. I'm organic now and I still have to worry about those corporate big wigs."

"How so?"

"What if seeds do blow onto my fields? They'll take me to court and sue me for everything I've got."

"How many acres do you farm?" Caleb asked.

"All told about 500, but here," Jim raised his arms wide and turned to show the expanse of his small farm, "maybe 15 acres on this homestead, here—"

He stopped in mid-sentence, turned and looked up. Delta and the others spun around; they gazed into the bright blue sky as they also heard the engine of the small plane and saw a crop duster, a biplane flying toward the fields.

"What the ..." Jim exclaimed as the plane came in low and began to spray a liquid on his crops. Jim began yelling, shouting as high as the sky—"Hey, Stop!" He flailed and waved his arms at the crop duster to stop, but the pilot whizzed the plane overhead ignoring Jim's pleas.

"Did you order any dusting?" Caleb asked quickly.

"No, like I said, I'm organic. Besides, it's not time to spray," Jim began to race after the plane.

Mona and Delta began coughing. Devika wheezed like an asthmatic. Jim suddenly realized what was happening. "Quick get in the house and close the windows," he yelled back at them. They all ran toward the house. Delta and Susan grabbed the girls as they reached the porch and drew them quickly into the house. Mona and Devika followed. Jim ran into the fields screaming curses at the pilot.

Caleb yanked off his kerchief from around his neck, tied it over his mouth and nose, and then ran for his Harley.

The plane made another pass. Low and slow for a biplane. Maybe 100 mph. Covering the area with a clear-colored liquid that fell like a fine mist on Jim's crops, the plane swooped and sprayed. Jim continued screaming until his lungs burned and he dropped to his knees in the field. Susan screamed from behind the screen door. She pushed it open and ran to her husband. Delta told Devika and Mona to stay with the girls. She ran to the field to help Susan get Jim.

Caleb had started his motorcycle and was now chasing after the biplane. He drove the bike along the bumpy rows of soy beans as fast as he could. The bike hit a wet patch and spun, nearly falling on top of Caleb. He got the bike back up and went in pursuit again. From 0–60 in 7.5 seconds, the salesman had promised. Caleb was counting on it. He shifted into second, and then third, maneuvered the bike into a straight smooth track made by Jim's plow. He cranked the bike to 80 mph, 90, 100. *That's not fast enough*, Caleb thought. He squeezed a little harder, 105 mph, 110, 120. He had less than a few seconds to catch the plane before it would reach the end of the field and would soar into the air, curving and turning back to make another run at the fields, 130 mph. The Harley Davidson bounced in the bumpy ruts of the field, going faster and faster. Caleb caught up with the plane and then jumped onto the seat of the Harley, leaning forward and holding the handle bars as steady as possible until he was positioned just under the tire of the crop duster. He stood up and let go of the handle bars.

Caleb leapt into the air.

CHAPTER 36

Saturday, August 28, 2010—outskirts of Lafayette, IN

Grabbing the metal strut with both hands, Caleb hung onto the biplane's chassis that connected the tires to the belly of the plane. The bike went flying across the soybean field; dirt flew feverishly into swirling clouds of mini-tornadoes. Caleb's hands held tightly to the metal, his arms burned, his legs dangled in the air. He strained every muscle in his upper body. The wind slapped his hair against his face. The biplane tipped. The pilot yelled, "What the fuck are you doing?"

Caleb swung one leg up and then the other, maneuvering onto the top edge of the landing gear. The pilot tried to stabilize the plane that dipped erratically. From the tire, Caleb quickly climbed upward, swinging one leg and then the other onto the lower wing. Once on the wing, he reached for the metal rod that supports the upper wing. The lower wing's slippery surface forced his legs to slide about, but his hand held firm to the metal grip. Pulling the weight of his body forward, Caleb inched closer to the inner stabilizing rod. The plane tipped and bounced from his weight. The pilot yelled again. The wind swallowed his words. Caleb gripped the metal connecting rods between the levels of the biplane's wings within the aileron of the two-bay biplane. He pulled himself to a standing position between the wings by holding the strut that connected the two wings. Caleb started to make his way toward the cockpit. The wind whipped his hair; his shirt billowed like a sail. The pilot turned fast trying to make Caleb slip.

He hung on.

The plane climbed higher; Caleb could see the entire farm below him. The Wildcat Creek sparkled in the distance and the words, *Jim loves Susan* appeared before him on the roof of the barn. It wasn't painted on as Delta had written, instead the words were more permanent, tiles far thicker than shingles had been laid in place and

227

attached by metal fasteners. Caleb could see Jim's love for Susan, tenacious and eternal. Caleb edged closer to the pilot. He shouted:

"Take it down, damn it!"

"You idiot, get off of my plane," the pilot yelled back.

"Take it down!" Caleb yelled again, his words fighting against the wind. The pilot ignored him. "If you want to live to fly again, land this plane," Caleb shouted as he inched closer, stretched out his arm and grabbed the pilot around the neck. The pilot tried to fight him off with one hand.

Caleb threw himself sideways wrapping his arms completely around the pilot's neck. The pilot began choking. He took both hands off the controls in an attempt to peel Caleb's hands from his throat. The nose of the plane tipped downward, much too fast.

Caleb yelled, "Turn off the applicator!" The pilot's eyes bulged as he fought back, struggling against Caleb's grip. The plane dove faster.

"Let go!" the pilot screamed. "Are you crazy?" the pilot yelled. The plants were much too close. Caleb leaned into the cockpit and flipped the switch, turning off the release valve. As he looked up, he saw the earth, the soybeans, the dirt coming at him fast and faster. The nose of the plane nearly touched the ground. The colors were much too vivid. Caleb loosened his grip on the pilot. Both Caleb and the pilot yanked up on the stick, simultaneously. They narrowly missed slamming into the ground. The plane headed forward and upward. The house! They faced the farmhouse; its white walls, stained with age, covered their view like the White Cliffs of Dover.

The pilot pulled back on the joystick. The biplane creased the roof. A shingle flew through the air as the tire of the plane scraped its surface. The plane soared into blue sky and white clouds.

"Now, land it, you son of a dick," Caleb ordered through gritted teeth as he tugged on the pilot's throat one more time.

"Okay, okay," the pilot surrendered. Caleb released his grip on the aviator, but held tight to the cockpit. The pilot brought the crop duster in for a more than bumpy landing, shredding soybean plants with the sheer force of the wind as he came to a stop on the county road at the edge of Jim and Susan's field. As the biplane slowed to a stop, Jim met them, rifle in hand. Delta and Susan came running just behind Jim.

"I want to know one thing," Caleb shouted at the man, breathing hard between syllables. Jim listened, his 22 caliber rifle pointed and cocked, waiting with seething anger for the pilot's response to Caleb's question. "Who paid you?"

CHAPTER 37

Sunday, August 29, 2010—Chicago, IL

The half court game was two on two—Reuben and Joe against Caleb and Ani—shirts against skins, respectively. They played on an outdoor court in Joe's old neighborhood, near Cicero. The ritual game had started in college when they used it to sweat alcohol from their bodies, to burn off their hangovers. At least that was the case for Caleb and Joe; Reuben and Ani were not big drinkers. This is also why the teams were divided—one hangover player teamed with one healthy athlete, each one a temple of their respective gods. The game never started before noon as Reuben always went to Sunday service and Joe said he had to service his headache until at least noon.

"You were too hard on her," Reuben said as he dribbled the ball down the inside sideline of the court. They had already been playing for nearly twenty minutes. Sweat dripped from his upper lip.

"I know," Caleb said, exhaling hard.

"No, I mean it. You don't know what the sheriff told her or what she said to him." Reuben dribbled across the key.

"I know," Caleb agreed as he swung his arms attempting to block Reuben's shot, but Reuben faked and then bounce passed the ball to Joe. It went under Caleb's arm; he lunged for it. Too late, Joe caught the ball.

"But you had the right stuff, my man. You told that sheriff where to put his racist bullshit," Joe praised Reuben as he dribbled. Ani tried to block Joe's layup, but it hit the backboard and then the rim and fell through. Ani quickly took it out of bounds.

"I know," Reuben agreed. "I did what I should've, but Caleb didn't need to take it out on Delta."

"Yeah, for chrissake, she's the first nice girl you've dated in ages, not to mention she lives in a church," Joe added as he waved his arms in front of Ani, who said, "If you aren't going to mention that she lives in a church, then why do you mention it?" Ani used a bounce pass to get the ball to Caleb. "She's not the first *nice* girl he's dated in a while; she's the *only* girl he's dated in a while."

"I know, I know," Caleb told them as he dribbled down court. "Mona called me." Caleb took a shot; nothing but net. Reuben took the ball out, threw it to Joe and set up a pick behind Ani. Ani turned right into Reuben.

Caleb yelled at Ani, "You fall for that every time, Ani."

"It is a mean maneuver," Ani announced.

"Mean or not, watch out for it," Caleb warned him. Joe shot. Two points. Caleb took the ball out.

"Speaking of mean, you were mean to Delta, she should watch out for you," Ani scolded in a kidding manner. Caleb threw the ball to Ani. Joe hammered it free with one hard pound to the ball.

"We made up," Caleb told them while guarding Reuben.

"You made out?" Joe twisted the words on purpose.

"Made up."

"Grow up," Ani told Joe.

"You grow up," Joe retorted. They both laughed.

"Really? You made up?" Reuben asked dribbling the ball behind and through his legs. This time Ani snatched it away from Reuben.

"Yes, really," Caleb said panting for air. "By the way, she said to tell you both she's sorry." Reuben went straight at Ani, but Ani dodged, shot and then jumped toward the rim tipping his own shot through the hoop. Reuben caught the ball as it fell through the net, took it out of bounds and passed the ball back to Joe. Joe dribbled down the sideline, shot the ball, and made the basket.

"That's game. You each owe me a fiver," he announced to the losing team—Caleb and Ani. Joe threw the ball at Caleb, who shot anyway, making a three point basket.

"So ask her out," Joe told him.

Reuben and Ani took their towels from their gym bags that lay under the basketball pole. Joe used his shirt tail to wipe sweat from his upper lip. Caleb stretched before sitting with his friends under a leafy maple tree that shaded the court. As they sat in the grass next to the court downing bottled water, Caleb told them how Mona had berated him for being too hard on Delta. Mona had reminded him of how the sheriff's description of the two suspects had matched that of

Reuben and Joe "roughly." Reuben scoffed. Joe added, "I don't know; we are pretty suspicious looking characters."

Reuben spit into the dirt.

"I know, I know. I agree with you, but that's what the sheriff told her." It was the best Caleb had to offer Reuben. "Anyway," Caleb began describing the events of Saturday morning on Jim and Susan Hack's farm, including the biplane, the spraying, and his aerial acrobatics from his Harley to the plane.

"Wow! How's your bike?" Joe asked.

"Leave it to Joe to ask about your bike before he asks about everybody else," Ani chided his friend.

"It'll live and everybody else is fine. But I could've killed that pilot with my bare hands. For chrissake, there were kids on that farm. He saw us standing in the field. He knew exactly what he was doing. Sure, times are bad for crop dusters—retired pilots with antique planes, but times are bad for everybody. You don't go around spraying pesticide on little kids." Caleb continued to tell Joe and the others about the terminator seed and Delta's attempt to re-collect her data. "I called Reuben last night and gave him a heads up. But anyway, she's trying to find out about a terminator seed. Ani, I tried to call you last night—"

"I know about the terminator seed," Ani interrupted.

"You do? What do you know?" Caleb quickly queried.

"There's a moratorium on the terminator seed. European countries outlawed it. Indian and South Korean activists led a movement to ban the terminator seed, as well. I heard Vandana Shiva speak on the matter in 2004 at the University of California, Santa Barbara. She's a gifted speaker, a scientist and a nonviolent activist who tells us *Seeds are our mother*. She leads women to civil disobedience in the image of Mahatma Gandhi. Yes, everyone loves her."

"Not everyone." Reuben interrupted. "I'll bet RichField doesn't love her. They have offices in India and they are trying to sell the terminator seed there. I also looked into some of the court cases," Reuben told them, adding, "RichField's been hit hard with lawsuits for everything from dumping toxic waste to claims about them bailing on taxes. But they're also hitting back. They've filed lawsuits against farmers for patent infringement."

"I know," Caleb told them.

"But why would they want Delta's research so badly, if everybody already knows about the terminator seed and there's a moratorium on it?" Reuben wondered aloud.

"Maybe they started using the terminator seed again after saying they wouldn't?" Ani offered.

"Maybe," Caleb said, only half-persuaded, suspecting that there is more to this than bringing the terminator seed back to market.

"I don't know, Caleb, with the terminator seed you could control the entire market. The market share must be in the billions—"

"But only if they establish a monopoly," Ani suggested, adding, "That way they could rake in the money. They might find that worth the risk of an anti-trust suit."

"They could have killed us; is it worth killing for?"

"People have killed for far less," Joe retorted.

"Maybe so, but I think there's something else going on here," Caleb asserted. "Think about it, they use the terminator seed and the herbicide or pesticide, make millions, even billions. They create a monopoly; they play the game as long as they can, then the government steps in with an anti-trust suit and *Bam,* the game is over. This is standard operating practice for giant corporations today. Why is this one worth killing over? No, Joe, I'm telling you, something else is going on here. It's more than the money for one patent. Power, I think. Some kind of political power game ..." Caleb mused.

"For people like that, it's always all about the money," Joe said, adding, "You wanna bet on it?" Joe laughed at the irony, spit on his hand and held it out to Caleb, who did the same before shaking it. "Another fiver?"

After they shook hands, Caleb said, "By the way, after the pilot told us who paid him to spray the farm field, he said, 'What's the big deal?' Just like that. And that's when Delta hauled off and punched him in the jaw."

"No shit?" Joe commented incredulously. "She's Delta Force!"

"She's got spunk, that one does," Reuben assessed.

"Gandhi she is not, but I respect her just the same," Ani agreed.

CHAPTER 38

Sunday evening, August 29, 2010—Chicago, IL

"Forgive me, Monsignor, for I have sinned."

The monsignor recognized the young man's voice, but even if he hadn't he knew who was in the adjacent, confessional cubicle. The young Father Brandon Langer had requested a special confession.

"Surely you haven't had time to finish two novenas, my son."

"No, Monsignor, I haven't." His words hung with shame; his eyes cast downward.

"Tell me, why have you returned to the confessional? It's only been a few days since your last confession. Is the Irish girl still skipping through your dreams?"

"It's more serious than that," Father Brandon Langer admitted to his superior. "I didn't feel right taking communion this morning."

"Have you killed anyone?" the white-haired monsignor asked.

"No, Monsignor."

"Well then, I think we can deal with it, whatever it is," the Monsignor tried to reassure his sinner. His hands, as usual, rested on his rosary. Kind words came easily to him. The Monsignor had celebrated his 80th birthday last January; he felt that he had heard every sin that marked humanity's frailty. This young priest would not shock him.

Although the Monsignor had to admit to himself that Delta's story, *The Probable and the Magical: The Secret Story of the Not-So-Virgin Virgin,* had caused him to awaken in the middle of the night. It wasn't that she suggested the virgin was not a virgin that troubled him. He had read the stories of Panthera the Roman soldier who was stationed in the Holy Land and had reportedly raped the virgin. No, this didn't cause his insomnia as he had previously judged the story false and had adhered to papal doctrine on the matter. It was the story of Joseph being a gay man who needed to hide his sexual orientation that bothered the elder priest. Delta had argued it within the story with such ease that the Monsignor had dreamt that it was true and that he himself gave a lecture on such matters. He awoke with a shudder and forced himself to find a valid argument against it. Such blasphemy had never before been asserted. The old priest had tossed and turned the thoughts around in his mind. Eventually, he had risen from his bed, slid his bony feet into a pair of slippers and gathered a robe about him. In the middle of the night the monsignor had gone to the kitchen and prepared himself a cup of warm milk as he thought only about Joseph. *True enough, early Judaism had laws about sexual activities that specifically denied the pleasures in which the Greeks and Romans had engaged. Plato described Socrates as offering to dance nude for a younger man's pleasure at the mere hint of the other man's interest, sometimes without any provocation at all; Socrates just liked dancing nude and he clearly enjoyed the pleasure of men. But the Jews needed men to sleep with women in order to procreate, to build their numbers, to advance their religion. They even had laws to that effect.* The elderly priest had sipped his warm milk and wondered if it could be true. It seemed possible, he thought. *Possible, but not probable,* he had thought to himself as he walked the lonely hallway of the priests' house. He stood momentarily in front of a mirror, looking at his pale and wrinkled visage. *Who is this man I see in the mirror,* he asked himself, *to be questioning doctrine at my age?* And then the Monsignor had gone back to bed to tussle with a tiny lingering doubt, like a pea under his mattress.

Now, he sat in the confessional listening, waiting, for the young priest who had brought him the manuscript to speak his peace, to confess whatever else weighed on his soul.

"Go ahead, my son, unburden yourself," Monsignor coaxed.

"I didn't tell you the whole truth during my last confession," Father Langer confessed.

"I suspected as much, my son … Go on then, tell me the whole truth."

CHAPTER 39

Monday morning, 6:00 a.m., August 30, 2010—outskirts of Lafayette, IN

Susan Hack stepped from the front porch of the old Sear's house. "C'mon, girls," she called to her daughters as she headed toward the long yellow school bus parked in the scraggy grass next to the barn. "We've got children waiting."

Jim looked up and smiled as he saw his wife getting ready to board the bus. Susan had been a part-time school bus driver for several years. Jim always told her she didn't have to drive and she always said she just wanted a little pin money, mostly to buy gifts for other people. They had picked up the bus on Sunday from the city garage. Both were grateful for the chore as they wanted to keep their minds off what had happened on Saturday morning when the biplane had soared above dusting their fields.

Having recovered from the effects of the pesticide, the girls came bounding from the porch each one having let the screen door bang behind them. The younger one dragged her backpack across the floor of the porch and down the steps; the older girl had her backpack secured over one shoulder. They called out, "Bye Daddy, see you later."

"Bye, girls. Drive safe now, ya hear, Susan."

"No other way," she called back and then they boarded the bus.

Jim momentarily stopped his chore of clearing some scrub from the field and watched them pull out of the driveway. He waved again. Susan smiled from behind the big wheel while looking into the oversized, rear-view mirror.

Jim left the scrub behind as he headed to the barn to milk the cows. Susan usually did the milking, but with school starting they shifted chores. Jim entered the barn and said hello to the animals, "Molly, howdy do, girl? You ready to give me some milk." The cow mooed as if she understood, but was annoyed by the prospect. Jim gathered up his pail and stool. Crazy Horse kicked his stall, making a banging noise. "Settle down, Crazy Horse. Molly and I got business to take care—" But just then Jim heard another sound; it was coming from the driveway.

He stopped, listened, and thought he heard a motor, tires on the gravel driveway. Susan must have forgotten something. He left his stool and started to go outside to see, but before he even stepped out of the barn he heard a car door shut. *Buses don't have doors that bang shut*, he thought to himself. Jim stood still for moment, thinking, *Damn, my rifle's in the house.* He looked around, spied the pitchfork and grabbed it. Only then did Jim step boldly into the early morning sunlight.

A tan car had pulled into the driveway and two men had gotten out of the car. One of the men already stood in his field, bending over, doing something that Jim couldn't make out. The other man was tall, 6'2 and about 200 lbs., maybe a bit more. He stood closer to the car, watching. The man spotted Jim. Jim called out, confronting him from where he stood.

"What are you doing on my property? This is private property! You're trespassing." Jim walked toward the bigger man with his pitchfork gripped tightly.

"No need for that," the African-American looking man told Jim in a deep voice. "We're just about done."

"Done with what? What's he doin' in my field? Get away from there!" Jim shouted to the Caucasian man with the blond hair.

The blond man stood up holding a gallon-size plastic-baggy in his hand, full of soybean plants and dirt. He walked without a word toward their car.

"What're you doin' with my crops? You thievin'—"

"Just taking a little sample," the first man told the farmer, "We're inspectors." The man pulled a camera phone out of his pocket. "Hey, now hold it up so we have a picture of exactly where this came from," he told the other man who stood with his back to Jim with the Sears house in the background, holding the baggy up high for good measure.

"Did you get my good side?" the blond man laughed. The man with the camera phone quickly snapped a picture of Jim for good measure.

Jim looked at them with disbelief. "Inspectors my ass! I don't know who you are but get off of my property!"

"You do understand, don't you, Mr. Hack? We actually are investigators. We'll have this crop tested for chemicals, herbicides and pesticides. We'll report our findings. Weren't you selling to a chain of health food stores up north? Your buyers might be interested in knowing that your organic fields aren't all that organic after all."

Jim turned white hot with anger. "You might think about what this pitchfork will look like right between your eyes," he shouted, turning the pitchfork to point it at them. "Get the hell off my property," he commanded as he considered whether to stab them or the tire of the car, or both. The first man swung his door wide open and leapt into the driver's side of the car. The other man jumped into the passenger's side, the engine still running afforded them a quick getaway. They absconded with the bagful of contaminated soybeans—soybeans saturated in glyphosate, leaving Jim standing in the driveway, feeling angry, frustrated, and defeated.

CHAPTER 40

Monday morning, 8:00 a.m., August 30, 2010—Chicago, IL

Zandie Tan sat at her receptionist desk, a cup of tea beside her keyboard. Ray Little passed by the glass exterior of the gallery on his way to the security station across the hallway; he waved to Zandie.

"Good morning, Ray," she greeted him, calling through the open doorway. "Are you ready for another week of securing the Thompson Center?" Zandie Tan's English was so impeccable one would have thought that she had been born and reared in the U.S. "We have a special collection of farm photographs coming in tomorrow. We're all going to be working on the 17th floor in the lay-out room. They're huge, poster-size images. We wouldn't want anybody to steal those."

"I'll take good care of your posters, Zandie."

Zandie smiled and returned to viewing her computer screen. The *China Daily News* appeared before her. Zandie Tan was born in Beijing and had traveled to the U.S. to study. Being accepted into graduate school in the U.S. was like hitting the lottery, except for the fact that she had worked hard for the prize. Good grades and great GRE scores, perfect English, and the desire to succeed coupled with intense dedication to her studies had advanced her to the short list and eventually acceptance into a master's program. Her parents, a music teacher and a pharmacy clerk living in Beijing, were thrilled for their daughter. Tuition paid by the university in return for teaching services and a small stipend in addition meant their daughter would get an education in the States. They hoped that when she returned to Beijing this would put her in the running for a very good job, a career. Upon completion of her master's degree she had been hired by the ISM—gallery, not simply as a receptionist, although she did indeed help in that capacity, but as the assistant archivist of international agricultural reports. She had been working with Dr. Goldman for nearly a year, first as an intern and now as an assistant. Zandie had been hired when the department realized that Chinese farmers had a history both in the U.S. and in China and that with trade opening so dramatically in the last few years a whole new set of narratives would be worth documenting. Zandie Tan would be there to collect them, to translate related documents if necessary, to organize them and finally, to archive them.

She took a sip of her tea and continued reading, when suddenly she leaned in closer to the screen as a headline caught her eye—*Experts warn of GM foods*. Zandie read the article. She then began googling news stories about genetically-modified crops. Article after article laid out the continuing debate. GM crops appear to be safe, but some scientists in Europe have found that GM corn may cause liver and kidney damage to test animals, other scientists found damage to the immune system of animal subjects. Others say it must be tested on a case by case basis. Still others lauded the numbers of people who can be fed when GM crops are used. Another article talked about how China has begun testing the crop with regard to how well it will grow, but is taking cautious steps because they want to be able to export their rice to Europe and Europeans have banned genetically-modified crops.

Zandie Tan picked up her tea and held it in midair as she continued to scan articles until she came across the term "terminator seed," which jolted her further forward. Even more unnerving, "zombie seed" appeared in one line of one article. "Zombie seed," she said it out loud and set her tea cup down so that she could use both hands to type. After typing *zombie seed;* she read furiously. Zandie Tan's fingers flew across the keyboard even faster than before, calling up article after article.

CHAPTER 41

Monday, August 30, 2010—West Lafayette, IN

On Monday morning, Delta sat down at her computer in her office in the west wing of Beering Hall, and typed in her ID and password. She watched as big, black, sharply edged letters appeared on the screen:

Saturday was a warning! Stop your research!

And then the letters disintegrated.

Delta was less surprised this time and far more angry than fearful. A tinge of guilt for placing the Hack family in harm's way bracketed her emotions, but mostly she was infuriated that anyone would spray Jim's fields with herbicides or pesticides, putting the girls at risk, placing Susan and Jim in danger and damaging their crops, jeopardizing their livelihood.

Delta waited for her system to come back on line and then promptly emailed a note to Caleb. She told him about the warning message and asked how anybody would have known that they were going to be at Jim and Susan's farm. She told Caleb that she had spent all day Sunday researching reports on the corporation in question, Richfield, and about the scientific research that the company is conducting. She added that she'll be damned if she'll quit her research. In fact, more determined than ever, Delta hit the send button.

Delta didn't have time to wait for a reply from Caleb. She had her Monday morning meeting and then her back-to-back classes to teach. She gathered her materials and headed for the meeting. During the faculty discussion of curriculum matters, Delta kept reading print outs that she had stashed in her folder. She read about court case after court case, plus, information on the history and development of the terminator seed. When the meeting ended she shoved the materials back in her oversized bag before leaving for class.

The first class went well. Delta quickly headed for her second class—Critical and Rhetorical Approaches to Public Relations. When she arrived, she found the room abuzz with students talking. Delta noticed that two of the students were especially dramatic and animated in their conversation, allowing her to overhear. One student said to the other, "No, you tell her." Each glanced up at her.

"Let me take attendance before we do anything else," Delta told them more than asked.

As soon as she was done taking roll call, Drew Underwood, whose name, coincidentally, was last on the roster, raised his hand. "I've got you checked in," Delta said seeing his hand come up again.

"No not that," he said lowering his arm.

"What then?"

"Professor Quinn, we found something that we think you should see," Drew told her. Lisa, the girl sitting next to Drew, continued.

"Yeah, Drew and I were in the lab last night; we were searching the internet for the *terminator seed* and ..." Drew picked up the thread from there.

"And we found something that we think you will want to know."

"What's that, Drew?"

"May I?" Drew said pointing to the computer in the front of the room.

"By all means," Delta waved him to the front of the room. She stepped back.

Drew turned on the projector, clicked the keys, and typed into the barren block under google:

Patent holders for the terminator seed

Delta watched, at first without expectations; suddenly she sat up straight—her shoulders pulled back, her head lifted, her eyes widened with shock as the words appeared in bold, black headlines:

Purdue University Holds Patent for Terminator Seed

Her eyes widened even further and her jaw fell open. She tried to control her muscles but her arms wouldn't move and her legs felt heavy, her feet felt glued to the floor. It was hard to breathe as if she had just been violently punched in the gut, like when she took a blow once in Karate class from an overzealous fellow student. *I thought we were the good guys?* She questioned the ethics of her own institution—Purdue University?! *How can this be?* A million questions raced through her brain; *Why hadn't I known this? What about Devika, wouldn't Devika Sharma have had an inkling that Purdue holds a terminator seed patent? Why didn't she tell me? How could it be with all the research that I've been reading, that this, this hadn't surfaced? Why hadn't any of the farmers mentioned this to me? Is this why they were so standoffish?*

"Should I read the article, Professor?" Drew was asking her.

She nodded, unable to verbalize her assent with words.

As he read, she tried to come to grips with the feelings of betrayal, of guilt for being a part of an organization that holds a patent for the terminator seed. She suddenly felt complicit in the suicides in India. What would she say to the students? Delta's mind blazed with questions and concerns. Following the shock and confusion a sense of embarrassment arose from inside her and then washed over her. *I'm the professor*, she thought, *my students shouldn't be teaching me; I should be teaching them. How is it that they found this bit of crucial information? How is it that I missed it?* She struggled to recover her composure. *Well*, she thought, *ethics, we'll discuss ethics.* Delta simply couldn't fathom how Purdue University could hold a patent on the terminator seed. She shook her head, took a deep breath and tried to compose herself.

When Drew completed reading the article, Delta stood to face the class.

"Incredible. This is certainly a good example of how ethics are a part of everyday experiences; they're not just abstract concepts that we talk about in class. I want you to work in groups asking yourselves what you would do; *what will you do?*" she emphasized, adding, "now that *you know, that I know,* that Purdue University holds a patent for a terminator seed."

Delta swallowed hard and spent the next forty minutes walking from group to group listening as they confronted each other on ethical practices. At Delta's request, they all used their phones or laptops to search for more information. Delta's face was still hot with guilt and embarrassment, when she asked herself, *what will I do now that I know Purdue holds a patent for the terminator seed?*

"But doesn't the superior seed help to feed larger populations?" one student asked. Delta listened as the group struggled with different arguments.

"Yeah, but organic farming is sustainable," a young man said and added, "I know, I'm taking an agricultural reporting class. We had a speaker in who explained it."

"But it's more expensive," another student said.

"What happens when you compare expense to lives, like the farmers in India?" someone else added. Delta swallowed hard, her stomach still felt queasy.

"It's not more expensive," another student said showing Delta a one page article by Howard Buffett.

In another group, the students were discussing the risk factors for the environment. "What will happen to the butterflies?" one young woman queried with serious concern only to have another laugh at her. "I'm serious, what if the butterflies eat the pesticides or the herbicides?" The other student considered the comment. "You're right it could have an effect, I suppose." A different group found an article about a zombie seed. They told the others.

"Do you think genetically-modified seeds could have an effect on birds that eat the seed, too?"

"Or eat the butterflies."

"My cat eats butterflies and moths."

"What?"

"Yeah, she loves them. Goes after them at night."

"The butterflies?"

"No, the moths."

"Cats don't eat moths!"

"But if they did, and if they eat terminator moths, or zombie moths, then they'll turn into zombies. Zombie cats," a student in the back of the room quipped, kidding the others.

"Don't forget," another student said, "that genetically-modified seeds are not all terminator seeds."

"But they could be," another student shot back.

"Do you think that will happen?" two students questioned in unison. So the conversation went with many intriguing questions and only a few answers. Delta's head was swimming with questions, as well.

As the class period drew to a close, Delta called for the students' attention from the front of the room. "Based on what I've heard from the different groups, I suggest that we all do more research. What do you say?" The students nodded in agreement as they packed their books and shuffled out of the room. Delta's embarrassment had eased somewhat allowing her to take a moment to thank Drew and Lisa as they passed by her.

"Good job. Thanks for finding that information."

"No problem, Professor."

Delta gathered her materials, left the room and headed upstairs. She stopped at the main office to pick up her mail.

"Professor Quinn." One of the secretaries called to her as if she had been saying Professor Quinn's name for the second or third time.

"Oh yes, I'm sorry. What is it?"

"This message came for you."

Delta took the message from the secretary and read it: *I found a copy of what you've been looking for. Can you meet me today at the ISM gallery? Zandie Tan, on behalf of Danielle Goldman.*

"You took this message?" Delta turned to the secretary with the question.

"Yes; why? Is something wrong?"

"Did she say specifically what she found a copy of?"

"No, she made it sound like you would know."

"Okay. Thanks." With note in hand, Delta rushed to her office.

Once there, she quickly typed an email to Danielle Goldman and cc'd her assistant Zandie Tan. It read as follows:

Dear Dr. Goldman,

It is my understanding that you have found a copy of my farm interviews per a phone message that I received. I am thrilled at the news. I wish that I could meet you today, but that's impossible. I can drive there tomorrow morning. Is 10:00 a.m. good for you?"

Prof. Delta Quinn

After sending this message, Delta quickly emailed Caleb telling him the good news. She had all but forgotten the bad news about Purdue University holding a patent for the terminator seed. Now, she began to think about where she might borrow or rent a car on such short notice. Maybe Mona would loan her car to Delta again, however this thought brought bad memories to Delta's mind. *No way is Mona going to jeopardize her little green Geo by entrusting it to me again.*

Just then she heard the familiar ping sound, signaling that she had email. She looked up; it was from Caleb. Delta opened the message.

No worries. I'll pick them up for you and drive to Lafayette with them tomorrow—later, KB

Delta sent an email to Danielle Goldman and Zandie Tan to let them know that her friend, Caleb Barthes would pick up the package in the morning around 10:00 a.m.

CHAPTER 42

Delta slept late on Tuesday morning. She had no classes and no meetings scheduled. Last week, Delta had practically fallen into a coma due to exhaustion, but that Tuesday night's sleep had been filled with confusing dreams and had been abruptly disrupted when Mona had arrived to pick her up for Wednesday morning's classes. Now, having slept the deepest and dreamt the longest of any night in the last two weeks, she emerged from her bedroom, dressed in a tank top and pajama bottoms, feeling well rested. Delta swept her ruffled hair from in front of her face and took a deep, clear breath. The world felt good again. After all, Caleb had stopped the pilot from doing extensive damage to Jim and Susan's crops and he had learned who had paid the pilot, plus Danielle and Zandie had found a copy of the farm interviews. This information would go a long way in figuring out who had been trying to stop her research, she thought. And now, Caleb was going to pick up the interview transcripts and bring them to Lafayette. Delta also smiled at the thought of seeing Caleb again.

Delta fixed a cup tea and carried it to her office under the choir loft. Her habit of looking at the stained-glass portrayal of the Annunciation every morning was hard to break, but her glance in that direction provided no more than the view of the plywood paneling Joe Jaworski had installed for her temporary protection. She felt better about her situation with Joe and Reuben after punching the pilot. *Displaced aggression, perhaps, but it worked like a charm*, she decided. Besides, she wasn't sure who she had actually wanted to punch, the sheriff for questioning Reuben and Joe, Caleb for blaming her, or the pilot for spraying the field with pesticide while they—Jim and Susan and the girls, Mona and Devika, and Caleb, stood below. She suddenly thought of the husband and wife in India who had drunk the glyphosate, ending their lives, obliterating a family, leaving a child orphaned. She glanced down at her purple knuckles. The bruises were worth it. Even more so, she knew that she'd also done it for Caleb and Jim, who both wanted to punch the pilot, but controlled their anger. She set her tea down by the computer and rubbed her swollen knuckles. It hurt to touch them. The pain felt good.

Delta sat down and flicked the computer on. Eleven o'clock. She hadn't realized that she had slept quite that late. *Eleven o'clock*, she thought again, *that's 10:00 a.m. in Chicago.* She quickly checked her email. There was a message from Zandie Tan.

Delta,

Your friend, Caleb, arrived and picked up the package of interviews.

Zandie

The message had been sent only moments ago—9:58 a.m. Central time. Delta closed the message and opened a new one to Caleb:

Caleb,

Thanks. Zandie told me you picked up the interviews. You're wonderful!

Delta

Delta sent the message and then stood to stretch, contemplating whether to shower or eat first. Stomach pangs motivated her toward the fruit basket on the counter where she retrieved a banana, but before Delta had peeled the banana halfway, she heard another ping coming from her computer.

She sat back down, banana in hand, reading the message from Caleb.

Delta,

I just got off the escalator. Be there in a minute. I haven't been there yet. Am I still wonderful?

Caleb

Delta emailed back.

Then who picked up the interview transcripts?!

PART IV

PART II

ANOTHER INTERLUDE

There are No Zombies, only Butterflies

An indigo scarf tamed the woman's unruly hair and a wheat-colored, loose sack dress hung over her lean body. She mixed easily with the small gathering of mostly men under a grove of juniper trees in the secret location north of the Port-au-Prince plantations. Near Gonaives, on the side of a mountain, close to a cave entrance, the men gathered along with a handful of women. The slave ships had always arrived with more men than women. The few women who arrived rarely lived long enough to bear children. She too had come from Africa, the woman with the indigo head wrap, specifically from Guinea. She brought the knowledge of the homeland and over the years had learned to mix the African religion well with the white man's religion. The more gods the better, she thought as she looked about her at the secret gathering of slaves who had learned how to slip away in the dead of night. The day after the secret meetings, they worked like the living dead, exhausted, with vacant stares, but in their hearts, each slave carried a secret which gave them the strength to pull their hoes. Specifically, the woman wearing an indigo head wrap carried a secret more powerful than any of the others. The houngan had taught her how to follow the trinity of stones before he had died. More importantly, he had bequeathed to her the secret seed, the *butterfly seed*. She was the woman who had discovered the field of zombies. And she had assisted the houngan in laying the dead to rest again. Now, she carried it—*the butterfly seed*, the most special seed from Afrique—sewn into the callous of her left heel. She carried it this very night—August 14, 1791—to a meeting with the Maroons.

She didn't need to brew the mysterious tea from the plant that grows on the island of Haiti where the houngan had secretly cultivated it; she needed only to bring the seed, as a part of her being, to the meeting. The gods would do the rest. But she needed all the gods and their cohort, including the Virgin Mary, for this to work. Most importantly, she needed to give herself up to Damballah and

Mary and then all would fall into place. She had to let them enter her body. All of this, she had told to the leader of the Maroons, the one-armed slave who had escaped and spent his evenings righteously raiding plantations, stealing back livestock in order to feed his followers, and confiscating weapons and ammunition in order to support the dream of revolution. He gave them hope. He told her, on more than one occasion, that he was ready. She had told him that the gods decide when we are ready.

At midnight when the night gave way to the next day, the Feast of the Assumption, the woman without a name, for she had refused to tell anyone her name, who wore the indigo wrap about her hair, would give the people the sign they had been awaiting. She watched as the moon reached its peak, high and full, with sultry black clouds whispering, *a storm is on the way*. She gave up her mind and body to the gods. She slumped at her place. Someone nearby noticed and nudged the others to pay attention. Those Maroons close-by watched as her body began to rise up and she made her way through the crowd.

As she languidly moved forward, as if a snake had entered her body, slowly curving its way through every part of her being, beginning with her head and neck which moved in a slithering fashion, followed by her shoulders and hips, she disappeared into the bidding of the gods. The irises of her eyeballs rolled back into her head and with each step that she took another Maroon moved back, aghast at her white and blood shot eyeballs leading her forward. The Maroons, clearing a path for her, fell silent. Only the one-armed leader seemed ready to receive her.

The gods in the form of the woman moved closer to the leader. That is when one of the other men saw that she held a knife within her hand. He gasped. Then sent warning to the leader by way of glancing at the weapon and then at him. The leader remained calm, unperturbed, and most certainly unafraid; he actually welcomed the zombie of the gods as she came closer. He held out his hands to her. She spoke:

"Haiti, I, Damballah's Daughter,

Entice Nightfall!

Zombies, Oh, My Barone,

I'm Eternity!"

She held up the knife as she spoke. Now all could see it gleaming high above her head. What message would the gods communicate? What had her words meant? The people wondered as they watched her come closer to their leader. He held up his hand for the crowd to stay back. The drums beat a ferocious rhythm. She danced in a circle, twirling, twirling. Faster and faster, while holding the shimmering blade over her head with two hands gripped around the hilt. It flashed repeatedly in front of the face of the one-armed man. She pulled the knife back; the people held their breath. She swung around in one last circle, her indigo scarf flying free. The drums beat faster yet. The knife, glistening with sharpness, full of death and full of possibilities, glimmered under the stars. Suddenly she thrust the knife downward. The people gasped in unison as her knife struck flesh. Blood flew, spraying the people.

The pig squealed a tormented cry as the blood gushed from its throat. The nameless woman collapsed. The gods had sent their message. That very night the Maroons attacked the plantations, not one, but all of the plantations on the near side of the island. They slayed the masters of slavery as the rich plantation owners lay sleeping in their beds. Pools of blood soaked their pillows. Surprised eyes, shocked eyes, ignorant, lifeless eyes stared into eternity. The gods had spoken.

Near daybreak, the nameless woman regained consciousness; finding her wheat-colored dress and indigo turban covered in blood, she looked up to see, first, the pink flesh of the dead pig and then the sun dawning. She stood and took a step. She felt the seed burning brightly in her heel and she knew that Haiti had begun its trek toward freedom. The pain had never felt so good.

CHAPTER 43

Tuesday, 10:02 a.m., August 31, 2010—Central Standard Time—
Chicago, IL

Caleb put his phone back in his pocket after sending the message to Delta asking if he was still wonderful. He arrived within seconds only to find the gallery doors locked, putting his status of *wonderful* in jeopardy. Just then, he heard the familiar sound of his phone alerting him to another message and without even looking at it, he knew what it would say, he knew its importance.

Like a flash of lightning activating every neuron in his brain, he now realized as he pulled on the locked doors to the gallery that Delta had written, *Zandie told me you picked up the interviews.* Someone had beaten him to the gallery; someone had gotten Delta's transcripts. He spun around.

"I have to see Zandie Tan and Dr. Goldman. I have an appointment," he said to the guard.

"Yes, well they're working on the 17th floor today. You have to go back down to the first floor and go through security and then you can take an elevator up," Ray Little informed him, adding, "That way," pointing Caleb toward the down escalator. "When you get to the 17th floor, circle around the promenade." He pointed again.

"You don't understand. I'm supposed to pick up important papers for Professor Delta Quinn and I think somebody else has picked them up!" His voice was full of urgency.

"So somebody else picked them up. Minor mix up." Ray tried to calm him down as he simultaneously thought the name, Delta, sounded familiar. Then Ray remembered Delta, or at least he thought he remembered her.

"What's her middle name?" Ray called out to Caleb, but Caleb didn't have time for superfluous questions. He had already taken off running back down the hallway toward the escalator.

Reaching the escalator, Caleb took the steps three at a time and at the bottom swung around the base and ran to the security area where fortunately the last person in line had just passed through. Caleb tore off his shoes, tossed them into a plastic tub and pulled his phone from his pocket. He held his arms up and the security guard scanned him. He then walked through the metal detector, grabbed his items and hustled to the elevator.

Once inside the glass elevator he struggled to get his shoes back on while keeping an eye on the floors as they passed. A huge American flag hung above the bay of elevators. He pulled out his phone and read her latest message—*Then who picked up the interview transcripts?!* He sent Delta a message—*I'm on it.* She sent a message back, *If it helps, the security guard's name is Ray Little. He works on the second level.* He shut the phone and put it back in his pocket. The elevator shimmied its way up until, at last, Caleb exited on the 17th floor. He glanced around quickly, turned back to the security guard in the elevator, "Zandie Tan and Danielle Goldman?"

"That way. Room 1734."

A man entered the elevator as Caleb exited; a small smile crossed the man's face.

Caleb burst through the doors of room 1734 where Danielle Goldman and her assistant Zandie Tan were working on labeling enlarged photographs—posters of farms and farmers. Caleb pushed the doors so hard they crashed against the wall. Zandie recoiled against her chair in fear of the mad man who had banged the doors open and had begun yelling.

"I'm Caleb! I'm Caleb Barthes! I'm Delta's friend who's supposed to pick up the interviews."

Danielle Goldman stood at the sound of the commotion. Her confusion passed almost instantaneously. She looked at the distressed Caleb and decided he was telling the truth.

"Who?" he shouted at them, almost out of breath, "Who did you give the transcripts to?"

Danielle nodded to Zandie to tell him.

"He said he was you," she pleaded her innocence.

"Just tell me; what did he look like? When did he leave? Which way did he go?"

Poor Zandie felt confused but blurted out answers to each of his questions. "Tall, dark, African-American, no Arabian, no I'm not sure. But you just missed him. You may have passed him. He was wearing a light weight, navy blue windbreaker with green trim. He's about your height, a bit heavier."

Caleb dashed out of the office. He scanned the Thompson Center from his 17th floor aerial view. He spotted him. The dark man in the navy-blue windbreaker was descending in one of the glass elevators, the one Caleb had just exited. The man was more than half-way to the bottom.

Caleb assessed his alternatives. He couldn't take an elevator, they were too slow. He urgently scanned the area. The exit stairs were not in open sight. He looked at the man in the elevator. He zeroed in on him and just then the man's eyes met Caleb's stare—each one realizing, without a doubt, who the other one was.

From Bobby Brown's perspective, Caleb's arms appeared outstretched on the railing of the balcony, his head illuminated by the light of the dome, and two massive girders crisscrossed behind his shoulders.

Caleb couldn't wait a second longer. He jumped onto the balcony railing and then leapt into the air landing on the top of one of the elevators. The sound brought guards running from every direction to get to the elevator bay. Ray Little ran to the edge of the balcony on the second floor to see what was happening. Caleb crouched on the top of the elevator. He had jumped from the seventeenth floor; the elevator had been making its way down from the sixteenth to fifteenth floor; it was moving to the fourteenth, thirteenth, twelfth; he regained his balance.

"Hey, what are you doing?" a guard yelled.

The elevator is too slow, Caleb thought, completely ignoring the guard. From his position on top of the elevator, Caleb could no longer see the culprit, he only knew that he was still in the elevator. The man in the windbreaker would get away. Caleb imagined the cocky, confident expression that probably crossed the man's face, the man who was getting away with the transcripts. Caleb couldn't let that happen. Just then the elevator that Bobby Brown was riding in stopped on the 7th floor to let people on. Caleb watched with satisfaction and now pictured the man's arrogant facial expression deflate and then twist into anxiety. Caleb was energized; he could catch up if ...

Caleb leapt again, this time grabbing hold of an elevator pole, sliding down like a fireman's pole. Looking up, Ray yelled a warning for Caleb to stop.

Guards were pulling their guns from their holsters. Caleb slid faster down the shaft. He was just above Ray. Ray pointed his gun at Caleb.

"No Ray, I swear, I'm a good guy. It's that guy we have to stop." Caleb pointed at the man exiting the elevator.

Ray kept his gun aimed at Caleb, but glanced the other way, toward the man in the blue windbreaker only to see him exit the elevator among a group of other people. Ray watched as the man shot a quick sardonic look at Caleb. Ray sized up the glare immediately; it was pure malevolence, without a doubt. Ray had given the man directions to Danielle and Zandie's work space on the seventeenth floor earlier—just minutes before Caleb had arrived. He remembered him because of his New York accent. Ray watched with one eye as the man headed for the street exit. With the other eye, he kept tabs on Caleb. Ray noticed the New Yorker smirk smugly once again at Caleb before exiting the building.

The elevator, upon which Caleb had been sliding down its pole, finally reached the first floor. Caleb jumped off and raced ahead in an attempt to catch up with the thief, the man who had posed as him and taken the transcripts—the man in the blue windbreaker. But two guards abruptly intervened. They grabbed Caleb and spun him around. Caleb looked with pleading eyes toward the security guard, Ray Little.

CHAPTER 44

Tuesday, 10:12 a.m., August 31, 2010—Chicago, IL

"What's her middle name?" Ray demanded. At first confused, Caleb suddenly realized Ray wanted to verify that Caleb really did know Delta. *Fuck*, he thought, *what is her middle name?* And in that instant Caleb remembered seeing her name in the by-line of the article that she had written—Delta River Quinn. "River!" he yelled out. "River!"

"Let him go," Ray yelled to the other guards. "He's a friend of mine. Crazy, I know. He did it on a dare." Then Ray looked at Caleb, and shouted down to the first floor, "Get outta here before I have you arrested."

Caleb darted out of the building.

He scanned the street—left, then right. *Think. Think,* he said to himself. And then it came to him, the parking lot—there was only one lot close by. Caleb rushed to the parking lot; he spied the tan-colored rental getting ready to pull out. It had to be him. Caleb raced full speed toward the car.

By then, Bobby Brown was in the car, engine running and waiting to pull into traffic. Caleb grabbed at the door handle. The door opened. Caleb pulled at the driver who pressed the accelerator, jerking the whole car forward, knocking Caleb to the ground.

"You son of a dick," Caleb yelled as the man broke free and his car sped out of the parking lot.

Caleb jumped up and ran to his Harley, started it and raced after the thief. After zigzagging through traffic, Caleb found himself within a car length of the tan car. A red light ahead provided the opportunity that Caleb needed. He revved the engine and pulled alongside of the car. The tan vehicle was trapped between a truck and a taxi stopped for the light. The driver looked furtively around him. Caleb pulled up just behind the tan car. He jumped off his bike, thrust the Harley between a pole and a mailbox on the sidewalk, turned and lunged for the door handle of the tan car. The door flew open. Caleb reached for the man's jacket to pull him toward him, but the driver surprised Caleb, slashing him across the forearm with a single, stinging slice of a knife blade.

Caleb jerked back. Brown pushed him from the car with riveting force. The light changed. Caleb struggled to get back in the car, but the driver pulled forward and then turned the wheel hard to the right. Caleb went sliding out.

Caleb ripped the buttons on his shirt as he tore it off and tied it around his bleeding forearm. He was only a few feet from where he'd left his bike. He scrambled for it, got back on; he had a pretty good idea of where the man was headed. Dodging pedestrians, Caleb rode over the sidewalk and around the corner onto W. Randolph.

Continuing down W. Randolph until he saw the signs for I 90/ W I 94, he slipped back into traffic. In less than a couple of minutes Caleb had caught up to the tan car. He cruised up behind it, not caring whether the driver saw him or not. Bobby Brown glanced in his rear view mirror. Caleb taunted him by driving closer, alongside of him. The driver held his phone in his hand and began texting. *Text all you want*, Caleb thought, *I know where you're going and I'm going to be your escort from hell.*

The driver of the tan car slowed slightly, keeping to a speed just a bit over the limit. *Doesn't want to attract the police*, Caleb thought. Caleb backed off slightly; he didn't want the driver to slam on his brakes, as that would send his bike crashing into the back of the car. Caleb followed at a safer distance, weaving into traffic in the next lane, angling his bike just to the side of the tan car's rear bumper, trying to stay in his blind spot. Caleb glanced up. The Kennedy Expressway was just ahead. *Without a doubt, this guy is headed for O'Hare Airport*, Caleb concluded.

Caleb saw the driver continue to glance in his rear view mirror while appearing to be fumbling with something. Caleb glanced over his shoulder—*nothing unusual, no police cars, just semis, cars, and taxis; everyday traffic headed for the airport*. Caleb looked up. The man had rolled down his window and stuck his arm out; his hand held a collection of papers that rattled in the wind.

Jesus, the transcripts, Caleb thought. *He's going to let them fly!*

Caleb raced toward the open window, extending his arm to grab the papers before the driver could let go, but just then he caught a glimpse of the taxi pulling alongside of him in the next lane over. The passenger in the taxi was riding in the front seat next to the driver not in the back as usual. The taxi pulled directly to the left of Caleb; the tan car directly to the right. *Damn,* Caleb thought, as he realized what was about to happen. He sped up. The blond man seated next to the cabbie, rolled down his window as if to say something to Caleb, but at the last second, to the cabby's surprise, he grabbed the wheel and turned the cab into Caleb's motorcycle. Caleb jumped to the seat; the cab just missed crunching his leg. The bike swerved under the pressure and began to tailspin. It was squished forward like cream out of an éclair. Caleb leapt to the front of the tan car; he was suddenly flying through the air, his arms and legs spread eagle. He landed on the windshield. His hands slid downward. Caleb caught himself by his fingertips in the groove that housed the windshield wipers.

The driver turned on the wipers. Caleb tensed his muscles as the metal-base of the window wiper raked the skin from his knuckles. Still holding onto the moving car with his left hand, Caleb ripped the metal wiper blade from the groove with his right hand. Instantly, the wiper blade turned into a weapon.

Caleb reached around with the blade in his right hand, stabbing at the face of the driver through the open window. Caleb hit him in the eye. Bobby Brown screamed. Caleb stabbed again. The car swerved. The determined reporter held tight, grabbing the grip again with both hands but not relinquishing his new found weapon. The driver threw the package down on the car seat and pressed the button to roll the window back up.

Brown swerved the car back and forth trying to shake Caleb loose, but Caleb wouldn't let go. They had already entered the Kennedy Expressway and were almost at the airport exit. The driver saw his chance. As the exit curved, he banged the car against a guard rail, with such force that Caleb lost his grip and flew off the hood of the car. The reporter's body sailed over the guard rail onto the grassy knoll, landing like a candy wrapper tossed from a moving vehicle;

his body bounced and rolled down an embankment with unforgiving force.

CHAPTER 45

Ani sat within his office at the Policy Institute of Chicago placing the final touches onto an email he was preparing to send to Delta. Ani had attached several documents along with a bibliography of references for Delta. Now he reread it for typos. Ani was a careful man; it was his attention to detail and the exacting care with which he approached his work that led to his being hired at the Policy Institute, the youngest lead researcher to date.

Ani reread the message a third time. It was the introduction that baffled him. Should it be formal or informal? Professor Quinn or Delta? He decided on the following:

Dear Prof. Quinn (Delta),

I have only had time to do the barest of bones research for you. That can, of course, be a dangerous thing, as I am sure I don't need to remind you. Nevertheless, based on what I have gathered and read so far, I can share the following: –

– Many countries have been involved in obtaining patents for genetically-modified organisms, including, and in addition to the United States, there is Belgium, Germany, Denmark, Switzerland, and Hungary, to name a few.

– Studies indicate interesting but mixed results with respect to the claim that GMOs will radically revolutionize agriculture, offering significant benefits to society.

– Studies also offer mixed results with respect to the claim that GMOs are insidious plants that are dangerous for human consumption.

– Concerns come from several camps: Evolutionary Biologists fear that inserting the pesticide into the plant will result in insect species that will adapt, causing a new set of problems; Ecologists fear the development of super weeds as they grow resistant to GM crops; Entomologists fear the loss of certain insects as the result of genetically-modified plants' resistance to herbicide being over sprayed. The spray doesn't harm the plant, but kills the surrounding weeds. Some of those weeds (like milkweed) are home to other insects like monarch butterflies. (And yes, the butterflies did die as a result of eating genetically-modified plant pollen, or they died from the eating the surrounding weeds which had been sprayed with chemicals, well actually I think it was the caterpillars, not the butterflies, but you get my point.) Dieticians fear the new plants will have weakened immune systems and poorer nutrient quality.

– Support comes from several camps, as well: Agro-economists support the use of GMOs which have already cost companies billions of dollars; these companies need to recoup the losses. The chemical companies pass the cost along to seed companies (or they buy the seed companies) charging them and the farmers more money. Genetic scientists are suggesting that the lower levels of nutrients can not only be ameliorated but enhanced. Vitamins can be genetically added to crops (Kind of like fortified white bread).

Representatives from these various positions were invited to a conference in Germany. According to Daniel Charles (2001) they were asked to hammer out a report that *provided the truth, the yet to be discovered truth, and the indeterminable about GMOs.*

The group labored under the rhetoric of risk. That is, they framed their discussions in light of risks to people, to the environment, and to insects. When all the studies were reviewed they found that GMOs are unpredictable, sometimes collapsing under a heat wave, but they noted that natural organisms are also unpredictable. They noted that some studies found the GMOs to cause illness but then follow-up studies found them to be harmless. At the end of the day, [Ani was most pleased with this expression—*at the end of the day*, as politicians use this phrase to summarize an argument, as if the final word really exists. Ani simply liked the Washington D.C. sound of it—very American].

Both sides realized that the rhetoric of risk didn't match with their goals.

The activists called for a rhetoric of democracy—simply label the GMOs so that people know what they are eating, they demanded. American companies sell genetically-modified products without telling the consumer. The companies, on the other hand, refused to support this solution. They called for a rhetoric of capitalist rights to frame the dialogue. Talks broke down.

In 1995, a massive infestation of tobacco-budworms ravaged cotton in the southern United States. The spraying of past pesticides had resulted in a worm that was resistant and no matter how much pesticide was sprayed the worms kept on eating. Farmers lost everything. The following year the EPA allowed farmers to plant GM cotton. It alone survived the ravages of the budworm.* This practice opened the door for all GMO products. Businesses sold the seed at reasonable prices much to RichField's dismay—the seed companies paid royalties to RichField, but RichField didn't think these seed companies were charging enough. They instituted a "perfidious scheme" (Daniel Charles, p. 152) to charge the farmers a technology fee and lock them into a contract that would forbid them from saving seeds from their harvest for the following year. RichField tried to get every seed company on board, leaving the farmers with no alternatives. Only one company stood in the way of "world domination" (p. 159). Oh, and most of Europe. But it would seem a little pressure from the U.S. government helped to soap the skids, so eventually it was predicted RichField GM soybeans would slide into Europe, too. It would seem RichField execs know Washington politicians by their first name. Eventually, the one other seed company that was holding out, reluctantly came on board.

But after mad cow disease the British people didn't trust the government to tell them what was safe and what was not safe, since the government had said beef was safe. Most of the European governments may have signed onto genetic crops, but the people had not. So they lost the European market. Activists were quite persuasive. Starlink was the final straw for people opposed to GM seeds. Starlink, a genetically-modified corn created by European scientists to compete with RichField's modified corn, demonstrated problems related to human consumption. When the corn kernels were placed in a solution of acid equivalent to stomach acids, the corn failed to breakdown; it was indigestible. Government agencies determined Starlink unsafe for human consumption. But it was granted the okay to be produced as feed corn for cattle. It would have to be isolated from corn meant for human consumption. However, this solution deteriorated—the feed corn somehow contaminated other corn products in silos. So much so that products in the U.S.—packaged corn bread, corn oil, processed food with corn syrup—were tested at an independent lab where it was discovered they contained Starlink corn. So people were eating the corn that had been declared unsafe for human consumption. Absolutely, a point for the activists opposed to GMOs.

Genetically-modified organisms (modified crops) struggled in other countries as well. For example in India, activists demonstrated concern for farmers who were facing the 'terminator seed.' China is still testing some small plots and has not committed to the genetically-modified soybeans seeds, yet. However, the illegal distribution of the seeds is taking place currently, giving some farmers an unfair advantage and possibly getting them hooked on GMOs.

In the U.S., with respect to corn, the genetically-modified crop fought off corn borers, but the corn borers only attack once every four years or so. Nevertheless, farmers bought the seed every year and at higher and higher prices. They signed contracts promising not to replant their seed, but some farmers broke that promise and planted seed that they had saved, which meant there wasn't a level playing field. So some farmers snitched on other farmers. RichField tried to get a Congressional bill passed to stop farmers from replanting. They were unsuccessful. Anyway, at the end of the day [and here, Ani was happy again with his use of the phrase], this became cumbersome for RichField which is when they went to work developing the terminator seed.

A RichField buying spree allowed them to control the market on GM seeds and hybrid plants. They began making the global move, but that's when they came face-to-face (figuratively speaking) with Greenpeace. They also failed to merge with a larger company which they hoped would help them recoup the millions of dollars they had poured into the project.

So if a company cannot find a larger company to help them out of the crisis and they have played their best cards in the business world, then the strategy usually goes something like this:

When all else fails, sell it to the military.

If that doesn't work, declare bankruptcy and get a bailout package.

I'll keep researching, but for now, here are some articles that you might find interesting (see attachments).

Sincerely,

Ani

P.S. Caleb is worth getting to know. You won't regret it.

P.S.S. *Note the GM product contains the pesticide for the budworm, but not for other destructive insects like the bollworm— farmers still had to spray. However, they sprayed less.

After rereading his own email several times, Ani leaned back in his chair and tapped a finger against his lower lip. He said, "I wonder what the farmers had to say, the one's Delta interviewed." He wondered, *what could be so dangerous in those stories to provoke burglary and threats*? In addition to sending the message to Delta, he copied the message to Caleb; Ani tapped the send button. His words flew on internet wings to Caleb and Delta.

But neither Caleb nor Delta, for very different reasons, was in any position to read Ani's email.

CHAPTER 46

Once Caleb had regained consciousness, he found himself lying face down next to a storm drain. An empty potato chip bag flapped next to his ear; a plastic bag blew over him. He began to feel sensations, which he would come to regret. His body ached; his arm was bleeding; his knuckles scraped and bruised. He stood up with great effort, reached into his back pocket and pulled out his phone. It was cracked; the face fractured like a thousand rays of light spreading from a single point in the center. *Oh God, not my phone*, Caleb lamented. He turned it on. It miraculously powered up. The reporter quickly scanned his documents, his notes, the story; it was all still there.

Before even attempting to climb the side of the ravine back up to the Kennedy Expressway, Caleb made a phone call. And it was not to Delta.

CHAPTER 47

Tuesday, 11:00 p.m., August 31, 2010—Washington D.C.

The two men, who had burglarized Delta's apartment in order to get the transcripts, had crashed into the Geo, and had sent Caleb flying from the hood of a rental car, held out the package to Ruby Carmichael. She ignored it at first, looked past it. With a nod of her head, and glance of her eye, she directed the two men to follow her.

Her stately figure was lit by the atrium lights of the lobby of the hotel. The two men had greeted her at the reservation desk and then the three retreated to a more discreet corner of the imposing lobby. Chandeliers sparkled overhead and huge tapestries donned the walls of the lobby. But this more sequestered corner of the hotel was lit by a stained-glass, ceiling light. Gentle shadows bathed the seating area. Ruby Carmichael had walked with the grace of a monarch across the marble floor to the set of leather chairs in the secluded corner, her high heels clicking crisply against the stone floor. Now she sat regally, a Nubian Queen, her hand extended.

Her height diminished little as she sat with her back straight and her head held high. The two men, Robert Cornelius Brown and Jason Slaughtery, had taken seats at her indication, a wave of her arm, a turn of her wrist. Only then did she accept the package. "Are these the interviews?" she wanted confirmation.

"Yes, of course," Bobby Brown told her.

Ruby Carmichael opened the package and extracted the papers. She began reading, then scanning more quickly. Eventually, she had flipped through all of the pages. Both men waited patiently. Carmichael gave no sign of her approval or disapproval, making both men a bit nervous.

"Are these the only copies?"

"Yes, absolutely," Bobby Brown told her, his voice deep and assured.

"How can you convince me of that?"

"You don't believe me?"

"I never believe anyone," she said as a matter of fact.

"We ran a scan program on both of her computers, using a known random sentence program from the actual interviews that were mailed to Tom Bradford weeks ago. I'm referring to the first package that he received that had the note on it about the zombie seed, the one that came from Danielle Goldman. We ran those sentences through the software program which then thoroughly checked her files. All her files," he emphasized. "We completely scanned both computers. Those particular sentences appeared nowhere. And we tracked her emails. Nothing. We scanned her deleted emails and her current emails. There is absolutely no indication of another set."

"So this copy from the ISM is absolutely the last copy?"

"Yes," he told her.

"Did you run a scan on the ISM computers?

Both men suddenly became quiet. Each looked at the other.

Carmichael sighed with disappointment. "You fools," she said under her breath.

"Do you have reason to believe that Danielle Goldman would make another copy?" the first man asked in their defense.

"Wouldn't you?"

"What should we do?" the second man asked her sincerely.

"Nothing," she said slipping the papers back into the manila envelope. "I've sent Tom Bradford to Chicago to get any remaining copies." Ruby Carmichael stood. Both men responded by standing up. "If I need anything else, I'll call you," she said. Then Ruby Carmichael, bio-technology weapons expert for the DOD, and recently named liaison to the CIA, simply turned and walked away without further word.

Bobby Brown and Jason Slaughtery, without saying a word to one another, left the hotel, wondering if they would get paid the full amount promised. Ruby Carmichael watched them depart from behind a shadowed, marble pillar in the lobby of the hotel. Once she was sure they were out of sight she took the elevator to the penthouse.

She watched the small television mounted in the upper corner of the elevator. *Washington D.C. talking heads, nonstop talking mouths.* Ethics committee members were investigating another senator.

Outrage over sexual harassment or campaign fund fraud or misuse and abuse of taxpayers' money—it was always something, which became more prominent the closer came Election Day. *Corruption is everywhere*, Ruby thought in an injudicious way, adding *anyone who gets caught is an idiot who deserves the penalties.* Ruby had no intention of ever getting caught. The elevator doors opened onto a long hallway with plush, red carpet lit by the rays of ornate sconces that hung on the wall opposite the elevators. Ruby stepped out. She walked past the antique couch-table that was embellished with lacy wrought iron, an enormous arrangement of fresh cut flowers sat on top, intended to welcome elite 'guests' of the hotel. Continuing down the hallway, Ruby didn't stop until she came to the door where a security guard in a dark blue suit kept vigil. They didn't speak to one another, simply nodded. Ruby knocked on the door.

"The door's open, Ruby," the voice from inside called.

Dr. Carmichael walked into the spacious living room area of the penthouse hotel room. The lights of D.C. twinkled beyond the sliding glass doors that led to a balcony. Reflected firelight intertwined with city lights appearing luminously magical on the glass panels. Deep within the reflection, Ruby saw the image of the face of her benefactor, who sat across the room by the fireplace. Ruby closed the hotel door behind her and turned toward the Senator. Flames from the gas fireplace gave the room a warm glow. She walked to the side of the high-backed, leather chair.

An outstretched hand waited for the package. Palm up. A starched white shirt sleeve with a gold cuff link with diamond inlays appeared at the edge of a dark blue suit jacket sleeve. An expensive watch appeared on his wrist.

"Are we sure this it?"

"Absolutely."

"Are you sure there aren't any other copies?"

"I have Tom Bradford double checking."

"Nice job, Ruby."

"Thank you, Senator."

Then Senator Searle leaned forward toward the fire and tossed the entire package into the flames.

"Aren't you going to read them?" Ruby asked.

"Now, Ruby, you and I both know if things go south, I'm better off not knowing what's in those interviews. Sometimes, it's better not to know the truth, don't you agree. If asked, I've never seen the interviews." He spoke calmly. She realized it was her job to take the heat if anything went wrong. She alone had seen the interviews; she alone would pay for having knowledge of them if anyone found out. She watched as the transcripts within the folder curled and melted under the red glow of the flames. Nearly ash, the interviews disappeared.

"Feel better now, Senator?"

"I never felt badly."

"Not even when you paid the pilot to spray that poor farmer's field with pesticide?" Ruby took the opportunity to remind him of his own culpability.

"Ruby, Ruby, whose credit card do you think I used?"

Suddenly stunned by the thought of it, Ruby looked down at her pursue, wondering if he had lifted one of her cards. When she looked up again she saw him holding out his hand, another credit card appeared between his fingers. "Take it, Ruby. It's yours." His words dripped with maliciousness. His tone said it all; he was giving her what she didn't want and he was enjoying it. "Go on, take it." Although she hadn't understood at first, she realized now that he had opened an account in her name and paid the pilot with 'her' new credit card. She took it from him and put it in her purse. She would deal with this later, cancel the card without payment, she thought. "I paid it off already," he said with a smile, knowing exactly what her next thought would be. "No need to thank me."

"Ruby, don't take it too much to heart, you're new at this game. I just had to make sure that you are committed to pursuing the project. You understand?"

Still Ruby didn't speak.

"Ruby, let me tell you a story." His voice was deep, his tempo slow, the tone was neither cruel nor smug at this point; instead it sounded nearly paternal. He lifted a Waterford crystal glass filled with bourbon toward his lips, poised in preparation, and began the story. "Once upon a time there were monarchs, kings and queens, royalty who ruled the world. Today, there are politicians and corporations. Right now, in history, the corporations have the edge. They rule the world. I know my place in this story. I work for the corporations. I wonder, Ruby, do you know who you work for?" He sipped the warm liquor, licked his lips and set the drink down. The glass of golden whiskey reflected the flames of the fire. The farmers' stories curled and melted into ash and sparks that quickly disappeared. "That's it, Ruby; that's the story we live by. The wealthy and the powerful always win in the end."

"And if they don't?" Ruby countered.

"Then it's not the end yet."

They both quietly watched the transcripts turn to flames.

"Good night, Ruby."

Ruby saw herself out of the Senator's suite. She rode the elevator back to the majestic lobby and took a seat in the same niche where she had met with Brown and Slaughtery earlier. Ruby pulled out her phone. She made two calls: one for a taxi and the other to Robert Cornelius Brown (a.k.a. Downtown Bobby Brown).

"Bobby, I need one more thing."

"Are you still mad about the—

"No, no, but I need your help with one more detail."

"Name it"

"Purchase 10,000 shares of RichField in the name of Jacob Searle."

"How do you want me to pay for it?"

"Could you open a credit card in his name?"

"Absolutely."

"Good."

"I can do it right away. Do you have Searle's personal info, social security, etc."

"I'll call you in the morning with the information. Working at the DOD and for the CIA has its advantages. You can pick up your payment in the usual place."

"Always good doing business with you, Ruby."

Ruby ended the call. Her taxi pulled up. It was beginning to rain. She left the lobby. A doorman opened the taxi door; Ruby slid into the backseat. She watched the rain dot across the windshield, making little rivers of water, blurring the view. The driver turned on the wipers, washing the water to one side and momentarily providing a clear view. Ruby Carmichael replayed the senator's words in her head: *Ruby, do you know who you work for?* And then she smiled as she thought to herself, *I work for myself, Senator, not for you. 'God Bless the child that's got his own. He just worry 'bout nothin' cause he's got his own.*

"Where to?" the taxi driver asked.

CHAPTER 48

Wednesday morning, September 1, 2010—Washington D.C.

Senator Jacob Searle's assistant set the phone receiver back in its cradle as she told the visitor in the dark suit, "The Senator will see you now." Knowing he would be received immediately, corporate executive, Stephen S. Miles, hadn't bothered to sit down, and now he moved from the reception area toward the senator's office door. The door was opening; the senator met the executive with a wide smile and outstretched hand. They shook hands aggressively; each expressing a strong grip.

Miles meeting Searle in his office was unprecedented. The two men never met outside of golf, when they *just happened* to be in the same place at the same time; intermediaries always set up the *happenstance* meetings. The intermediaries were always from the corporation. It wasn't difficult to find out the Senator's schedule and adjust Miles' schedule accordingly. As CEO, Miles would fly on the corporate jet. Searle never realized just how carefully planned the initial meetings had been; it was better that way, Miles thought.

Searle enjoyed a good round of golf. He especially liked playing with Miles, a worthy opponent, but not quite as good as himself, Searle thought. The senator considered Miles a fair golfer, but a brilliant businessman. Searle more than respected Miles' business savvy; actually he was in awe of Miles' organizational genius, but he would never say so.

Stephen S. Miles, CEO, thought Searle was nearly a cliché, not a caricature of a senator, but certainly not unique. Miles recognized that Searle managed to get what he wanted by working within the law, usually. Miles considered the senator smart, but not very creative. Miles felt that the senator waited for projects to come his way. Little initiative and less aggressive than what suited Miles. If the senator had had any passionate reason for entering politics, it had disappeared long ago. He had learned how to stay in office. Probably has a mistress, but has been smart enough not to get caught, Miles

279

decided. Exposure of an extra marital affair would be a hard blow to a man who'd built his campaign on "family" values. Probably takes a few vacations on taxpayers' dollars, but nothing that his voters would find too grandiose. Miles saw the senator as having developed a mild addiction to golf, four-star restaurants, fine wine, and especially the stage and applause that came with the *speaking engagements* that indirectly paid for the golf vacations, the fine food and wine. Miles saw an opportunity and seized it.

One day Senator Searle would write his memoir; and, thought Miles, it would have little to say. His constituents liked him well enough as Searle managed to give back to the people through pork barrel initiatives; thus, he had little fear of not being re-elected, Miles thought, and that was a good thing for Miles, as well. Searle could be maneuvered, manipulated easily enough, but not naively. Not a patsy, but not a partner either, the perfect accomplice, neither a crony, nor an idiot, the kind of man that you can lead without having to tug the reins; this is what Stephen S. Miles thought of Senator Searle who now offered him a seat.

"To what do I owe this pleasure?" Searle asked in a full, throaty baritone.

"Just in town for a meeting and I thought I'd see if you had time for a game of golf, my friend."

"Oh, if only..." Senator Searle said lifting the phone receiver and pressing one button. "Lilly, would you bring us a couple of cups of coffee..." he held his hand over the receiver from habit, "Cream? Sugar?"

"Black's good."

"Black and strong, Lilly." Senator Searle hung up the phone.

"How are *things*?" Miles asked.

"*Things* are fine. Couldn't be better."

"Great. That's good to know."

"But that didn't bring you all the way to Washington D.C."

"I have another request," the CEO added.

"Which is?"

"Well, I know it's very early to be asking this, but I don't want someone else to scoop you up. You're such a dynamic speaker. I want to give a donation of say one hundred thousand dollars to my alma mater to have you, specifically you, be there graduation speaker."

"Stephen, I'm honored. Of course, your secretary will have to get the dates to Lilly so she can check my schedule."

"Of course, of course. But you'll do it?"

"I'll certainly look into the possibility." Senator Searle knew how it worked. Miles gives a donation to the university. The university pays for the flights, accommodations, food and lodging. In addition, Searle's name gets added to a list of V.I.P.s each of whom receives invitations to golf outings in Hawaii in January, Florida in March, and California in April. Speaker's fees for Senators may have been banned a decade ago, but everybody on Capitol Hill knew there were ways around that problem. He was being coy for another reason. He waited to hear Miles' explanation.

"Well, good. You look into it and get back to me. I know how busy your schedule is. We've been busy, as well. Very exciting things happening at corporate headquarters. Have I told you about our latest project?"

"Latest project? No, I don't think so."

"Well, you know we took some heat for our genetically-modified seed that included a genetic sequence that, well, finalized fertility." Miles never called it the terminator seed.

"Yes, from Greenpeace … and others. But you promised not to use it anymore." Senator Searle was becoming quite curious as to where CEO Stephen S. Miles was taking this conversation. After all, Searle had just assured him that *things* were taken care of. No one would find out about the zombie seed having been tested in U.S. fields. Ruby had managed to get the transcripts and he had burned them himself.

"Yes, and organic farmers," Miles pointed out.

"You mean in addition to Greenpeace?"

"Yes. It has come to our attention that perhaps we should revitalize the V-GURT seed program. We're concerned about the organic farmers."

"How so?" Searle controlled his urge to laugh or to use sarcasm in his response, but his head was nearly exploding with commentary like: *Stephen S. Miles concerned about organic farmers, that'll be the day. He thinks they're idiots trapped in a narrative of nostalgia and technophobia.*

"Well, as you know, we've been sued a few times for having herbicides, pesticides and genetically-modified seeds contaminate organic farmers' fields when the wind blows." Searle kept an unemotional countenance as he thought, *a few times, you mean nearly fifty times.* The tables had turned; RichField was now losing the courtroom battles as more farmers were proving the contaminated seeds had blown onto their property. Miles continued, "We can hardly be held accountable for an act of God—the wind," Miles added with feigned sincerity. "But these kinds of courtroom interruptions are becoming quite a nuisance. Honestly, no one likes lawsuits," Miles determined.

"Except the winners," Senator Searle added. He paused before adding, "And you've won quite few, as well, haven't you?"

"We did win some, but the sympathy is leaning toward the small-holder farmer, right now. But, we think we've come up with the perfect solution." Miles paused for effect. "A win-win situation for everybody."

Senator Searle leaned forward, also for effect.

"Even better than win-win; it will be phenomenal for everybody." Miles looked excited. He continued, "We bring the V-GURT with a T-GURT twist to market on the grounds that it will keep organic farming safe. That is, if the wind blows our genetically-modified seed into the organic farmers' fields, the seed, whatever kind of genetically-modified seed, won't grow until it is allowed to do so via an application of a specific spray. Say we genetically modify corn to be healthier, you know add nutrients to it, then we will add what you call 'the terminator technology' *and* we'll add what's referred to as the 'zombie technology' to it so that the modified seed can never contaminate the organic fields. It won't grow until we supply the special fertilizer."

"Fertilizer?"

"It's very technical," Miles told him.

Senator Searle was not stupid. The room went quiet. Searle sat back, taking in the idea as well as its implications. The terminator seed had caused massive suicides in India. It had wreaked havoc, politically and socially, in underdeveloped nations. It had bankrupted a number of farmers in the U.S. and had put seed cleaners out of work, some of whom lived in Searle's state; plus it had put other seed manufacturers out of business. Miles had been actively creating a seed monopoly and Searle knew it, even if no one else did. Searle had to walk a fine line. Currently, he was receiving hundreds of thousands of dollars-worth of perks via the *speaking engagements* from RichField, but he had no other connection with them. If this plan went belly up, he could easily detach himself from the seed giant. On the other hand, if it worked it could be a billion dollar idea. *It might be worth it*, Searle mused. He knew where Miles was headed with this.

"You'd be helping the organic farmers," Stephen S. Miles interrupted Searle's thoughts. Searle dismissed this as ridiculous, and read between the lines. However, it could help his image, Searle thought; that is, both that he cares about all farmers and he could build an eco-friendly platform while supporting big business. *This might not be such a bad idea. But would the farmers fall for it?*

"You could mention it in the graduation speech at my alma mater," Miles added.

At first, Searle had figured the speaking offer of one hundred thousand dollars had been a thank you for taking care of *things*— destroying the interviews about the zombie seed—now he realized it represented an *advance* connected to Miles' most recent scheme.

"Just think of how it would protect organic farming. We could make the terminator seed and the zombie seed legal, mandatory even." Miles' excitement got away from him, he actually used the terms—terminator and zombie—aloud in a sentence.

My god, Searle thought, *he's not only talking about legalizing the terminator seed and the zombie seed, but actually forcing anyone who is not organic to be required by law to use his product.*

"Who would it hurt?" Miles added. "It would provide people with the knowledge they've been demanding—a right to know if their crops are genetically-modified. It will be the most commonplace practice. People will accept it as normal in no time at all. Plus, it will protect farmers. I think Bradford should announce the benefits of the

V-GURT and T-GURT technologies *and* I think you should propose the legislation. This is an opportunity for you to take the lead."

Perhaps, he's right, Searle thought. *It could be an opportunity. And if I don't do it, he'll move it ahead with someone else.*

"But not Bradford."

"No?"

"Of course you need a Senator like myself to move the legislation forward, but as for who came up with the idea—you need somebody from Greenpeace or maybe a professor from a university, someone less connected, more innocent. I'm afraid people would see through Bradford's connection too easily."

"But the Department of Agriculture is a perfect—"

"Bradford and I play golf. He's helping with the *other matter*. I think I know a researcher I can get on board, but really if you could sell the idea to some Greenpeace advocates, make them think it's their idea ..."

"Senator, you surprise me," the CEO said smiling. Truly, this did surprise Miles as he hadn't thought of Searle as being smart enough or devious enough to contribute to the plan. He liked the idea of using a professor or an activist, but felt getting someone from Greenpeace on board would be too much of a stretch. *A professor, on the other hand, now that might work,* Miles nodded. Miles could hardly control his enthusiasm, if this works every farmer in the country will be required to buy *parch, parch-prepped* seeds and the latest products that Richfield was rolling out.

"What about the *other thing*?" the senator said, shifting his posture and the topic in order to mask his hubris over his own clever idea of bringing a professor on board. The senator knew better than to crow over his own contribution. First, Miles was always far more clever than he; and second, people who look pleased with themselves betray their own surprise that they'd come up with a good idea. Good ideas should appear as second nature. But he did feel as though he had just dropped a hole in one for a championship match.

"Nothing like having this sort of thing supported by a university," Miles complimented Searle and then addressed the *other issue*.

"Now on the *other matter*—"

"You mean T-Gurt technology as weaponry?" Searle wanted confirmation.

"Yes. Absolutely, I think you should proceed as planned, take the idea to the committee on biological weapons. Do you still have your friendly expert on T-GURTS."

"Yes, she's ready to support the use of the zombie-seed technology."

"Good. Sounds like everything is falling into place."

"You don't think launching two projects would appear suspicious?" the Senator reconsidered his collusion, had he jumped in too fast? He wondered, suddenly feeling a bit wary, would promoting the latest invention by RichField be a bit dangerous for himself. Sometimes, his brain moved with a detrimental swiftness.

A knock at the door jarred his thoughts. "Come in," the senator called out.

Lilly opened the door with one hand and held two cups of coffee on a tray in the other.

Turning his wrist over and glancing at his watch, Stephen S. Miles, CEO of Richfield, announced, "Oh, I didn't realize the time. I wish I could stay, but I have to be off. Great catching up with you, Senator. Do think about that speaking engagement. We'd love to have you. And there are a lot more of those engagements in your future. You, my friend, have a way with words, not to mention novel ideas," Miles proclaimed with a smile as he saw himself out. "Lilly," he nodded, "sorry to have to rush off without the coffee, especially after you went to all that trouble."

"Oh, no trouble at all," she said. Miles took large, confident steps as he exited. Calling over his shoulder, "Golf next time, Senator."

"You bet," the senator added. But Miles was out the door.

"What a nice man," Lilly commented, enjoying the attention he had given her, and then she smiled at the thought of the executive's compliment of her boss. She handed Senator Searle a cup of coffee. "You do have a way with words," she added.

CHAPTER 49

Delta finished another interview for her project on the communicative framing of abusive relationships, and as she packed her worn, dusty, black canvas bag she forced herself not to think of the desperate situations these women face. For now, she pushed her thoughts toward a proper set of hopeful propositions, inspired by the window displays that lined the long hallway of Stewart Center, she thought—*people can reframe their experiences, rewrite their stories; people are resilient.*

The hallway was flanked with display windows, each one announcing various attractions—upcoming musical events, plays, speakers, student fundraisers. The displays were brightly illuminated and were studded with colorful backdrops. Delta paused at one display filled with a green backdrop which was covered in photos of Haiti. Sponsored by the agronomy club, the motif supported sending seeds to Haiti to reforest the hillside and promote local agriculture. The pictures taken by the group showed busloads of Haitians moving from the cities to the country, people planting trees on a hillside to help stop erosion, and others hoeing in a field of their own making. Inside the window-box display were a row of pots with little green shoots emerging from the dirt. In the center of the display read the words: *Helping Haiti: One Seedling at a Time* and underneath, contact information had been provided for how to help. Delta stood still for a moment to take in the image of the little seedlings sprouting into green leaves. These testaments to the resilience of life lightened Delta's dark mood. She continued on her way, passing the snack store and newspaper stand—closed for the night. Farther down the hallway, she found the computer lab quietly deserted for the night.

As Delta reached the exit and the darkness beyond the glass doors, she suddenly remembered the attack that had followed her exiting the building just last Wednesday. She told herself to be alert, be ready.

She carried her bag in her hand instead of over her shoulder, so that it would be low to the ground, easy to drop or to swing if necessary. Although the thought of having to report another broken tape-recorder to the university wasn't something she'd look forward to either, she knew she wouldn't hesitate to use it as a weapon. She opened the heavy glass door slowly and looked to either side before taking a step.

Indeed, her caution paid off. She could see a figure in the bushes. For a split second she considered going back in and calling the police. But instead, she claimed her right, *damn it*, to walk through the night. She had spent the week reviewing American Kenpo karate moves, which she retained in her muscle memory. She had studied karate for a short time nearly ten years ago. But some things do indeed stick with a person—stance, salutation, and the five-star block series. She had been embarrassed to have been caught off guard last week. That wouldn't happen again. She felt ready for him. She took the first step with confidence and the next steps down with caution and then turned past the bush. Her karate background was limited, barely a purple belt, but she knew that it would only take the appearance of confidence to scare off a coward. She stood her ground. On the brink of physical defense, adrenaline-laced acuity and intense accuracy flooded into her mind and her muscles, preparing her for assault. She was ready. She took another step forward. Steady, easy, ready.

She kept walking. She tightened her grip on her black bag. Ready. The bushes rustled. She took a deep breath. And then took another step. She walked further.

Delta stepped beyond the shadowy figure. He hadn't attacked. She became more curious than suspicious, more angry than fearful. She stopped. Turned around and took three steps back.

"Come out from behind that bush!"

The shadow cowered.

"Who do you think you are anyway? And why didn't you attack?" The adrenaline was talking. "Suddenly shy? You weren't shy last week," Delta blasted the darkly clad figure.

"Come out of those bushes, right now!" she demanded.

Too her surprise a wiry young man sheepishly held the bush aside and stepped out, looking left and then right before completely stepping into the light of the street lamp. He wore a bandana around his arm and held something behind his back; otherwise, he appeared perfectly ordinary, dressed in a dark T-shirt and jeans. He stood there, waiting for Delta to say something else. The silence became awkward.

"Who are you?" she finally demanded. "And what do you want?"

"I, I'm Ryan Campbell and I don't want anything."

"Why were you hiding in the bushes and why didn't you attack me?"

"Because you're not a zombie," he said, looking perplexed by the question.

Delta was equally confused by their exchange. Ryan Campbell wasn't the man who had attacked her last week; Ryan was shorter, thinner, even the hair was different, but then what was he doing in the bushes waiting for her, she wondered. Ryan Campbell spoke up, also trying to make sense of the encounter, "Hey, are you a moderator? You're not a zombie."

"Moderator? Zombie?"

"No, I can see you're not a zombie. Hey, I don't see a moderator's bandana either. So, who are you?" he now sounded defiant, as if, if she were neither a moderator nor a zombie, she had no right to call him out.

"I'm Professor Delta Quinn."

"Oh jeez, professors are off limits." His voice became acquiescent again, "I'm sorry."

"What're you holding behind your back? What's this all about?"

Ryan Campbell brought both hands around in front of himself for Delta to see—in one hand he held a bright yellow nerf gun and in the other hand, a rolled tube sock.

"What's in the sock?" she asked, but before he could answer they both turned at the strange sound coming from beyond the building "Za, za, zazaza."

"Well, what's in the sock?"

"Just more socks. That's the rule—nerf guns and socks with rolled up socks inside, nothing that could hurt anybody, especially not professors and I can clearly see that you're not a zombie." He spoke quickly and glanced around appearing agitated, paranoid. The young man became more desperate at the sound which was drawing closer, "ZA, ZA, ZAZAZA!"

"What's that?" Delta asked him.

"The Zombies. They just got another human. They're celebrating. Please, can I go now?"

"I take it you're a human?"

"Yes, please, please, can I go now?"

"Yes," Delta excused him just as an outburst of 'zombies' poured into the area between the two buildings. A running, screaming, flurry of activity took her by surprise. The noise surrounded her like a swarm of bees "ZA, ZA, ZAZAZA!" the zombies cried.

Ryan called for reinforcements, "Humans!" And as the zombies suddenly saw the 'humans' streaming into view their celebration song ceased. In order to stave off the attack, Ryan hid behind, Delta, yelling, "Professor. She's a professor." He spun her around as a human shield. Then he yelled, "Zombies. Zombies! Reinforcements!" More students appeared. A force of bodies poured from the bushes south of Purdue Memorial Union. 'Humans' flooded the area like a tsunami of bodies. Instead of the Za, za, zazaza song, 'zombies' shouted commands to organize. Nerf balls flew through the air. 'Humans' sent socks flinging and nerf balls zinging. Zap. Zap. Zap. Zapzapzap. Popping noises and screams of delight followed by peals of laughter which filled the night sky. In the end, somehow, the 'humans' rallied and scared the 'zombies' away. The 'humans' danced victoriously. "Za za zazaza zap!" they countered. Their cheers drifted away. The tsunami receded, only a few humans remained.

Delta watched them, still half in shock. Many of the 'zombies' wore make up. White faces with red eye-liner and fake blood dripping from their mouths. One student dressed in a Frankenstein costume, a suit with sleeves too short and floods for pant legs. A girl had make-up that made her nose look disjointed and seemed to have real blood dripping from her tongue. They each wore a bandana, but it was a different color from the one that Ryan wore.

Ryan stood amongst a group of 'humans' laughing and extolling their survival techniques. "Wake up! Look at me! Regardez moi! I am human. I do defeat, the za za zombies. Zap!" They slapped each other on the back while hooting their victory. He yelled, "Thank you, Professor." And he added, "I'm sorry; I hope I didn't scare you."

Delta relaxed, a smiled returned to her face, and after a moment of collecting herself, she realized what had just happened—*Zombie Tag.* She continued her walk to the bus stop. "I could have taken him," she said aloud. After another step or two she turned back toward the group which was disappearing into the mall, "I could've taken you," she yelled. Her whole body swelled with a sigh of relief.

The bus arrived shortly thereafter. Delta showed the driver her Purdue ID and took a seat, but before returning her ID to her purse she took a long, hard look at it—*indeed, I am not a zombie; I am a human.*

Delta's phone rang—it was Caleb.

CHAPTER 50

Thursday, 11:00 a.m., September 2, 2010—Chicago, IL

"Do I look all right?" Danielle Goldman asked her assistant Zandie Tan.

"You look perfect," Zandie assured the woman who stood straightening her mauve suit jacket and adjusting her brooch.

"It's been a long time since I've seen Tom Bradford. We went to college together, you know. Thirty years is a long time," Danielle added.

"You're fifty-something? Really? You don't look a day over forty-five," Zandie told her supervisor, Dr.Goldman. Danielle pursed her lips and glanced sideways wondering if that was a compliment or a veiled insult. It didn't matter, she didn't have time to give the thought another second as a knock sounded on the door of the 17th floor archival office of the ISM gallery in Chicago and a man walked in without waiting to be invited.

"Tom, you look wonderful," Danielle told him enthusiastically, before adding, "I was so surprised that you decided to make a special trip to Chicago."

"You're too kind, Danielle. I wasn't bald the last time I saw you. But like I said, I wanted to thank you in person," he told her before glancing toward Zandie Tan, without giving any further details in front of Danielle's assistant.

"Oh, this is my assistant Zandie Tan," Danielle introduced them and then turned toward her office. Bradford gave Zandie a slight nod, not a hello.

"Well, come in, come in and tell me what it is you want to thank me for."

Danielle led Tom Bradford to her office. She waved him in and left the door ajar.

He closed it.

"Danielle, I wanted to thank you in person for sending the package to me, the one with the note about the zombie seed."

"Oh, Tom if I'd known that was why you wanted to thank me, believe me I would have told you not to make the trip. For heaven's sake, I sent it to you because I don't want to have anything to do with the terminator seed."

"Danielle, this is not the terminator seed," Tom confided. "This is different."

"But you told me the zombie seed was just another name for the terminator seed. How is it different?" she asked.

"It's far more advanced. It's the T-GURT technology."

"The zombie seed?"

"Danielle, this has to do with top secret security. But I've obtained special permission to discuss it with you."

"With me? Why me?"

"First, you need to understand the power of what you call the zombie seed, the T-GURT technology. And second, you need to know how you can help your country."

"I'm listening," she matched his serious intensity in tone.

Tom Bradford and Danielle Goldman sat adjacent from each other at a small work table in her office. Tom leaned forward.

"For a decade scientists have been working on developing the V-GURT, the terminator seed."

"For financial gain," she interrupted.

"Yes, of course, the terminator seed protected any and all genetically-modified seeds from being used by just anybody without any protection for the company, but also for the future of genetically-modified plants. This is a breakthrough. I mean, we could feed millions and millions of starving people with further development of genetically-modified crops. We at the U.S. Department of Agriculture support these efforts."

"Financially?"

"Yes, we've given grants and such to one or two companies, plus one or two universities."

"Did they know what you planned to do with the terminator seed? Test it on farmers in India?" Danielle's voice increased a half octave. She didn't attempt to hide her contempt. Tom took a deep breath.

"Okay, I realize the terminator seed had problems," Tom offered. Danielle rolled her eyes at the understatement.

"Following the development of the terminator seed, and recognizing its social implications, we encouraged different research." He cocked his head and tipped it slightly begging her to consider the possibility of a change of heart at their headquarters.

"And RichField was all the more willing to help out as they reaped the benefits, no pun intended," Danielle regained the calm in her voice with this judgmental determination and sarcastic statement. Tom readjusted himself in the seat. *She isn't going to be an easy sell*, he thought.

"Danielle, what you call the zombie seed is genetically superior in every way. It will flourish in the fields. It will not result in farmer suicides, I assure you."

"The terminator seed needed double the water. People in countries undergoing droughts had no clue to this property of the seed. So tell the families of the one thousand four hundred Indian farmers who committed suicide that this seed is new and improved. Tell the environmentalists that this ameliorated seed is the answer to all their problems."

"Danielle, we have perfected it. The zombie seed can be turned on and off at will. It's a T-GURT not a V-GURT." He punctuated his words with emphasis.

"What on earth do you mean?"

"The farmer plants the seed, and let's just say, something goes wrong, for example, there's a drought so the seed won't grow. The seed company can restore it. They can give them the means to bring the seed back to life. It's not a terminator seed; it's a resurrection seed." Here Bradford hoped she wasn't paying too much attention.

"Tom, it could still have problems. It sounds like it's a sister seed to the terminator seed. And how much will it cost farmers to bring this seed back to life? What will they have to *pay* to have the seed *resurrected*?" A patina of sarcasm coated the words *pay* and *resurrected*.

"Of course, the companies will charge. We can't get corporations on board without letting them make a profit. They need the money to pay for more research."

"Why on earth would you want a seed that would, for all intents and purposes, be dead and then come back to life? Tom, is it glyphosate that brings it back to life?"

"No, it's not glyphosate. It's something safe, even good for people." Tom Bradford didn't give details.

"Like what?" Danielle wanted to know, clearly still skeptical.

"Tetracycline can restore it. A simple antibiotic. It won't hurt anyone."

"But why, Tom? Why? You saw what murderous effect this had on Indian farmers. I'm not talking about food harvests; I'm talking about social implications."

"I know what you're talking about, Danielle, but if we can control the seeds that are sold world-wide, we can control crop production world-wide. We can turn seeds on, or we can turn seeds off. Instead of using embargos or armies, or nuclear weapons, or drones, we can keep whole populations under control with the zombie seed."

He paused, perhaps realizing that he had said too much. She remained stock still. Suddenly she breathed in as if the wind had been knocked out of her.

"Oh, my god, Tom. You're talking about controlling the whole world's food production! Doesn't that amount to having a weapon of mass destruction?"

"Only if our hand is forced in that direction," he told her, but as he saw her jaw drop, he added quickly, "No, no we're thinking more along the lines of how to save whole populations from starvation, that way we'll win the hearts and minds, we'll win over friends. Danielle, friendly nations make good neighbors. Starving people are susceptible to terrorists, to cults, to communism. Danielle, I must get you to understand the significance of this. We need this scientific advancement. This is progress of the best kind. If we don't have it, then other countries will develop it, and then we'll be subject to someone else using it on us. We can't let anyone get a hold of the terminator seed or the zombie seed. We're talking about the balance of power. We need to have a U.S. company control the market through V-GURTs and T-GURTs, what you call the terminator seed and zombie seed, respectively. The technology must be ours. The process is already being applied to and tested on animals. Think of it,

Danielle. It's not inconceivable to think that one day it will be applied to people. Can you imagine if an astronaut went into space dormant, so to speak, and could be awakened, brought back to life decades or even eons later? The possibilities are staggering. It will make cryogenics passé. The T-GURTs technology could be the cure to death itself. It's the Lazarus technology; not the zombie seed. Now do you see how important this is to your government, to your country?" Tom's eyes were pleading with Danielle to understand. "Can you imagine if this fell into the wrong hands?"

She remained quiet, serious. Then Danielle stood up and turned away from Tom Bradford, Assistant Secretary at the USDA. She took a deep breath. And then she faced him.

"You really think other countries are moving toward this technology?"

"Absolutely." A pause followed.

Danielle stared intently into his eyes. She swallowed hard. He softened his voice, "Please, you must believe me."

She sighed and with a heavy voice added, "I do believe you. That's the problem."

"Danielle, you must understand if we don't control the technology, others will. And that could be devastating. Just think what could happen if our enemies cornered the market and controlled plant production," Bradford let her think about it; she in turn took another deep breath. He continued, "Can you imagine if our seed were substituted with terminator seeds and we didn't have the antidote—the T-GURT, the resurrection seed planted and the antibiotic waiting." He continued, "There are children starving in Sudan, mothers who can't breastfeed in Haiti due to malnutrition, there are—"

"Okay. Stop," she raised her hand as she spoke. "I understand. But only because I do believe you'll have to do a lot of good before you can commit acts of hostility. I assume you'll need to prove the power of the zombie seed by making it work in impoverished nations before you can control countries' economies? You'll feed whole nations, right?" He was nodding emphatically, "Yes, exactly. Poor countries will be fed while enemy nations won't be able to disable us by way of genetically-modified warfare."

"All right then, but what can I do to help? Why come to me?" she questioned.

"I just need to know if you kept a copy of the transcripts, the ones that came with the zombie seed note. The farmer interviews that you sent to me; I need to know if there's a back up. We can't have them falling into the wrong hands."

"Is that what those transcripts were about? The zombie seed was tested on U.S. farms?"

"Yes."

"Is that how you know it's not dangerous? Is that how you tested the tetracycline?"

"Yes, yes. That's why this is top secret. The government can't have anyone else finding out about this. Did you keep a copy of the interviews?"

"Yes, we keep a back up of everything that comes through the office."

"May I have it?"

Danielle hesitated. Tom Bradford reached out for her hand.

"The transcripts detail stories of several farmers whose crops failed to grow. The same crops were rejuvenated following a spraying by the company who sold them the seed—what you call the zombie seed. Yes, it was tested on Midwestern farms. We had to test here; we couldn't risk having it fall into another country's hands. Senator Searle will present a report to the Committee on Foreign Relations on how advantageous the development of the zombie seed will be—both for humanitarian reasons and for U.S. defense. Do you see how important this is now?"

"Yes." She then asked, "What more do you need?"

"Just the copy of the transcripts that you made," he concluded. Danielle appeared surprised that her part in this top secret venture would be so simple.

"That's it?"

Tom nodded and Danielle Goldman opened the door of her office and called Zandie Tan to her side. She instructed Zandie to pull the copy of the farm transcripts that had arrived with the zombie seed note several weeks ago. Zandie raised her eyebrows at the instructions. "Do as I say," Danielle told the young woman.

While they waited, Tom relaxed and turned to Danielle, "You look good, Danielle. I've missed you."

"That was a long time ago, Tom. And we discovered rather quickly that we're very different people."

CHAPTER 51

Thursday, early afternoon, September 2, 2010—Chicago, IL

Dr. Danielle Goldman stood at the window of her outer office. She peeked through the blinds, watching Tom Bradford exit the lobby of the H.R. Thompson Center with a folder under his arm. She dropped her finger from between the slats of the blinds.

"All clear," she loudly announced.

From an adjacent office, several people spilled forth, including a bandaged Caleb Barthes and a beaming Delta Quinn. Following Caleb and Delta, Lindsey Polacheck stepped from the office, joined by her friend, Zandie Tan. Finally, a handsome man wearing a suit and tie walked from his hiding place toward Danielle Goldman. He pulled an earpiece from his ear.

"Thank you, Danielle. We couldn't have done it without you." He held out his hand, palm up. "You were great. Very believable. So very believable. Honestly, it was the best performance I've seen in a long time."

Danielle reached down the front of her blouse and fished out a wire. She then unhooked the microphone from the brooch on the lapel of her suit. She wound the wire carefully around the transmitter and placed it in the waiting palm of the man dressed in a navy blue suit.

"I've been on this case for almost five years."

"Well, you've got them now, Len," Danielle said to Leonard Masterson of the U.S. Department of Justice. "I can't believe how high this goes," she added.

"Was there any truth to what he was telling me?" Danielle asked.

"The only truth is that they want a monopoly on the seed so that they can control the world food market. The stuff about replacing cryogenics, is definitely gibberish. The only top secret part of this is by RichField. As for Bradford caring about feeding the hungry children of the world, I doubt it. No, Bradford is in cahoots with RichField. Plus, those claims about the government protecting you from terrorists were meant to get you to turn over the copies of the transcripts that prove they illegally tested genetically-modified seeds in U.S. farmers' fields. Why? Not just so they can control the market. No, there's more to it than that. With the help of Caleb Barthes and his friend, Craig Richards at the *Chicago Tribune*, we were able to finish putting the pieces of the puzzle together. You weren't kidding, Caleb; they don't call him "Tracker" for nothing," referring to Caleb's mentor. Caleb smiled. Leonard Masterson continued to explain everything to Danielle, "Tracker was able to trace the phone call by which somebody purchased a credit card in the name of Ruby Carmichael. And that credit card was used to pay the crop duster who sprayed Jim Hack's farm. One would have thought that tracing the call would have led to Ruby Carmichael's cellphone, but instead it led to Senator Jacob Searle."

"What was the Senator planning?" Delta asked. Leonard Masterson of the Justice Department answered, "The meeting he has scheduled with the Foreign Relations Committee, which Bradford mentioned, is real. It's scheduled for next week, which is when Senator Searle plans to ask for twenty-five billion dollars to support research into the most promising and important chemical weapon of all time—the zombie seed. He couldn't afford to have it linked to any scandals, like illegally testing it on U.S. farmers or that it is a variation of the terminator seed. Nor could he afford to have himself linked to anyone at the RichField Company. That would reek of bribery and collusion."

"Bribery and collusion?"

"I found out this morning that Searle owns over 10,000 shares of RichField stock. Not to mention the thousands of dollars he's taken from them in 'speaking fees', indirectly that is."

"What about the claims that it could help starving children?"

"The starving children in Sudan will likely be starving even if they get the zombie seed to market. Saving children is not on their slate. The history of the terminator seed proves that. As for the part about controlling other countries, well, it's possible the Pentagon is in on this, after all, Ruby Carmichael is connected in some way and she's from the DOD with links to the CIA."

"Wow, if farmers thought they had it rough with the terminator seed then imagine what would happen if the zombie seed made it to market?" Zandi Tan remarked. "The seed companies could charge astronomical amounts for the seed."

"Not to mention that they would also charge for specially formulated tetracycline," Danielle added.

"Yeah, like we need more antibiotics out there. Jeez, talk about antibiotic resistance problems; just imagine the havoc if every farmer in America started spraying the fields with antibiotics!" Mona shook her head after making this observation.

"Sadly, corporations control the world," Caleb said to no one in particular.

"Not if I can help it," Len told them, adding. "And we couldn't have done it without all of you."

It suddenly dawned on Delta that the copy of the transcripts that Danielle and Zandie had given to Tom Bradford, had been in their office the entire time. Delta asked, "But Zandie, if you had an extra copy of the transcripts, why didn't you give those to Caleb instead of sending him after those thugs? He might not have been hurled from a car."

"Oh, she didn't have an extra copy, Professor Quinn," Lindsey Polacheck of the Newberry Library piped up, "I did." Lindsey continued, "Zandie was telling me all about what happened at lunch one day, that's when I told Zandie that I had an extra copy."

"But Lindsey, if you had an extra copy, why didn't *you* give us a copy when we came to see Dr. Gold?"

"I didn't know you wanted a copy."

Delta thought back to their visit to the Newberry Library; she remembered that Lindsey had not been in the room when they made their actual request. She had given them the tour, "Ta-da," and then left them with Dr. Gold, "Ta-da," who also never explained the reason for their visit to Lindsey, at least not in any detail.

"So was that the last copy?"

"Of course not," Danielle Goldman said with a smile. "But that's not what Tom Bradford asked me. He asked if I had kept *a* copy. I actually had kept several copies, once Lindsey and Zandie brought them to my attention I decided a few more copies might be in order."

303

"So did I," Lindsey said with impish enthusiasm. Lindsey reached into her bag and pulled out yet another copy of the transcripts. She handed the folder to Delta, saying, "Ta-da!"

"So do you know who all is involved in the scheme?" Caleb asked Len Masterson.

"We're not sure yet, but what we do believe is that they were testing the zombie seed on unsuspecting farmers in the Midwest and that they were trying to create a monopoly. They have lobbyists dripping from the walls of the House and the Senate, Republicans and Democrats alike, judges and who knows who else. It goes very high. Ruby Carmichael and Senator Searle may not be the only ones in on this scheme and there may be more to the scheme than we currently know. We have a good deal to look into with regard to the zombie seed and some possible new schemes with respect to the terminator seed. Delta's transcripts are going to help support the investigation."

"There is one thing I still don't quite understand, Professor Quinn."

"What's that Mr. Masterson?"

"Please, call me Len."

"Len"

"How did you come to use the expression, zombie seed? No one else knew that the expression *zombie seed* was their code name for this latest genetically-modified seed? At least not until recently."

"Oh, Len, that's quite a different story," Delta blushed slightly at having to explain the religious zombie seed story to everyone. "Let's just say, the other coincidence is that Tom Bradford called it the resurrection seed."

Len cocked his head, not understanding. Caleb changed the topic.

"Len," Caleb interrupted. "What about the two guys who broke into Delta's apartment and crashed her stained-glass window?"

"And sliced Caleb's arm and sent him flying off the hood of a car?" Delta added.

"And wrecked my Geo," Mona reminded them.

"I hate to tell you this, but they're the small fish. We'll bring them in and probably cut a deal with them. Their testimony will corroborate what we have here. They provide the link between

RichField and Bradford and then Bradford to Carmichael. Ruby Carmichael links the whole thing to Senator Searle. Yeah, sorry, but those two guys are small fish, one is Robert Cornelius Brown , a.k.a. Downtown Bobby Brown who works for RichField and the other, a friend of his named Jason Slaughtery. We'll throw them back in the pond in order to get them to turn evidence, which is a shame because we think they were tracking Delta since she'd been in New York City at a conference."

"What about the RichField Corporation? Will they be handed a get-out-of-jail-free card?"

"No, I plan to open an investigation into anti-trust violations and who knows maybe illegal testing of agro-chemicals, if we have enough evidence."

"I wish we could get everybody including the small fish, but I guess we can't have it all," Mona concluded.

"I'm sorry about your car," Len Masterson added. "But I'm especially sorry that you two suffered at the hands of those two idiots," he said turning to Delta and Caleb. "If there were anything I could do, I would," he added.

"Well, there may be one thing you can do for me, Len. Let me walk you to your car," Caleb offered.

CHAPTER 52

Friday afternoon, September 3, 2010—Lafayette, IN

Mona dropped Delta off at her remodeled church apartment on Friday afternoon following classes and a late faculty meeting. The graduate advisee promised to pick up her advisor the next morning, so the two could drive back to Chicago. Caleb had promised to take them to another Sox game on Saturday. After putting her work away, Delta stepped back outside to get her mail. Mrs. Rushka waved from her apartment as she took her little dog inside. Delta waved back before flipping through the stack, mostly junk mail that she had extracted from the mailbox, and then she turned to go inside, but stopped abruptly.

The sight of a yellow Hummer pulling into the parking lot left her immobilized. She could neither move forward nor backward. The Hummer came to a stop. She stared as the door of the monstrous vehicle opened and a man got out. Delta recognized him.

He walked slowly toward Delta.

"Can we talk?"

Delta still couldn't speak. It didn't make sense. She nodded. The man followed as she led the way into her apartment.

"Brandon, I mean, Father Langer. Should I call you Father Langer?"

"No, Delta. Oh, no. We've been friends far too long for that kind of formality. I've come to confess something and to ask your forgiveness."

"Please, sit down," she said motioning him toward the couch, concern covering her face.

"I was very distraught over the story that you sent to me. The one about the Virgin Mary not being a virgin and especially the part about the zombie seed that the Virgin uses during the crucifixion," he told her as she sat down next to him.

"Do you mean the part where Mary soaks the veil with the herbal tincture and gives it to Veronica so that when Veronica wipes Jesus' face, she is able to apply the resurrection herbs to his parched lips?"

"Yes, and the rest."

"That the mixture eases his pain, allowing him to fall into a coma, and then Mary's tears awaken him three days later."

"Yes, yes."

"A little too hokey?" she asked, adding. "Kind of contrived, huh? I thought that would be the hardest part for people to believe."

Father Brandon Langer sat quietly, only now realizing that he was sitting in a remodeled church. He looked around at the stained-glass windows that were still intact, one of which portrayed Mary suffering at the loss of her son to Pontius Pilate. Fr. Langer gathered his thoughts into words.

"How could you say the Virgin wasn't a virgin?"

"Narrative probability," Delta answered. "I stand by that being the most believable."

"I don't understand," Brandon looked seriously concerned.

"Do you know how many girls are raped before the age of twenty?" Delta asked him without flinching. Delta had done her research, all part of understanding domestic abuse and violence against women. Father Brandon shook his head.

"I do," Delta continued. "And it's far higher than the number of girls who are impregnated by God."

"But Delta, why would you want to take the sacred story away from those who do believe?"

"To expose the sequestered story. To give the victimized women of the world a little hope. To let them know that perhaps, just maybe, the story was otherwise. That it may have been possible for a woman to turn her victimization into the greatest resistance movement in the history of the world. It wasn't Jesus who saved the world; it was Mary who created a resistance movement through Jesus. "

"Revenge?"

"What you call revenge, I call justice."

"Delta, what justice is there in calling Joseph gay?"

"The justice lies in its probability. Can't you see that? Why else would Joseph have married the girl?"

"Maybe, he loved her," Brandon offered. His eyes pled to be understood. A silence filled the room. His vulnerability was in her hands. Delta didn't know what to say, "Brandon, I—

The embarrassed young priest felt her sympathy was about to turn into words like, *I had no idea. I uh, I want us to continue to be friends.* Unable to bear such pity, he quickly interrupted her, saying, "Why would *you* of all people destroy the image of the Holy Family?"

"What's that supposed to mean, 'me of all people'?

"You would think someone who had been orphaned as a child would recognize the value of maintaining the story of the Holy Family, intact, not with an illegitimate status hanging over the Savior's head or with a gay father in the picture. Delta, honestly, you, of all people, should understand the sanctity of family."

Delta fell speechless for a moment as she suddenly envisioned herself in the orphanage again, feeling utterly alone, feeling stripped of who she had been, not knowing how to defend herself or how to define herself until she began taking care of her younger brother and sister. Her only connection to the world as she had known it existed in the brief moments of caring for her younger siblings, holding their hands, finding them clothes, rocking them when they cried at night— caring for them. Without them she would have been a zombie, walking through life without meaning or purpose or definition. Holy family?! She just wanted a *whole* family.

"Delta?" She didn't answer him. "Delta, I'm sorry. I didn't mean to bring up—"

"Brandon, this is what I do. I study stories, sequestered stories." Delta regained her voice and her presence. "When a story speaks of injustice, I attempt to understand it and maybe even rewrite the story. I hope that my work gives voice to the victims." Delta's voice was calm and strong. Father Langer became quiet, respectful. Delta continued, "I'm sorry that I bothered you with my Gnostic story and that you drove all the way here to—"

"Delta, I drove here to West Lafayette, to the University, about three weeks ago to see you, to talk to you," he interrupted. She looked perplexed. He continued, "I saw you get into your car at the university and I followed you. On the way, I became distracted and accidentally rammed our Hummer into your car."

"Our Hummer?"

"It belongs to the parish. A car dealer gave it to us for the priests to use. I was too embarrassed to have you find out that I was following you *and* that I hit your car. What would you think of me? I panicked and drove off. I abandoned the Hummer and took the train back to Chicago. I phoned the Hummer in as stolen. What a mess I made of everything." He slumped.

Delta nodded in agreement, but her silence was filled with sympathy, as well. Brandon continued his confessional tale.

"The police called the monsignor and told him that the Hummer had been found. They also told him that it had been used in a hit and run. I didn't know that he knew. He kept waiting for me to confess. Once I confessed my sin, he sent me to see you. He gave me instructions to tell you that it is now your vehicle. So here I am and here are the keys." Brandon put the keys into her palm and then pulled out the title and registration. He tried to hand over the paperwork to Delta, but she resisted.

"No, you should keep it. Besides it's not quite my style." Delta backed away from the registration and Brandon's outstretched offer.

"The Monsignor insists. He said to tell you, you can sell it, if you like. The police told him how your car was totaled in the accident and about your concussion. Can you ever forgive me, Delta?"

Delta tilted her head; a slight, soft smile crossed her face. "A Hummer, eh? Well, maybe I could get used to a Hummer. Lord, knows a girl like me needs something as big as a tank to stay safe." She considered the possibility of driving the Hummer.

"Hey, how did you get back to Chicago?" She was curious.

"It's a long story, filled with generous and unsuspecting people who loaned me money and gave me a ride to the train station. I need to make amends to more than you. But mostly, it was one serendipitous encounter after another. I didn't plan a thing; it just all happened."

"Well, that's actually good to hear," she decided.

"Why?"

"It's good to hear that you're not a practiced thief."

"That's an understatement. Plus, one lie after another ate away at me."

"You did make a bit of a mess, didn't you?" she said it with a smile.

"A favor?"

"Sure."

"Could you give me a ride to the sheriff's department? I want to make things right."

"You know I won't press charges."

Nodding, he took the words that he didn't want her to say to him earlier, and said them, "I hope we can remain friends."

"Absolutely, I wouldn't have it any other way." She hugged her long-time friend; he swallowed back tears that she would never see.

Impressed by Brandon's effort to set things straight, Delta not only agreed to take him to the sheriff's department, but added, "I need to make something right, as well. I'll pick you up later to take you to the train depot, okay?"

CHAPTER 53

Friday, September 3, 2010—outskirts of Lafayette, IN

After dropping Father Brandon Langer at the sheriff's department and promising to pick him up later to give him a ride to the train depot, Delta made a phone call and set up a meeting.

The meeting took place in their usual spot, a corner library table in the Stewart Center. Karyn's eye was healing; the bruise had begun to change from blue to yellowish green.

"I owe you an apology," Delta told the girl.

"For what?"

"For handing you resource information, for expecting you to go to a counselor, or the Crisis Center or the police and expecting it to be simple. I knew better."

Karyn tipped her head and furrowed her brow. "What do you mean?"

"I didn't do any of those things when it happened to me, but I expected you to do just that, go to the police."

"What are you talking about, Professor? What happened to you?"

Delta told the girl with the multi-studded earrings and the choppy hair how a man had attacked her, shook her like a child, and told her to quit doing her research. She confessed to Karyn that she didn't report him to the police.

"Why not?" the girl asked intently while tugging on a lock of hair and pulling it over her bruised eye. Her royal blue painted fingernails were bitten to the quick.

"First, because it all happened so fast. I mean, I just couldn't believe it was happening."

"Yeah, it's jolting, isn't it?"

"I mean it's a shock to the system. Like where did that come from?"

"But once the shock wore off, then what?"

"Then I realized that he had shaken me by the shoulders as if I were a child." Delta paused for a second before continuing, "He took my dignity away. I was embarrassed. He treated me like a child and I couldn't do a thing about it. He said, quit doing your research, you're only—"

"Only making things worse," Karyn finished Delta's sentence. Delta looked surprised. Karyn reached into her purse that hung from the back of the chair. Pulling out her wallet she produced a snapshot. "Did he look like this?"

Karyn handed Delta the picture of a happy couple in goth prom attire—a snapshot of herself and her boyfriend in High School during happier days.

"Is this the guy?" she asked Delta again.

Delta nodded. "I should have reported it, but I felt like the police might laugh. I mean he only shook me, right?"

"And he dragged you into the bushes, took away your dignity and embarrassed you," Karyn's ire was up. Her words corrected Delta's dismissal of the event as trivial, reminding Delta that he did more than shake her a little. Karyn found strength in protecting Delta. Delta didn't stop to think about how she had just framed the event.

"I should report it," Delta said tentatively, now knowing for sure that it was Karyn's boyfriend. She had suspected but hadn't been sure until now.

Karyn sat up, straightening her shoulders. Her eyes met Delta's eyes, on par, not from tilted head or from behind a lock of hair. "You should report it. He had no right to hurt you in any way. I'll go with you."

Delta reached across the table and laid her hand on Karyn's hand, "That's what I should've said to you weeks ago."

"Better late than never," Karyn smiled.

"We'll go together then?" Delta offered.

"Sounds like a plan," Karyn placed the prom picture on the table. She slid it away from her, determined to leave it behind.

Both stood up, gathered their possessions and pushed in their chairs. Karyn stuck her gum underneath the table top before they left, at which, Delta couldn't help but smile.

"I got another tattoo," Karyn said as they exited the library.

"Yeah, what of?"

"*Love hurts*. I put it next to my butterfly."

314

"I'm thinking of getting another one, too" Delta told her new friend.

"Really? What?"

"A simple sentence—'There is no Truth that can't be changed.'"

"I like it," Karyn told Delta.

They both laughed.

"Hey, do you like baseball?" Delta asked putting her arm around the girl as they left the building.

"Yeah, I do. Hey, do you have car yet?" Karyn asked.

"As a matter of fact, I do. Need a ride?"

CHAPTER 54

Friday, September 3, 2010—outskirts of Lafayette, IN

"So, I think I know what you did wrong," Delta said as she pulled into the warehouse parking lot.

"What I did wrong?! He wronged me," Karyn protested while folding a fresh stick of gum and plopping it into her mouth.

"Yeah, yeah, sorry, I didn't mean it that way. What I mean is you were trying to create a home. You know, you were defining the relationship like a married couple who goes grocery shopping together after writing a list. You took a sandwich to him at work. You were like a little wife who wanted a home and a family."

"Yeah, so?" Karyn pointed for Delta to park close to, but not next to, a truck in the back row of the parking lot.

"So, he didn't. He didn't even want the grocery list. He didn't want two plants on the railing or two cats in the yard or flowers in the vase. You get what I'm saying?"

"Park here," Karyn told the professor. Delta brought the Hummer to a stop.

"Do you get what I mean, that he didn't want to be defined as a family man?"

"Well, he doesn't have to worry about that anymore. And, wouldn't it have been easier if he had just said so?"

"I think he thought he was saying so. But yes, talking trumps hitting any day."

"He wasn't trying to say anything. He's a zombie. He works all night and sits in front of the TV all day except when he picks a fight with me. Otherwise, a zombie, who's not doing anything with his life, except picking up fifty pound seed and grain bags and moving them from one spot to another." Karyn jumped out of the Hummer. Delta followed her lead.

"I bet you're right."

"Of course I am," Karyn slipped closer to the truck.

317

"No, I mean about the zombie thing. I'll bet the only time he felt alive was when he was fighting with you. That's why he always apologized afterward. So you'd come back to him." Delta spoke as she followed Karyn along the back row of the warehouse parking lot. Farther down, a lamppost lit the night air. Swarms of insects filled the ray of light.

"So our relationship could live to fight another day?"

"Something like that."

"Are you sure it wasn't his job that drove him crazy?"

Delta wondered how much his job had to do with it. *Some people just aren't meant to be working in warehouses or factories. Take Jim Hack, the farmer, for example. He nearly went crazy while working in a factory, but he had a dream. He had a future to focus on— buying a tractor and starting his own farm. Karyn's boyfriend was proud of his job when he first landed it, but in time the monotony wore on him and unlike Jim Hack, Karyn's boyfriend didn't have a dream. Maybe that's what makes a zombie a zombie, hopelessness, a dreamless state of being. On the other hand, lots of people would consider the warehouse a great job to have, a real job, one that contributes to society and pays a salary that allows a person to support a family. There are a number of people who would be grateful for any job.* Delta had another thought, "Do you think—"

"Shh! This is his truck," Karyn whispered in a stage voice, cutting off Delta's comment.

"What do you need to get out of the truck?" Delta asked.

"Nothing, really." Karyn pulled a tube of super glue from her purse.

"Then what are we doing here?"

"This." Karyn bit off the cap of the glue. She spit the tip onto the asphalt. "Thanks for stopping at the drug store." Karyn squirted super glue into the keyhole of the driver's side door of the truck.

"I know it's sort of a high school kind of thing to do, to get even …" Karyn spoke these words as she rounded the other side of the truck and squirted the sticky substance into the other lock. Next, she took the moist gum from her mouth and stretched it until it tore into two pieces. She jammed half of it into the first lock and then she did the same with the rest of the gum into the lock on the passenger side.

After that, she took a toothpick from her purse, spit on it, forced the gum deeper into the lock and then shoved the toothpick in as well; finally, she broke off the toothpick at the nub. She repeated the process to the other lock, saying, "… but you have no idea how good it feels to lock him out."

CHAPTER 55

Saturday, September 4, 2010, BAT DAY—Chicago, IL

Delta arrived at the stadium parking lot in the yellow Hummer. Caleb was waiting for her. He shook his head at the sight of the mammoth yellow machine.

"That's insane," he told her.

"I know, I know," she said, "Besides being huge, I'm too eco-friendly to keep it, but it proved useful in getting everybody here. I brought a few friends," she said turning to Mona, Devika, Jim and Susan Hack and their two little girls who were all exiting the Hummer. "I hope you meant it when you said I could bring as many people as I wanted to help us celebrate." The last one out of the yellow Hummer was Karyn.

"Absolutely. Tickets are on me." He had a handful of tickets in his fist.

The group entered the stadium and Caleb bought hot dogs for the girls and a hotdog bun for Delta on the way to their seats. They greeted Joe, Reuben, and Ani. Delta made the introductions at which time she couldn't help but notice Ani's eyes alight when he saw Devika Sharma. Joe noticed, as well.

"Karma brings Dharma through Sharma," Joe teased. "Hey, Caleb, you're a big spender today what are you celebrating?"

"I sold the article idea about the zombie seed and they want a whole series on what's going on with the terminator technology."

"Way to go," Joe added and Reuben high-fived Caleb.

"I owe it all to Delta," Caleb added.

"Around the horn," Delta called. In response, Reuben high-fived Ani, who high-fived Joe, who high-fived Mona, who high-fived Delta.

"I invited a few more friends," Caleb nodded in the direction of the entrance. Zandie Tan and Danielle Goldman as well as Lindsey Polacheck waved from the entrance as they made their way toward the group.

"Play ball!" the announcer shouted.

The group watched the game with intense excitement, but Delta couldn't help but notice that Caleb used the binoculars more than he had the last game. She watched to see what he was looking at and it didn't seem to be the players.

At the seventh inning stretch, Caleb stood and nodded to Reuben, Ani, and Joe.

Then turning to Delta, he said, "We'll be back. Beer run and a pit stop. Do you want anything?"

Delta shook her head no. Once Caleb was gone, she picked up the binoculars and scanned the crowd in the direction that Caleb had been looking.

CHAPTER 56

Saturday, September 4, 2010—Chicago, IL

Caleb stopped at the concession stand where he bought a tray of beers and gave them to Ani to carry. Next, he headed to the gift stand where he bought two signed bats for Joe and himself. They continued on to a section on the opposite side of the stadium. Caleb stood at the archway and pointed the way for Ani who walked down the stadium steps to row Q, seats 1 & 2. Once there, Ani spilled the beers all over the front of two men seating in row Q, seats 1 & 2.

"Oh, my most sincere apologies," Ani said with his thick Indian accent, and as he attempted to wipe the beer off their shirts, he spilled more.

The two disgruntled baseball fans brushed Ani aside as they made their way for the men's room to get paper towel. Once they entered, Reuben came from around the corner and set up a bright yellow, plastic horse stand that read, "wet floor;" he then stood guard outside the restroom When a fan tried to enter the restroom despite the 'wet floor' sign, Reuben said, "Oh man, you don't want to go in there right now. Some guy upchucked in there in the worst way." The stranger headed to the next restroom. Reuben kept guard for the next ten minutes while Caleb and Joe, who had entered the restroom, had a word with the two men from the opposite side of the stadium.

As the two men turned around from the sinks, they found themselves face-to-face with Caleb Barthes and Joe 'The Hammer' Jaworski. Their eyes widened as Joe lightly beat the small bat against his own palm. The taller of the two men tried to push by Caleb and Joe, but Joe pulled the bat up horizontally blocking their path.

"Gentlemen, a word," Caleb said. "I see you received that thank you note from Tom Bradford for a job well done and the round trip tickets to Chicago to watch the Sox beat the Yankees."

The two men fell silent as they processed the fact that the note from Tom Bradford had been a forgery.

"Give me your phone," Caleb said to the man with the blond hair.

"Give it to him," the taller man said. The man with the blond hair pulled his phone from his pocket and handed it over, reluctantly, to Caleb. Caleb had not forgotten that Downtown Bobby Brown carries a concealed knife; he wouldn't put it past him to have gotten one into the stadium. Caleb kept more than a half an eye on the two men as he scanned the phone list, until he found it.

"Delta Quinn. Just as I thought," he said. Caleb held the phone in his palm. He popped the back off and pulled out the sim card. "And yours," he said to other man.

"He doesn't have her number," Slaughtery said.

"Give it to me," Caleb told Bobby Brown who reluctantly handed over his phone.

Caleb scanned it. Then he held it up for Slaughtery to see; Delta's name and number appeared on the list.

Caleb pressed another application—pictures. He scanned them until he found the one he was looking for; he held it up for all to see. In the photo, Slaughtery is standing in front of Jim and Susan Hack's farm holding a bag of soybeans in his hand. Caleb shook his head, dropped both phones to the floor and then smashed each one with his baseball bat.

"I'd invite you to stay, but your tickets are forgeries. You may have gotten into the stadium, but I'll point out to the police that those are counterfeit tickets. I think you have a plane to catch anyway, don't you? Come on, we'll escort you to the exit. Sorry, you can't stay to see the Sox beat the Yankees."

After escorting Downtown Bobby Brown and Jason Slaughtery to the exit, Joe turned to Caleb, "That was an expensive way to get even. You should've at least let me hit them while we were at it. Now, they'll listen to the end of the game in the airport and then catch their flight."

"Well, that would be the case Joe, except for the fact that," Caleb paused and pulled his phone out to check the time, "at this very moment their names are being added to the "no fly" list by a certain friend of mine at the Justice Department."

When Caleb, Reuben, Joe and Ani returned to their seats, Mona wondered aloud, "You know, there's still one thing I don't understand. I realize it was Karyn's boyfriend who called Delta saying, quit doing your research, but—"

"Ex-boyfriend," Karyn corrected her.

"Yes, sorry. But who sent the 'Cease and Desist!' message?"

"That message is suspiciously bureaucratic sounding," Caleb added.

"I agree, very bureaucratic." Ani added, "It reminds me of the kind of messages that the government office might send to our policy institute, if something is amiss."

"Or something the university might send," Mona suggested.

"Some mysteries take longer to solve than others," Delta predicted.

"And some are never solved," Ani added. His words made Delta's thoughts land like a butterfly on memories of her father driving, driving forever, driving across a frozen tundra, frozen in place, frozen in time, frozen in her memory, a mystery never solved.

"Well, in the meantime you've got a whole posse watching your back," Mona told Delta. "But especially, you have one hell of an investigative reporter on your side," she said of her brother.

"That reminds me," Jim Hack said, "I have something for you two." He held out his hand, "Both of you." Delta and Caleb both held out an open palm which is when Jim dropped a smooth stone into each of their hands. The couple looked quizzically at the small rocks and then back at Jim. "You know, like the *Chicago Tribune* building—rocks from my farm for your walls—a memento of your first story together."

"How did you know this would make the perfect gift?" Delta asked. Jim glanced at Mona who smiled and gave them a wink.

CHAPTER 57

Saturday, September 4, 2010—Chicago, IL

"How 'bout those Sox?!" the crowd cheered. "Good guys wear black!" they chanted. "Yankees go home," others shouted.

"I still love New York City," Delta told Caleb. Joe piped in, "I told you Delta, you can love New York, just not the Yankees." Caleb gave Joe a little shove and he headed off in the direction of Ani, Devika and Reuben. The others were trailing behind.

"Don't listen to him. You can love any team you want. Cubbies, Sox, Yankees, Mets, Indians, whichever team your heart desires." He smiled at her as they walked toward the bright yellow Hummer. She leaned against the side of the vehicle, facing Caleb. He placed the palm of his hand against the door. She noticed his outstretched arm, bandaged from where Downtown Bobby Brown had knifed Caleb when he tried to rescue the transcripts.

"Did he ruin your tattoo, 'Never quit searching for—"

Caleb finished the statement, 'Never quit searching for the Truth; it *lies* somewhere.' As for ruining the tattoo, the doc says, he only underlined it."

"Nice," Delta said with a smile. "Now that's poetic irony."

Caleb Barthes leaned forward and kissed Delta Quinn. She kissed him back. Their long, sweet kiss lingered, but once their lips parted, she looked deeply into his eyes and asked with a smile,

"So, do you want to know what I have planned for next week?"

CHAPTER 58

Friday, September 10, 2010—outskirts of Lafayette, IN

Delta had finished teaching her back-to-back classes, attended several afternoon meetings, packed her big, black canvas bag and picked up her mail from the main communication office before heading home. As she flipped through the mail, she had noticed that one business-sized envelope had no return address, plus the address to "Professor Quinn" had been handwritten. After sifting through the rest of the mail she slipped the bundle into the side pocket of her bag.

The drive home in the yellow Hummer under sunny skies felt relaxing. Delta barely noticed when she passed the spot on the road where she had been struck by a hit and run on August 10, 2010, one month ago.

Once home she set her bag aside and changed into her yoga pants and tank top.

She tousled her hair into a loose ponytail and prepared a snack. Delta laid out avocado and lactose-free cheese slices on a plate with a handful of crackers. She poured a glass of chardonnay. After watering her indoor plants, the barefoot professor pulled out her mail, tucked it under one arm and carried her mail, snack, and wine to the patio.

Each patio had a cement window box along the outside wall where Mrs. Rushka and Delta had added a carefully selected array of garden herbs, below that they had planted vegetables. As Delta came outside, balancing her mail, appetizer and wine, she greeted Mrs. Rushka who was tending the plants.

"There's an old Russian saying," Mrs. Rushka told Delta from across the wrought iron fence that divided their patios, "Why should a man die, if he has sage in his garden?"

"Indeed, why, and why should a *woman* die if she has sage in *her* garden?" Delta added.

"Always the feminist, my little Delta. I like that."

"Look," Mrs. Rushka said, pointing to an exquisite monarch butterfly with golden-orange mosaic wings, each section trimmed in a fine black line, "like a stained-glass window. Well," she said changing the subject, "I'll bring you some tea later. Sage and peppermint tea. You'll like it very much."

"I'm sure I will," Delta thanked her neighbor. Before sitting down, she plucked some arugula and basil. Butterflies fluttered upward from the English lavender that grew at the edge of the patio. Delta thought of something Mrs. Rushka had said some time ago when bemoaning the existence of butterfly houses: "How can they be who they're supposed to be, if they're trapped in those houses? Just like people, they need to be free to fulfill their destiny." Delta returned to the patio chair as Mrs. Rushka disappeared into her apartment.

She flipped through the mail, mostly annual announcements about conferences and other academic notices. However, the plain, white envelope with the handwritten address intrigued her; she opened it first, took a sip of wine and began to read:

Dear Professor Quinn,

You don't know me but I owe you an apology. I'm a scientist who works for RichField Corporation. I'm the one who sent you the "Cease and desist" message. I overheard management talking about your research; they said that it might jeopardize the T-GURT research and that's why I sent you the message—Cease and desist; your research may be dangerous! I didn't want my research interrupted, but now I'm not so sure. It's ironic, but perhaps it's my research that could be dangerous.

Recently, I discovered that four different types of weeds are now immune to the herbicides that I helped to create. Additional research confirms that both swallowtail and monarchs butterflies are dying from the pesticide.

I also learned that the genetically-altered food has a lower vitamin content than organic food; but, instead of promoting organic options, we scientists spend time and money trying to figure out how to genetically insert nutrients into the food that we made less nutritious. For example, scientists found a way to infuse daffodil genes, which carry vitamin A, into rice, making 'golden rice.' This could keep millions of children from going blind, but patent infringement keeps us from being able to supply it. In other words, the very companies that created it are keeping it from market. So maybe we should think about offering carrots or sweet potatoes, or fruits like cherries, or vegetables like turnips or dandelion greens.

We've created some wonderful products but we've also disrupted the socio-economic systems in developing countries. We've given farmers new agricultural methods, but we've also learned that genetically-engineered plant pollen can be carried as far away as 13 miles by wind to other plants, killing their future generations. We've created excellent herbicides, but we don't know how to control weed encroachment or superweeds. RichField advised farmers last week to "spray more." That hardly seems like the solution.

Professor Quinn, my eyes are open. You should continue to conduct your research. But I should continue to conduct mine, too. I just need to lift my head from the microscope every now and again to see the effects. Myopia doesn't suit scientists. Collaboration does. My research may move us forward technologically; but, it should be informed by your research, which will keep us honest

Again I apologize for sending the "Cease and desist" order. I hope you will pursue your research —see it through to the end.

Sincerely,

A Fellow Scientist

Delta folded the pages of the letter and returned them to the envelope. She felt a tickling sensation on her bare foot. Looking down, Delta Quinn spied a monarch butterfly resting on the tip of her toe. She was pleased that not all the monarchs have disappeared. Although she would never know who penned this letter to her, she felt as though she had made a new friend, albeit one more person who could hack into her computer.

Delta watched the butterfly until it took flight, eventually landing again in the milkweed bush that Mrs. Rushka had planted. Delta remembered that Mrs. Rushka had said, "The world needs butterflies," as she pressed soil around the milkweed plant's roots. Indeed, Delta thought, *we do need butterflies. And we need scientists. We need geneticists, biologists, environmentalists, and activists. We need to think ahead—what will happen seven generations from now. Not just one or two generations—*she pictured her students in her mind—*in the classroom, walking on campus or running about playing games like zombie tag.* She remembered the young man wearing the sign that says, *Wake up ... It's not a Game!* She remembered the student who had said, *you're not a zombie. That's right, I'm not a zombie,* she thought. Delta Quinn stood up.

She left her spot at the patio table and went into the apartment bedroom where she opened the top dresser drawer. Although she only meant to put away the anonymous letter, which she had just finished reading, she felt compelled to retrieve the envelope with the newspaper clipping about her mother's death. She lifted the envelope, removed the story and read:

Funeral for a Brave Woman

August 15, 1986   The funeral for Katherine (Beauvoir) Quinn was held at 10:00 a.m. in St. Thomas Catholic Church, where she and her husband were members. Katherine Quinn was of Cherokee and French descent. She is survived by her mother, Emma Walks-the-Ridge Beauvoir, who lives in Tennessee and a grandmother who lives on the Qualla Boundary. Katherine is also survived by her husband Daniel Quinn of Akron, Ohio. The couple met in Ohio when Katherine's father, Mr. Beauvoir brought the family north so that he could work in the Goodyear rubber factory. Katherine was killed trying to protect her neighbor from a violent attack of domestic abuse. Katherine (Walks-the-Ridge Beauvoir) Quinn, a brave woman, leaves behind five children; Jacqueline, 9, Nathan, 7, Delta, 4 ½, Carrie Ann, 3, and Tommy, 2.

Tears filled Delta's eyes as she folded the note and said aloud, as if her mother could hear her, "I wish I could be as brave as you." Then she thought to herself, *I only collect the stories of those in need—of farmers, of whistleblowers, of abused women—you, however, became a part of the story. You saved your neighbor's life.* She returned the yellowed newspaper clipping with the obituary to its envelope and then placed it back in the drawer. Before she shut the drawer she pulled out the police paperwork that had condemned the man who had shot her mother. She reread the pronouncement—manslaughter. Delta took that aging piece of paper into the living room, and with the angels in the stained-glass windows as her witnesses; she lit the corner of the paper and watched it turn to flame. As the heat approached her fingertips she dropped the flaming paper into a ceramic dish, where it curled into oblivion. Delta took a step forward, leaving the remains behind.

Sitting down at the computer, she typed the words, *terminator seed* and *Purdue*. She paused for a moment before adding, *world hunger*. She wanted to know what the University is doing about that problem. After all, if they hold a patent for the terminator seed, then they need to be held accountable. She read ferociously for several hours with the intention to speak out—to be a brave woman. Later that evening, after having read nonstop at the computer about the varying uses and effects of genetically-modified crops, including having read the materials that Ani had provided, and finally after carefully having reviewed the farmers' transcripts from the copy that she had been given by her new friends at the Illinois State Museum—Chicago Gallery and the Newberry Library, she composed the following letter to the President of Purdue University.

Dear President Córdova,

In the right hands, science can alter the world for the better, bringing about an end to world hunger. In the wrong hands, it can have devastating effects. It would seem Purdue University holds both a patent for the terminator seed as well as one of the keys to ending world hunger. Purdue has at least two stories to tell; the first will make you proud, the second one will give you pause. The first is about a Purdue professor.

Gebisa Ejeta, born in a rural village in Ethiopia, in 1950, took his first breaths within a mud hut. His mother encouraged him from the time he was a small boy to obtain an education, in order to overcome hardship and hunger. So, as a boy, he walked 20 kilometers to get to the school, staying all week, and then he trekked the 12 and ½ miles back home again. The devoted student eventually graduated and with financial assistance, later entered Jimma Agricultural and Technical School where he applied himself to his studies. His hard work and insightful mind led him to apply for college where he studied agronomy. One of his college mentors introduced him to Professor John Axtell of Purdue University. Axtell's specialty—developing a strong sorghum plant—intrigued the young Gebisa Ejeta. The grain, although native to Ethiopia, struggled in drought-like conditions, also common in Ethiopia, but if a way could be found to breed a heartier plant, then Ethiopians would be less dependent on what had provided such an inconsistent harvest. Ejeta entered Purdue University's Ph.D. program. His research studies focused on the sorghum plant, so vital to the African people's diet. Not until after exhausting all hybrid options to protect the sorghum plant from a virulent weed—striga, did the scientist turn to genetic modification. Then he discovered a means to protect the plant from striga, which attacks sorghum in a stealth manner, through the root before any evidence on the surface is visible. One cannot pull striga that one cannot see. Ejeta worked long hours, alongside his lab assistants and his colleagues, each contributing in important ways, until they found the answer and with it came the World Hunger Prize. Since then Ejeta has teamed with organizations, specifically World Vision International and Sasakawa2000, as well as USAID to deliver eight tons of seed to Ethiopia and surrounding countries. This is a story in which Purdue University can take great pride.

Foods have been genetically modified in the United States to benefit people by providing crops that are more resilient, foods that have longer ripening times and plants that can genetically fight off diseases. But there have been problems as well. For instance, well-intended researchers inserted the Brazilian nut protein gene into soy beans which caused allergic reactions for those who are allergic to nuts. Genetically-modified cotton crops need double the water than their non-genetically modified counterpart crops. Researchers inserted pesticide genes into plants; the pollen they exude allowed farmers to reduce spraying, but it also killed monarch butterflies. In other fields, the farmers sprayed more herbicide because their plants were modified to resist the spray, causing the surrounding foliage to become resistant. Now, the weeds are fighting back.

Eddy Anderson, a farmer living in Dyersburg, Tennessee, who has spent the last fifteen years using no-till agriculture, protecting the soil, keeping the environment safe from pesticide run-off, and eagerly using the latest genetically-modified crops, now faces superweeds. I am not invoking hyperbole. These weeds grow at an alarming rate—three inches a day and to a top height of seven feet, and they are resistant to herbicides. They have infected over twenty states in the U.S. growing cotton, corn and soybeans. The President of the Arkansas Association of Conservation districts said, "It is the single largest threat to production agriculture that we have ever seen."

The story of superweeds pales in comparison to what has been happening in India. Thousands of farmers are committing suicide each year because their crops have failed due to a combination of drought and genetically-modified plants' need for more water, as well as the high cost of seeds. The cost of seeds is exorbitant. The stranglehold that corporations have on small farmers is only reinforced by the terminator technology which has only made things worse. Purdue holds a terminator patent.

The terminator technology led to the development of the T-GURT—the zombie seed which could lead to market domination by the patent holders which in turn will surely squeeze small-farm farmers out of the agricultural business. Furthermore, it relies on antibiotics to restore life; we simply do not yet know the consequences of what will happen if this technology is put to use.

Beyond the terminator seed, beyond the zombie seed, I found an article tonight that tells the story of the exorcist gene. This genetic modification enables the plant to discard its modified gene after harvest, like shedding leaves, only some of these leaves will be poisonous. What are we leaving behind? Where are we going in the future?

I recommend you publicly declare a moratorium on terminator, zombie, and exorcist seeds, until we know more about the material and social consequences. I encourage you to help the farmers of Indiana as well as the farmers of India. I beg you to speak out against monopolies that have the potential to destroy the American way life, of fair competition. I ask you to lead the university toward its mission—to educate, to research, and to give back to the people.

Sincerely,

Prof. Delta Quinn

Without hesitation, Delta Quinn hit the send button. As the message disappeared, she heard the dinging sound alerting her to a new incoming email. She looked at the list in her inbox. The latest message was from one of her students, Drew Underwood. She clicked on the message and read the contents:

Prof. Quinn,

We're starting a new game of zombie tag next week. Do you wanna play on our team? Usually professors aren't allowed to play, but in your case we'll make an exception. C'mon, we'll let you be a Human or a Zombie, whatever you want. It'll be fun.

Drew Underwood, Zombie Tag Organizer Extraordinaire

Delta read the message and smiled at the invitation. Then she glanced at the clock—6:30 a.m. Had she been up all night? And what of Drew Underwood, had he been up all night? Or was he just getting up? Was he taking his zombie make-up off or putting it on? Was he hanging up his sign that says, WAKE UP—IT'S NOT A GAME or was he pulling it over his head to put it on? She had figured out his alter-ego the last time he spoke with her in class. His eyes gave him away. They were pleading with her to WAKE UP. They were thanking her for listening and learning about the terminator seed and its troubling history. She wrote a response to his invitation to play zombie tag and sent it. Next, she lifted her wine glass to her lips, took a sip and went back outside to watch the sunrise, to sit among the sleeping butterflies under the light of a full morning moon. Za za zazaza. Zap!

HAITI: THE EPILOGUE

Haitian Monarchs

On Monday, September 13, 2010, the children of a small orphanage in a rural area of Haiti gathered around a table to check on the seedlings they had planted in little Dixie cups filled with dirt. To their amazement the first shoots had sprouted and little green stems with bright shiny leaves had reached for the sunshine and found it. The children gathered around their teacher who led them along an ancient path to a secret place on a hillside. The teacher walked with a slight, barely perceptible, limp, as if she had a small pebble or a seed in her shoe, but that couldn't be it, since she was barefoot. After walking for some time, a boy called out.

"Look," the boy said, pointing to a colorful bush.

The youngest of the children stepped forward and reached out a fingertip to touch the bush. Just then a flutter of Haitian monarchs flew freely from the bush into the sky, delighting the children of St. Joseph's orphanage and their teacher. After they watched the butterflies alight, a girl looked down and found three stones, which she pointed out to the teacher, who said, "The Trinity."

"This is where we'll plant our seedlings," the teacher told them. There, the children dug into the dirt with their bare hands, freed the plants from the Dixie cups and carefully inserted them into mother earth.

"What is this plant called?" a child asked. The teacher answered, "Call it the butterfly plant."

APPENDIX

THE SECRET STORY OF THE NOT-SO-VIRGIN VIRGIN:
THE PROBABLE AND THE MAGICAL

Chapter One

A young girl with loose hair and dusty toes walked toward the village well. Her mother had sent her to fill an urn with water, an early morning chore. Like the dew-covered flowers, she greeted the morning with plump lips and sleepy eyes. Her veil began to slip from her head, but as she reached for the covering, she was jolted brusquely into the air and swung quickly into an alley. The urn flew in the opposite direction. Shock and surprise shot through her like lightning.

Her back hit the stone wall pushing the air from her lungs. A man's hand covered her mouth and nose, so that even if she had the breath she could not scream. Her eyes rolled upward. His armor dug sharply into her arms and thigh. "Don't make a sound," he threatened. She could not, for still she had not gasped the breath she needed. He swung his forearm against her chest, holding her in place. He grabbed her robes and shoved the fistful of cloth upward against her stomach laying bare her thighs. Upon seeing her nakedness he lost all control and forced himself upon her, over and over again, and she screamed out in pain. He was oblivious to her scream—loud and long and high. It meant nothing to him; but to her it meant everything.

Her scream turned into a searing white light, whose heat was bright enough to burn a hole in gold. The rays from the light traveled in every direction until pouring over the universe. At the center of the screaming light burst a creature made of flames with rays of golden light that flapped like giant wings. At first, the wings screeched like metal scraping metal, but then the noise transformed into an intense musical pitch, a high note beyond human capability, and the companion light was so bright it shamed the sun. The sound became so intense, and the light so ferocious, that the sound exploded into silence and the light contracted into a golden dot. Both burst into the essence of heaven; an enormous angel appeared before the girl. The golden winged being, spoke: "Mary, come with me. Don't stay here. Come with me."

Mary did as she was told. Turning around a moment later, Mary saw herself pressed against the stone wall, under the brute force of the Roman soldier. Having satisfied himself, the soldier adjusted his loin cloth and bluntly stated, "You can go now. I'm finished."

What the soldier didn't know was that Mary had already left with a golden angel, an angel who wisely advised Mary, "Don't look back. Come with me, Mary. I'll take you home."

Chapter Two

Mary stood in the archway, for that is where the golden angel left her. She didn't enter the home, as she was without reason. The home was without meaning to her. She stood there, hollowed by the experience. Empty. Her eyes vacant; her hands dangling at her sides, she simply stood.

This is how her mother found her. The mother of Mary fell silent at the sight of her daughter; her robes torn, her stare distant. There was no urn in her hands, no veil on her head. After taking in all of this, the mother took the girl by the hand and led her to the back courtyard. She lowered the girl into a sitting position onto a stone step and gently raised the girl's gown, to which the girl made a feeble attempt to raise her arms, but a weakness overcame the child, all the mother heard was a small whimper in protest. The mother studied the girl's thighs and discovered the pink, blood-stained semen dripping down her leg.

The mother felt her daughter's pain with such oneness that she too began to cry. Her salty tears stung her daughter's bleeding wounds, making the girl cry out. As the mother sobbed, each teardrop grew in size from a pebble, to a rock, to a boulder. Eventually, these boulder-size tears came crashing down on the child like a giant tsunami washing over her. The saltiness of the enormous tears caused profuse burning; a burning so hot it boiled the tears so that a cloud of steam raised into the air around the mother and daughter, in this cloud the mother remembered the first time that she felt oneness with her daughter.

The day the baby was born the midwife had taken the infant, washed her, and wrapped her in swaddling. Then the midwife handed the baby to the mother, who, in turn, unwrapped the swaddling and held the tiny, naked form to her breast. Following the feeding, the infant slept on the mother's chest and they were one again. Skin touching skin, warmth wafting around them as the mother placed the swaddling and her shawl over them both, not between them.

Now, in the misty vapors that enshrouded them, the mother touched her daughter's cheek and delicately moved a strand of hair from her face. The girl was cleaned from the ocean of tears and dried now from the steam that was quickly evaporating. The mother spoke, "You are a virgin. A virgin is a girl who has not consented nor freely joined together with a man. You have not consented. Do you understand me? You are a virgin. There is no other way that it can be."

"I have never consented to be with a man."

"I know," the mother agreed. "Therefore, you are a virgin."

"I am a virgin," the girl spoke as she had been told.

The mother embraced the girl who looked upward, seeing the golden angel in the distance. The golden angel said, "You are a virgin."

But the girl didn't care.

Chapter Three

Yosef sat quietly with a cup of tea. His fingers, the fingers of a carpenter, cradled the cup gently. He listened patiently first to the father and then to the mother. He occasionally glanced at the girl, who sat apart from them in the corner of the room.

"She is a good girl. She will make a devoted wife."

"She is a virgin and follows the laws of the Torah."

"We realize that she is young. Some would say a bit young for marriage, but really once a girl has become a woman, is she not ready to bear a child and care for her husband and children?"

Yosef sighed slightly, wondering what he would do with a wife. *And such a young wife, too.*

"You have always been a generous soul. A man with patience," the father said.

Yosef wondered now what was wrong with the girl.

"It really is time that you take a wife, Yosef. People are beginning to talk," the mother said.

"And this will keep them from talking?" Yosef said sarcastically, offended by the implications that Mary's mother had made. *Let them talk*, Yosef thought.

"What's wrong with her?" Yosef asked bluntly. It was the previous slight that aggravated his rude remark. He felt the shame of his comment as the girl looked up. He caught her glance. Her eyes held a glint, shiny as any polished stone. He could see that she was not lacking in intellect. Her eyes were not surrounded by whites. He could see that she was neither brain-damaged nor physically impaired, her hands had moved across the table with grace and ease as she had poured the tea. She was not plain, perhaps even lovely, if one were interested in women.

The father remained silent. The mother swallowed hard.

"She is with child."

"I thought you said—"

"She is a virgin. She has never agreed to have relations with any man."

Yosef leaned back in his seat. He rubbed his forehead. After a time he spoke again, "You ask a lot."

This time the father answered him, "She will come with a dowry, of course. One mule, several yards of the finest fabric, urns, pottery, candle wax, and oil."

Yosef did not speak. He wasn't trying to negotiate a better deal; he was trying to envision his life with a wife and child. Mary's mother could see the concern.

"She is a sweet girl and she will miss her mother very much. I would hope that you would allow her to come to us for extended stays. We have a kinswoman, Elizabeth in Judea, who is also with child and we should like to visit her often, taking Mary and the baby with us." Mary's mother's voice quavered slightly. Yosef remained still.

"You know what they will do to her," the mother finally said with desperation. "You alone can save her life."

Yosef looked at the girl. Her eyes did not in any way plead for her own life. Her eyes seemed to say, *Who can hurt me; I am of another world.*

Yosef took a deep breath and then nodded.

"The fabrics, will some of them be silks?" Yosef asked.

Mary's father smiled with delight. "Yes, yes, I will make many of them silk. As a matter of fact I have some now." With that said, he turned to his daughter, "Mary run and fetch the silks from the bags on the mule." The girl obediently left.

"You are a good man, Yosef. We will not let you regret this."

"How soon must the wedding take place?" Yosef asked.

"Two weeks." The mother told him.

"Two weeks?" Yosef was surprised. "She doesn't appear to be showing."

"She will soon."

"When will the baby come?"

"Winter's solstice."

"That soon?" Yosef's voice was unsteady.

"Everything will be fine," Mary's mother assured him.

Mary returned with fabrics over her arm.

"Well, leave me with my wife to be. I shall walk her home shortly. We shall walk through the market together and I may buy her a piece of fruit. I will be sure that many people see me with my betrothed."

Mary's mother thanked Yosef profusely as did her father, before they left.

Yosef took the silks from Mary's hand. He playfully wrapped one around her waist, tucking the end into the waistband. Then he selected a colorful piece of fabric for himself and wrapped it around his waist in much the same way. Then Yosef took another yard of fabric and made a veil for himself. He smiled. Next he hid his smile. He made his hands into imaginary castanets and began to do a belly dance, flirtatiously, coyly, with exaggerated femininity. Mary began to laugh. She tried to hide her laughter behind her hand shoving giggles back into her mouth.

"Feel free; laugh with me. Dance with me," Yosef told her as his movements became larger and the swirling fabric filled the room. At first, Mary could only watch with amazement, but then she joined him.

The silks began to billow outward as each twirled to the music that Yosef hummed. The swirling materials expanded as if the air under them were making them grow ever outward. Silks filled the small house and even floated into Yosef's workshop. Mary's smile grew wider as well. She leaned her head back in gentle abandon, smiling, laughing, twirling, as did he; until, each felt overwhelmed by silly, giddy dizziness and fell to the floor. Their fall was cushioned by the now hundreds of thousands of silk fabric that magically covered the floor. The betrothed couple lay in them as if they were the softest down pillows on earth. Yosef reached out his hand to Mary, "I may not be the husband you dreamed of, but I will be a friend to you and a father to your baby."

Good to his word, Yosef took Mary to the market. He made sure the gossips of the village saw them together and that they saw the billowing, brightly-colored silks that followed them. He looked upon Mary as if she were his greatest joy. She, in turn, looked at him with admiration. As they were about to leave the market, something changed the gaiety. Mary spied a Roman soldier, standing casually by a vegetable stand at the west end of the market. Her body stiffened. The wind ceased and the billowing silks fell abruptly to the ground. Her husband-to-be couldn't move her along. He looked up to see what she see saw. It gave him pause, as well. The soldier came toward them.

The village knew this soldier; his name was whispered in fear, Tiberius Julius Abdes Panthera. Panthera ate the core of his pear, stem and seeds, swallowing it all before he approached the betrothed couple.

"What's this? Two ladies out for a stroll in the market?"

Yosef and Mary remained silent.

"Panthera," another soldier called to him; he turned away from the couple to see his friend waving him in another direction. Panthera gave the couple one last suspicious look and left them. "I'm coming, my legionnaire," he called out. Once Panthera was out of ear shot, Yosef turned to Mary and spoke. "There will come a day when we shall awake and all the Roman soldiers will be gone," Yosef promised her. Mary nodded, but didn't believe Yosef. As the couple turned to leave, they stepped on the fallen silks which remained lifeless on the ground.

Chapter Four

A Visit to her Cousin

Following the marriage of Yosef the carpenter to Mary the daughter of Anne and Joachim, the girl's parents whisked her away to visit Elizabeth in Judea. The cousin, Elizabeth, welcomed the child into her home. Elizabeth was past the time of natural child-bearing and all were surprised to hear of her pregnancy.

"We both have fears," she said to Mary, "You because you are so young and me because I am so old. But fear not, the baby in my womb kicked for joy at your arrival. This is a good omen."

Mary did not answer; instead, she stood draped in shyness. Elizabeth turned to her cousin Anne and reassured her, "Worry not; I'll take care of the child." Anne, the mother of Mary, kissed the girl on the forehead and touched her cheek. Giving her away once again, brought tears to Anne's eyes. Mary realized from the touch of her mother's fingers that she would leave her again with strangers. Both the mother and daughter felt the anguish of that bitter sweet moment as they remembered when Mary had turned seven years old, the age of reason, and had entered the Temple of Mt. Carmel as a virgin ready to serve El. Anne and Joachim had been unable to conceive a baby and Anne had promised that if God were to bless them with a child, then she would send the child into his service. Thus, Mary served in the temple for five years, until her first menses came when she was twelve, at which time she was given back into her parents care. But the child knew little of the outer world. In the temple, she had spent her days carrying water from the well within the confines of the temple gardens or she had spent her time kneading, baking, and serving bread with the cooks of the temple to the rabbis. She had dusted the shelves and the furniture and carried the cloaks and tassels of the holy men. When not in service, Mary prayed to the god of David, the god of Abraham. But she had never spun wool, never laid a warp or pulled the bobbin for the weave, never guided sheep, never walked on a public road, and had never seen a Roman soldier.

Mary didn't know how to be a wife or a mother. In earnest, she entered into a domestic education guided by her kinswoman Elizabeth, but she would learn more than her parents expected. Her cousin Elizabeth would come to realize that the girl had an education of a different kind well beyond her years.

During the first few weeks, Mary shadowed her cousin Elizabeth in her daily tasks. Elizabeth being nearly forty moved with an elegant however, slow step. She had performed her duties for many years and now she engaged each task with meditative patience. She sliced fruit slowly and Mary watched as the woman closed her eyes, dipped her head slightly downward and then raised her head taking in the fragrance of an orange or a pear or a pomegranate. Each time a smile would cross Elizabeth's face. Elizabeth took clothes to the river, and swung the robes one at a time into the waters before bringing them up with vigor and slapping them against a flat rock. She sprayed the girl with water the first time and Mary jumped back with surprise but soon fell into laughter alongside her elderly cousin. "It's good to know that there is still laughter in your soul," Elizabeth said to the girl as a sanguine expression graced her face.

In the afternoon, Elizabeth spun wool, singing as she did so. Mary had never heard this kind of singing. She listened with joy as she helped Elizabeth twine rope on her thigh and weave baskets from reeds. One day as Elizabeth was showing her how to sew garments; she said to the girl, "What did they teach you at the temple? How did you serve the rabbis?"

"I served them bread dipped in honey that I helped to kneed and bake in the ovens. I dusted their shelves and tables and chairs; I swept their pathways. I hung their garments to dry after a servant washed them at the river. I folded their robes and laid them on their beds. I poured herb teas while they taught the boys. I served them stews and soups while they engaged in debate."

"Ah, what did the rabbis debate?"

"They debate everything," Mary said with a smile. Elizabeth responded in kind.

"And what did they teach the boys?"

"They taught the boys Genesis, Exodus, Leviticus, Numbers, Deuteronomy, the prophets Joshua, Samuel, all the way through to Malachi. They learned the Psalms and Song of Songs and the Story of Ruth and so much more." Mary's words flowed forth like a fresh water spring from a mountain's side. These were the narratives that this girl had also learned. These were the stories of her people.

"As a Temple Virgin you learned all this while attending the rabbis, yes?"

"Yes, but I am no longer a Temple Virgin." She hung her head.

"You are always a Temple Virgin. This is a title that recognizes the service you performed and the knowledge that you were given. Did you think that you were eavesdropping?" The girl looked up with surprise for indeed she did think that she had been stealing knowledge not meant for her.

"The rabbis are wise men, are they not?" Elizabeth asked and Mary nodded.

"They placed you exactly where they wanted you. They let you hear the sacred Word because you are blessed. They were preparing you for your role."

"I heard the rabbis say that one day a messiah will come. He will be flesh and blood, of this world, and he will lead the people, especially the poor and the oppressed out from under the Roman yoke of oppression. I heard the rabbis strategize from day-to-day how best to reclaim the land of their fathers, but their voices lacked meat and always disappeared into their wine glasses." The girl now confided more openly that she had had a dream the night before, which showed her the future. "I now believe that I am the voice, for an angel has told me, and I know the best way to save the people from Roman rule. I promise you that I will teach my son all that I have learned and all that may be." Mary spoke with such fierce determination while her eyes looked into the future that Elizabeth was taken aback. The older woman responded quickly, wanting to encourage the girl in her new found strength.

"Then, blessed art thou, Mary; I will rear my son to prepare the way for your son." Mary nodded with appreciation. Then Elizabeth told her, "And you will hold your head high with dignity when you return to your village."

After that, Mary spent many happy days with Elizabeth and her husband. She sang the songs with Elizabeth and worked alongside her. When at last, Elizabeth gave birth to a boy child, Mary assisted the midwife—she washed the boy clean and handed him to Elizabeth. Mary watched as the babe suckled and she felt her own babe kick within the womb. While Elizabeth spent hours sleeping or suckling her babe, Mary went about as the midwife's assistant, learning all she could, including how to turn a baby whose feet are coming first, how to clear the air ways so the infant can take its first breath, and even how to help a woman who is dying in child birth to feel no pain, helping her to slip into death when there is no other recourse. The midwife gave herbs to Mary to take back to her village.

Six full moons had come and gone since Mary's arrival at her cousin's home and now it was time for her to leave. She surrendered her days of joy in the house and returned to the home of her husband, Yosef. But before leaving she said to Elizabeth, "I feel gratitude for all that you have taught me and for the promise that your son will pave the way for mine. For I realize now the following:

My soul doth magnify the Lord.

And my spirit hath rejoiced in God my Saviour.

Because he hath regarded the humility of his handmaid;

for behold from henceforth all generations shall call me blessed.

Because he that is mighty,

hath done great things to me;

and holy is his name.

And his mercy is from generation unto generations,*

to them that fear him.

He hath shewed might in his arm:

he hath scattered the proud in the conceit of their heart.

He hath put down the mighty from their seat,

and hath exalted the humble.

He hath filled the hungry with good things;

and the rich he hath sent empty away.

He hath received Israel his servant,

being mindful of his mercy:

As he spoke to our fathers,

to Abraham and to his seed forever."**

*The Latin version reads 'from progenies to progenies' The English versions vary 'from generation unto generations' and 'from generations to generations'

**_Magnificat,_ Luke 1: 46-55

Following these words, Mary miraculously disappeared and then reappeared within the home of her husband. Whereupon she said to her husband, "Yosef, I will bring forth the son they seek. We will have much to teach him."

Chapter Five

The Star of Bethlehem

The command had come for the census to be conducted. Yosef and Mary were instructed to travel to the town of Yosef's birth in order to be counted like cattle for the satisfaction of the Roman Empire. This census, a regional undertaking, would pave the way for the great census to be conducted three years hence. The emperor liked to brag about the number of conquered and kept careful records of his subjects for purposes of taxation.

Mary was heavy with child when they undertook the trip to Bethlehem. Between the intermittent walking and riding on the mule her body began to fight against her. In the beginning, her abdomen tightened into a stiff, round ball. This sensation felt good in a strange way, but as they continued along the rocky path, a cramping came upon her and she was not as soothed by this sensation. The turmoil grew over the hours leaving her nauseated, and she suffered hot sweats which were followed by cold shivers. Her hands and chest became clammy; gripping pain racked her body every so often and without warning, until she finally cried out in pain.

"We're almost there," Yosef told her.

Once they reached the city, Yosef discovered there was no available shelter. Each time he returned after entering an inn, he reported that the inn was full. Mary began to see her husband as weak. Disappointment turned to frustration. At the fourth inn, Mary could tolerate Yosef's failure no longer. Frustration turned to anger. She dismounted the uncomfortable mule. As her feet landed with a thud on the solid earth, a searing pain nearly brought her to her knees. When the pain at last subsided, she walked past her husband brusquely shoving his shoulder aside with her shoulder. She entered the inn.

Desperate, she stood in front of the owner, who was surprised to see this girl at his table.

"Give me whatever lodging you have, but give me something, a place to birth my child, a child of God," she demanded of the inn keeper. Mary was suddenly overwhelmed by a pain so tremendous that her demand was punctuated by a screeching wail as if the night sky had opened, releasing a thousand screaming bats. The inn-keeper and his customers looked up to find the ceiling covered with screeching, winged rodents. Terrified that the winged vermin would send his customers scurrying, the inn-keeper grabbed the girl by the arm and quickly escorted her to the barn. There, Mary lay upon the straw. Alone. Writhing with pain. Yosef—nowhere in sight.

The straw pricked her skin raw with each turn and twist of her body. No position brought the comfort she sought. Her stomach squirmed and she felt a wave of black wash over her like a tidal wave made of tar. The pitch sealed her lungs, but once it had passed she drew a deep breath into herself. Then she pulled herself upward; she knelt and held onto the side of the manger. The pain shot through her being and she tossed her head back, looking upward through a hole in the roof. There she saw a star and the light of that star took away the sea of blackness.

The star's brilliance exploded and in it she saw the angel. "Come away, Mary. Don't stay here."

Mary left with the angel and floated gently into the night sky looking down on herself through the hole in the roof. The midwife had arrived and she set the baby on the prickly straw and laid Mary down on her back. Then the midwife removed a Persian cucumber from her haversack and expertly inserted it into Mary's vagina so that it wouldn't constrict before she could remove the afterbirth. The midwife bit the umbilical cord with her sturdy teeth, after which she saw to the infant, clearing the mucus and blood, beholding the miracle of life—the squirming infant let out a healthy cry. The midwife was saying something, but Mary was too far away to hear her. Mary began to return, floating back into her body. She returned to her place on the stable floor just as the midwife wrenched the afterbirth from her. Mary screamed a scream as sharp as broken glass. Then all became quiet.

Chapter Six

Seeds of Resistance

When Mary awoke she found her infant son sleeping next to her in the prickly straw. She rolled over on her side, feeling the stinging tip of shirred wheat, *once a seed*, she thought, *a seed that grew into a feathery plant, produced and reproduced itself, year after year when sown by hand.* The seed could be milled and turned into manna and the best seeds would be stored and sprinkled onto the fertilized fields come spring.

Her infant lay sleeping by her side. She raised herself on one elbow and glanced around by the light of the oil lantern. Beside her a flask of water and a gourd filled with millet and fruit. Mary ate and drank, replenishing her strength. Yosef was asleep on the far side of the barn, keeping his distance from the blood soaked straw that Mary would undoubtedly have to gather up herself. For now, she was too weak to stand. She wanted only to hold the infant, to smell his wet head and feel his soft skin. Her anger at Yosef subsided.

A donkey brayed and the babe beside her let out a small cry. Mary leaned toward him only to find her groin muscles wrench with pain. She tried to scoop him closer as his cry intensified. "Shh," the mother said.

With one hand she was eventually able to bring the baby to her breast. She lay on her side, her arm protecting the infant. She lowered her robe and brought the baby to her nipple, all the while stroking his cheek and like a baby bird his mouth opened in anticipation.

The child suckled heartily taking in the liquid of life that precedes milk. As he suckled, she spoke softly to him.

"You are the son of God; the child of a virgin mother. I have plans for you.

"I shall educate you so that you will see that your purpose is to save the people. You shall be a Messiah. You will gather the Israelites unto you and you will do it through the word, not the sword. You shall be the Prince of Peace. I shall rear you so that you may achieve a most glorious end and I shall stay with you every step of your journey.

"You shall begin with the meek and bring them to you. The poor, the sick, the lame, and build your flock. In time, you will reach out to the wayward, the sinners, the prostitutes, the slaves of the Roman households. You will offer them what no man or woman or child can argue against. You will offer them peace and serenity; you will offer them heaven after earth and forever more. In time, you will persuade the farmers, the fishermen, the salt vendors, and others to heed your parables and they will follow you. Finally, you will persuade the educated, the accountants, the lawyers, the tax collectors and the rabbis to be your disciples. You will drain the Roman Empire of its citizens drop by drop, until the Empire is dry. The great philosophers will be echoes of the past; the Greek and Roman gods will tumble from their pedestals; the Roman Emperor will quiver at the sound of your name—Jesus."

"You alone will lead the people in a great resistance against the enemies of our land, the men who have mocked your father and abused your mother, the greedy emperor who forces women to give birth alongside the road or in a stable just so he can claim and count his conquered people for taxation. Greed guides this tyrant; generosity will lead you forward. Give yourself to the people and teach them to do unto others as they would have others do unto to them." Mary's words fell on the child like seeds.

"Yes, Jesus, all this I will guide you toward—

"Mary, are you well?" Yosef asked her; his voice heavy with sleep.

"I'm fine. I've named our son. He will be called Jesus."

"Jesus." Yosef repeated the name before falling back to sleep.

Mary lowered the infant from her breast and pulled the swaddling blanket around him. She picked up a piece of straw that was caught in the folds of the baby's neck, which threatened to pierce his shoulder. She held it between her forefinger and thumb and suddenly pressed down, driving the sharp edge into her flesh. As the blood trickled from her finger, and continued to flow from her womb, she whispered in the shadows of the night, "I swear by my woman's blood and the oath blood pricked from my finger that all this shall come to pass."

She then opened her palm and witnessed that the straw had turned into a seed. The virgin mother delicately placed that seed into her herb pouch, knowing it was the seed of life, a seed that would be crucial to her plan.

The Last Chapter

Some say that is not exactly what happened; rather, seven days later, after the birth of Christ, four travelers arrived at the inn. Yosef and Mary had been invited into the inn to share dinner with the other travelers since a room had become available for them. The evenings were long and cold at this time of year and so the travelers passed the time by telling stories. Mary used this opportunity to usher in the story that her son would one day free the people of oppression, that he would use words instead of swords, generosity over greed, compassion over tyranny, and love over hate. She described great feats and miracles that he would perform, including the ability to turn water into wine and that he would be able to walk on water. She told the travelers these stories about her son and many more. At the end of the travelers' stay, they each in turn gave Mary a gift for they decided she was the best storyteller they had ever come across. One man gave her frankincense, another myrrh, and a third man gave her a few gold coins. But the fourth man, an African magi, took Mary aside allowing her to view as he cut the heel of his foot and extracted a magic seed, a seed so powerful that if anyone took her son's life, she could use it to restore his full humanity. He called the seed—the butterfly.

As the boy's life unfolded, the stories of miracles came true. In the end, when the Roman soldiers captured him and tortured him to the brink of death, Mary stayed by his side waiting with the mixture made from the leaves of the magical seed, along with the seeds of the seed. When she saw her opportunity she inserted the healing herbal medicine into Veronica's veil and instructed Veronica to wipe her son's face, to feed him the mixture and to insert the seed into his mouth. Following the crucifixion, Mary sat by her son's tomb for three days, and when nothing happened she entered the tomb, weeping, afraid that the butterfly seed had not worked. Indeed, the magic had not worked, at least not until the mother's tears accidentally fell upon her son's lips and he awakened.

That's probably what happened, but I suppose it took a great deal of magic.

AUTHOR'S NOTE

Dates used in this novel were altered and or compressed to fit within the confines of the story. Most importantly for baseball fans, The Sox v. Yankees games were scheduled for August 27, 28, and 29, 2010. I had to move their dates forward a week in order to fit the timeline of the story. The actual outcomes of those games are as follows: Friday August 27, 2010 – CHW 9 v. NYY 4; Saturday August 28, 2010 – NYY 12 v. CHW 9; and Sunday August 29, 2010 – NYY 2 v. CHW 1. Most importantly for those interested in the development of the terminator seed and the zombie seed is to note that the unfolding of these events has covered several years.

The novel, *Zombie Seed and the Butterfly Blues: A Case of Social Justice*, was inspired by the stories of farmers as told through farmers themselves plus the writings of brave activists, investigative reporters, scientists and other researchers, as well documentarians. I have provided twenty facts and a bibliography of useful sources (which were used in the writing of the novel) for readers who would like more information. In addition, for those who are interested in debates as to whether the V-GURTs (a.k.a. terminator/suicide seeds) and T-GURTs (a.k.a. zombie seeds) are harmful or helpful to society, I have included the citation for a 74 page report by Dr. Lemaux of the Department of Plant and Microbial Biology, University of California, Berkeley. However, it should be noted that mention of certain developments like 'golden rice' which Dr. Lemaux sees as a purely humanitarian development is hotly debated by others. I have added a list of a few sources on golden rice, as well. The references can be seen at the inserted link.

FACTS

FACT I
On January 15, 2010 the U.S. Department of Justice announced an official investigation into the business practices of Monsanto Corporation. The investigation continued for nearly three years (see references- U.S. Opens Inquiry into Monsanto, 2010 and see- Khan, March 15, 2013).

FACT II
Eddy Anderson's story about superweeds was published in the New York Times, May 3, 2010 (See references- Neuman & Pollack, 2010; Also see- Tom Philpott, 2013 for an update on the superweeds situation).

FACT III
Gebisa Ejeta, Purdue University Professor, received the World Food Prize on October 15, 2009 (See references- Ejeta, 2010).

FACT IV
The story of the suicide farmer in India is based on a true story (See references- Malone, 2008).

FACT V
The character of Jim Hack is a fictionalized representation of small-farm-holding farmers across the Midwestern United States. However, his character is based on a real person interviewed by the author for research purposes. Confidentiality was promised and Human Research Subject clearance obtained (See references- Clair, 2011).

FACT VI
In March 1998 the US Patent Office granted Patent No. 5,723,765 to Delta Pine & Land for a patent titled, Control of Plant Gene _Expression. The patent is owned jointly, according to Delta Pine's

Security & Exchange Commission 10K filing, 'by DP&L and the United States of America, as represented by the Secretary of Agriculture' (See references- Engdahl, 2006).

FACT VII
On August 16, 2006 *The New York Times* reported that Monsanto had reached terms of agreement with Delta and Pine Land for its acquisition of Delta and Pine Land for $1.5 billion and *The American Agriculture* announced that the deal is subject to regulations specifically mentioning that the U.S. Department of Justice required Monsanto to divest itself of several cotton seed assets *(See references- Pollack, 2006).* The deal was not completed until May 31, 2007 (See references- Staff, 2007).

FACT VIII
Women between the ages of 20-24 are most at risk for partner abuse (See references- U. S. Department of Justice, Bureau of Justice Statistics, "Intimate Partner Violence in the United States," 2006).

FACT VIX
Approximately 1.3 million women are abused by their partners annually in the U.S. (See references- Costs of Intimate Partner Violence, 2003).

FACT X
"On Graveyard Dirt and other Poisons," a chapter in anthropologist Zora Neale Hurston's book, it is pointed out that Sir Spencer Wells "found germs of scarlatina in the soil surrounding a grave after thirty years." He also found the germs of yellow fever, typhoid and other infectious diseases in the cemetery (See references- Hurston, 1938, pp. 251-252). Additional cites on this matter can be found in *The Journal of the Royal Society for the Promotion of Health* (See references- Bucknill, 1915 for full citation).

FACT XI

The Baroness, Catherine Doherty, was born on August 15, 1896 but she died on December 14, 1985, not 1986 (I took literary liberty with dates in order to make the storyline fit). However, her life story is based on a true story and it is a fact that the Baroness is currently being considered for canonization by the Catholic Church (See references- *Catherine Doherty*, 2011, also see *Edward J. Doherty, Jr.*, 1990).

FACT XII

UNICEF estimates the number of orphans in Haiti to be 440,000 as of 2009, that is, prior to the earthquake of January 12, 2010 in which thousands upon thousands of people were killed (See references- *UNICEF—At a Glance: Haiti (Statistics for 2009)*, 2010).

FACT XIII

The author spent four days in an orphanage in Combermere, Ontario, Canada when she was four years old, the same orphanage that was founded by The Baroness.

FACT XIV

February 4, 2012 Purdue Agriculture Alumni invite Howard G. Buffett, proponent of organic and no-till farming to be guest speaker at the annual fish fry dinner (See references- Purdue University Agricultural Alumni, 2012). Studies by Prof. Tony Vyn and his Purdue University team reported that no-till is better for the environment (See references- Wallheimer, 2010).

FACT XV

On September 11, 2012 a Chinese researcher was suspended pending investigation into collaboration with US researchers for illegally testing genetically-modified rice on Chinese children. (See references- Reuters, 2012).

FACT XVI
February 2013 U.S. Court of Appeals for the Federal Circuit Court prepares to hear the case of Vernon Hugh Bowman (A 75 year old farmer) v. Monsanto (See references- Harris, 2013).

FACT XVII
February 13, 2013 Problems with genetically-modified crops include giving questionable yields according to university studies. In general, organic crops provide higher yield than genetically-modified crops. Stacked genes (meaning terminator, zombie, exorcist) appear to have unintended consequences. And organic crops have better water holding capacity than genetically-modified crops, making organic less susceptible to drought damage (See references- Philpott, 2013).

FACT XVIII
February 19, 2013 U.S. Court of Appeals for the Federal Circuit Upheld Monsanto's right to apply patent restriction to the progeny seeds from genetically-modified crops (See references- Vernon Hughes Bowman v. Monsanto).

FACTXIX
March 14, 2013 Scientists report a 59% decline in the monarch butterfly population, in large part due to climate change and the overuse of glyphosate on GMOs (See references- McCauley, 2013).

FACT XX
Several businesses and universities, including Purdue Research Foundation, hold terminator technology patents (See references- Suicide seeds: Not dead yet!).

REFERENCES

Achbar, M. Abbott, J. & Bakan, J. (2003). *The corporation.* Zeitgeist Films.

Arendt, H. (February 25, 1967). Reflections: Truth and Politics. *The New Yorker.*

Baigent, M., Leigh, R., & Lincoln, H. (1982). *Holy blood, holy grail.* New York: Bantam Dell.

Bucknill, P.J.R. (1915). Cremation: The only rational means of the disposal of the dead. *The Journal of the Royal Society for the Promotion of Health, 36 (1), pp. 54-56.* Retrieved from http://rsh.sagepub.com/cgi/pdf_extract/36/1/54

Buffett, H. G. (2012). *In support of conservation agriculture for smallholder farmers* Retrieved on December 7, 2012 from http://www.thehowardgbuffettfoundation.org/wp-content/uploads/2012/07/Harvest-Advertorial-July-4-2012.pdf

Black, J. E. (2009). Native resistive rhetoric and the decolonization of American Indian removal discourse. *Quarterly Journal of Speech, 95*, 66-88.

Bucknill, P.J.R. (1915). Cremation: The only rational means of the disposal of the dead.

Caldwell, J. (October 3, 2011). Glyphosate-resistant waterhemp rising. Retrieved on 12-1-11 from http://www.agriculture.com/news/crops/glyphosateresist-waterhemp-rising2-ar19648

Carson, R. (1962). *Silent Spring.* Boston & New York: Houghton Mifflin.

Catherine Doherty (June, 26, 2011). Retrieved on October 28, 2011 from http://en.wikipedia.org/wiki/Catherine Doherty.

Charles, D. (2001). *Lords of the harvest: Biotech, big money, and the future of food.* Cambridge, MA: Perseus.

Clair, R. P. (2011). Reflexivity and rhetorical ethnography: From family farm to orphanage and back again. *Cultural Studies ←→Critical Methodologies, 11,* 117-128.

Conrad, C. (1992). Corporate communication as symbol and practice. In R. Heath & E.L. Toth (Eds.). *Rhetorical and critical perspectives on public relations* (pp. 187-204). New York: Lawrence Erlbaum.

Costs of Intimate Partner Violence against Women. (2003). Centers for Disease Control and Prevention, National Centers for Injury Prevention and Control, Atlanta, Georgia. Retrieved from http://www.ncadv.org/files/DomesticViolenceFactSheet(National). pdf

Crumb, M. J. (April 1, 2011). *Retired Purdue professor's biotech claims questioned by scientists.* The Associated Press. JCOnline.com. Retrieved from http://www.jconline.com/apps/ pbcs.dll/article?AID=/2011041156/NEWS09/110401014.

Crumb, M. J. (April 2, 2011). *Ex-Purdue professor's claims stir biotech pot.* The Associated Press. JCOnline.com. Retrieved from http://www.jconline.com/apps/pbcs.dll/article?AID=20110402020 0/NEWS0501/104020328.

Dechant, D. (April 30, 2002) "Transforming public research into exclusive rights: Purdue Defends Terminator" (*Cropchoice,* Guest Commentator) (also see *Farm News from Cropchoice*). Retrieved February 11, 2010 http://www.purefood.org/patent/ purdue050202.cfm and http://www.cropchoice.com/leadstrycf82. html?recid=688

Edward J. Doherty, Jr. (April 3, 1990). *Eddy Doherty: Co-Founder of Madonna House.* Retrieved on October 29, 2011 from http://www.madonnahouse.org/doherty/Eddy.html

Ejeta selected as featured speaker for commencement ceremony (April 20, 2010). Retrieved April 20, 2010 from http://www.purdue.edu/newsroom/purduetoday/faculty_staff_news /2010/100420

Engdahl, F. W. (August 27, 2006). Monsanto buys 'Terminator' seeds company. *Global Research.* http://www.globalresearch.ca/ monsanto-buys-terminator-seeds-company/3082.

Experts warn of GM foods. (February 24, 2010) *China Daily News. People's Daily Online.* http://english.people.com.cn/ 90001/90776/90882/6900888.html

Delta and Pine Land Company (January, 2000). *International Directory of Company Histories,* vol. 33, St. James Press, 2000. http://www.deltaandpine.com; http://www.deltapineseed.com

Genetic Engineering and Biotechnology-Agricultural Applications of Genetic Engineering. (2011). Retrieved on December 13, 2011 from http://www.libraryindex.com/pages/2267/Genetic-Engineering-Biotechnology-AGRICULTURAL-APPLICATIONS-OFGENETIC-ENGINEERING.html

Gillam, C. (April 13, 2010). *Special report: Are regulators dropping the ball on biocrops?* Thomson Reuters. Retrieved from http://www.google.com/#hl=en&sugexp=les%3B&gs_rn=1&gs_ri=hp&gs_mss=Gillam%202&cp=31&gs_id=4r&xhr=t&q=Gillam%202010%20are%20dropping%20the%20on%20biotech&es_nrs=true&pf=p&tbo=d&rlz=1W1GGHP_enUS487&sclient=psy-ab&oq=Gillam+2010+are+dropping+the+on+biotech&gs_l=&pbx=1&bav=on.2,or.r_gc.r_pw.r_qf.&bvm=bv.41248874,d.aWc&fp=8ca49b8c698010fc&biw=731&bih=385

Greenpeace: Wal-Mart illegally selling GM rice in China (March 19, 2010) Retrieved from http://www.chinacsr.com/en/2010/03/19/7321-greenpeace-wal-mart-illegally-selling-gm-rice-in-china/

Harris, P. (February 9, 2013). 75 Year Old Soybean Farmer Sees Monsanto Lawsuit Reach Supreme Court. *The Guardian: Guardian News and Media.* Retrieved from http://www.rawstory.com/rs/2013/02/09/75-year-old-soybean-farmer-sees-monsanto-lawsuit-reach-u-s-supreme-court/

Heinl, R. D., & Gordon Heinl, N. (1996). *Written in blood: The history of the Haitian people, 1492-1995.* Lantham, MD: University Press of America.

Herodotus. (1954). *Herodotus: The Histories.* (Trans. And Introduction by Aubrey De Sélincourt). Harmondsworth, Middlesex: Penguin Classics.

Hurston, Z. N. (1938). *Tell my horse.* Philadelphia, PA: J.P. Lippencott Company.

Kahn, L. (March 15, 2013). How Monsanto outfoxed the Obama Administration. *Salon.* Retrieved from http://www.salon.com/2013/03/15/how_did_monsanto_outfox_the_obama_administration/

Kilman, S., & Catan, T. (January 15, 2010). U.S. opens inquiry into Monsanto: Antitirust enforcers probe business practices surrounding biotech soybean seed. *The Wall*

Street Journal. Retrieved from http://online.wsj.com/article/ SB10001424052748704363504575002742582725272.html

Laureates: 2009 Laureate Gebisa Ejeta. Retrieved on April 20, 2010 from http://www.worldfoodprize.org/press_room/2009/june/ ejeta.htm.

Lemaux, P. D. (2008). Genetically-engineered plants and foods: A scientist's analysis of the issues (Part I). *Annual Review of Plant Biology, 59,* 771-812. Retrieved from http://arjournals.annualreviews.org/eprint/ESHx4FnZadAJZqvlsG Rg/full/1.0.1146/annuarev

Lemaux, P. D. (2009). Genetically-engineered plants and foods: A scientist's analysis of the issues (Part II). *Annual Review of Plant Biology, 60,* 511-559. Retrieved from http://arjournals.annualreviews.org/eprint/ESHx4FnZadAJZqvlsG Rg/full/1.0.1146/annuarev

Leonard, C. (December 14, 2009). *Monsanto stomps down budding seed competitors.* Associated Press. Retrieved from http://www.commondreams.org/headlines.

Magnificat Luke 1: 46-55 (Translated from the Latin to English version by Douay-Rheims), Reims, France 1582. Retrieved from http://en.wikipedia.org/wiki/Magnificat and follow-up information from http://en.wikipedia.org/wiki/Douay-Rheims.

Malone, A. (November 3, 2008). *The GM genocide: Thousands of Indian farmers are committing suicide after using genetically modified crops.* Retrieved January 29, 2010 from http://www.dailymail.co.uk/news/worldnews/article-1082559?The-GM.

McCauley, L. (March 14, 2013). Herbicides for GMOs driving monarch butterfly population to 'ominous' brink. *Common Dreams.* Retrieved from http://www.commondreams.org/ headline/2013/03/14-3

Monsanto (January 30, 2010). Retrieved from http://en.wikipedia.org/wiki/Monsanto.

Neumann, W. & Pollack, A. (May 3, 2010). "Farmers Cope with Roundup®*-Resistant Weeds." *The New York Times, Business Day Energy & Environment* retrieved from http://www.nytimes.com/2010/05/04/business/energy-environment/04weed.html?emc=etal.

Pagels, E. (2003). *Beyond belief: The secret gospel of Thomas*. New York: Vintage.

Peterson, B. H. (May 19, 2009). *Monsanto terminator making a comeback? Enter the Zombie!* Retrieved from http://www.AmericanChronicle.com/article/view/103033.

Philpott, T. (February 6, 2013). Nearly half of all US Farms now have Superweeds. *Mother Jones*. Retrieved from http://www.motherjones.com/tom-philpott/2013/02/report-spread-monsantos-superweeds-speeds-12-0

Philpott, T. (February 13, 2013). Do GMO crops really have higher yields? *Mother Jones*. Retrieved from http://m.motherjones.com/tom-philpott/2013/02/do-gmo-crops-have-lower-yields

Pollack, A. (August 16, 2006). Monsanto buys Delta and Pine Land, top supplier of cotton seeds in U.S. *The New York Times*. Retrieved from http://www.nytimes.com/2006/08/16/business/16seed.html?_r=0 also available at

Purdue Agricultural Alumni (2012). *The famous Purdue ag fish fry*. Center for Global Food Security, Purdue University. Retrieved from
https://www.purdue.edu/discoverypark/food/events/view.php?id=746

Reuters (2012). *China-US project allegedly tested genetically modified 'golden rice' on kids*. Retrieved from http://www.chinadaily.com.cn/china/2012-09/11/content_15751208.htm. Also see http://worldnews.nbcnews.com/_news/2012/09/11/13796926-china-us-project-allegedly-tested-genetically-modified-golden-rice-on-kids?lite

Schlosser, E., Pearce, R., & Robledo, M. (2009). *Food Inc*. (Directed by R. Kenner). Los Angeles, CA: Magnolia Entertainment.

"Seeds of resistance: Saving seeds is a political act." International Museum of Women, Power and Politics (2004). This article contains quotes from Vandana Shiva's 2004 lecture given at University of California, Santa Barbara. Retrieved from http://imow.org/wpp/stories/viewStory?storyid=1236.

Source Watch. (February 28, 2009) Retrieved from: http://www.sourcewatch.org/index.php?title=Monsanto_and_Term inator_Technology

Staff. (May 31, 2007). Monsanto to acquire Delta and Pine Land, Divest Nexgen and Stoneville. *Farm Futures.* Retrieved from: http://farmfutures.com/story-monsanto-to-acquire-delta-and-pine-land-divest-nexgen-and-stoneville-8-12117

Suicide seeds: Not dead yet! (January/February 2001). *Organic Consumers Association, 68.* Retrieved from http://www.organicconsumers.org/Patent/terminatorseeds.cfm

Tabor, J. D. (2006). *The Jesus Dynasty: The hidden history of Jesus, His royal family, and the birth of Christianity.* New York: Simon & Schuster.

Tally, S. (April 18, 2002). *Terminator tussle: Controversial technology needed, experts say.* Purdue News. Retrieved from http://news.uns.purdue.edu/html4ever/020418. Thompson.terminator.htm;

UNICEF—At a Glance: Haiti (Statistics for 2009) (March 2, 2010). Retrieved on October 29, 2011 from http://www.unicef.org/ infobycountry/haiti_statistics.html

U. S. Department of Justice, Bureau of Justice Statistics, "Intimate Partner Violence in the United States" (December, 2006). Retrieved January 2, 2011 from http://www.ncadv.org/files/ DomesticViolenceFactSheet(National).pdf

U.S. Opens Inquiry into Monsanto. (January 15, 2010). *The Wall Street Journal.* Retrieved from http://online.wsj.com/article/ SB10001424052748704363504575002742582725272.html

Vernon Hugh Bowman v. Monsanto. (February 19, 2013). Legal Information Institute. Retrieved from http://www.law.cornell.edu/supct/cert/11-796

Waddington, L. (December 31, 2009). Monsanto, big ag has 'troubling' control over seed market: Ten companies account for two-thirds of the world's proprietary, seed market, report. *Iowa Independent.* Retrieved from http://iowaindependent.com/24537/ monsanto-big-ag-has-troubling-control-over-seed-market-report-finds.

Wallheimer, B. (March 24, 2010). *Genome mapping technique speeds process of finding specific genes.* Retrieved from http://www.purdue.edu/newsroom/research/2010/100324Saltmapping.html

Wallheimer, B. (March 29, 2010). *Orange corn holds promise for reducing blindness, child death.* Retrieved March 30, 2010 from http://www.purdue.edu/newsroom/research/2010/100329RochefordBetacaroti.html

Wallheimer, B. (December 20, 2010). *No till, rotation can limit greenhouse emissions from farm fields.* Retrieved from http://www.purdue.edu/newsroom/research/2010/101220VynNitrous.html

Wallheimer, B. (November 28, 2011). *Herbicide may affect plants thought to be resistant.* Retrieved December 1, 2011 from http://www.purdue.edu/newsroom/research/2011/111122MurphyTransporter.html

Weise, E. (March 30, 2010). Monarchs no longer rule: The butterflies, already losing habitat, are being battered by bad weather. *USA Today*, Science section, 8d.

Xinhao (September 11, 2012). *China to further investigate GM rice case.* Retrieved from http://www.chinadaily.com.cn/china/2012-09/11/content_15751208.htm

Yan, Wang (April 4, 2010). Greenpeace worries GM rice about to be planted. Beijing: *Chinese Daily News.* Retrieved from http://www.genet-info.org/information-services/news/en/21957.html

*The word roundup® should have a trademark symbol placed next to it. I added the one in the references where it was missing.

*V-GURT—a.k.a. terminator seed technology
*T-GURT—a.k.a. zombie seed technology

Additional internet citations that provide information about 'golden rice' include:

http://www.bangmfood.org/feed-the-world/17-feeding-the-world/37-golden-rice-a-dangerous-experiment

REFERENCES

http://www.bangmfood.org/publications/4-short-leaflets/33-10-
reasons-why-we-dont-need-gm-foods
http://www.genecampaign.org/Publication/Article/GMtech/Story%20
of%20golden%20rice.pdf

Never quit searching for the truth; it *lies* somewhere.

You need to be free to follow your destiny.

There is no Truth that can't be changed.

Wake up ... It's not a Game!

Love hurts!

ABOUT THE AUTHOR

Robin Patric Clair is a Full Professor in the Brian Lamb School of Communication at Purdue University. Her research areas include organizational communication, narrative inquiry, sexual harassment, and diversity issues. She teaches classes in organizational communication, diversity and rhetoric with an emphasis in narrative studies and has also taught critical approaches to public relations. In addition, she teaches ethnography and critical interpretive methods classes. Professor Clair has been named a Diversity Fellow at Purdue University as well as a Fellow to the Center of Creative Endeavors from the College of Liberal Arts at Purdue University. She has published over 40 journal articles and book chapters and has published three nonfiction books. Her books include: *Organizing Silence: A World of Possibilities* (1998—SUNY), *Expressions of Ethnography: Novel Approaches to Qualitative Methods* (2003—SUNY) and *Why Work: The Perceptions of a "Real Job" and the Rhetoric of Work through the Ages* (2008—Purdue University Press). Professor Clair has received numerous awards for her research, including seven 'Top Paper' awards, two 'Research Article of the Year' awards, two 'Outstanding Book of the Year' awards, and the 'Golden Anniversary Award' from the National Communication Association. In addition to research awards, Professor Clair's poetry has received honorable mention from Writer's Digest as well as publication in *A Capella Zoo* and most recently in "The Best of *A Capella Zoo*" wherein the poetry was selected by author Gina Ochsner to represent the best poetry from the last five years of the magic realism literary journal's publications. *Zombie Seed and the Butterfly Blues: A Case of Social Justice* is Professor Clair's first published novel.

9 789462 093065